PRELUDE TO CATASTROPHE

BOOKS BY ROBERT SHOGAN

No Sense of Decency: The Army-McCarthy Hearings

Backlash: The Killing of the New Deal

*The Battle of Blair Mountain:
The Story of America's Largest Labor Uprising*

*War Without End: Cultural Conflict and the
Struggle for America's Political Future*

Bad News: Where the Press Goes Wrong in the Making of the President

*The Double-Edged Sword: How Character Makes and Ruins Presidents
from Washington to Clinton*

Fate of the Union: America's Rocky Road to Political Stalemate

*Hard Bargain: How FDR Twisted Churchill's Arm, Evaded the
Law, and Changed the Role of the American Presidency*

Riddle of Power: Presidential Leadership from Truman to Bush

None of the Above: Why Presidents Fail and What Can Be Done About It

Promises to Keep: Carter's First 100 Days

*A Question of Judgment: The Fortas Case and the
Struggle for the Supreme Court*

The Detroit Race Riot: A Study in Violence (with Tom Craig)

PRELUDE TO CATASTROPHE

FDR's Jews and the Menace of Nazism

ROBERT SHOGAN

CHICAGO   *Ivan R. Dee*   2010

PRELUDE TO CATASTROPHE. Copyright © 2010 by Robert Shogan.
All rights reserved, including the right to reproduce this book or portions
thereof in any form. For information, address: Ivan R. Dee, Publisher,
1332 North Halsted Street, Chicago 60642, a member of the Rowman &
Littlefield Publishing Group. Manufactured in the United States of America
and printed on acid-free paper.

www.ivanrdee.com

Library of Congress Cataloging-in-Publication Data:
Shogan, Robert.
Prelude to catastrophe : FDR's Jews and the menace of Nazism / Robert
Shogan.
p. cm.
Includes bibliographical references and index.
ISBN 978-1-56663-831-9 (cloth : alk. paper)—
ISBN 978-1-56663-909-5 (electronic)
1. Roosevelt, Franklin D. (Franklin Delano), 1882–1945—Relations with
Jews. 2. Political consultants—United States—Biography. 3. Jews—United
States—Biography. 4. Brandeis, Louis Dembitz, 1856–1941—Political and
social views. 5. Frankfurter, Felix, 1882–1965—Political and social views.
6. Rosenman, Samuel I. (Samuel Irving), 1896–1973—Political and social
views. 7. Morgenthau, Henry, 1856–1946—Political and social views.
8. Cohen, Benjamin V.—Political and social views. 9. National socialism—
Germany—History—20th century. 10. Jews—Europe—Social conditions—
20th century. I. Title.
E807.S49 2010
973.917092'3924—dc22   2010010179

For Ellen Shrewsbury Shogan
in loving memory
and for our daughters
Cynthia and Amelia

CONTENTS

PREFACE

FRANKLIN ROOSEVELT was the first great hero of American Jews. He was admired, even worshiped, to an extent far exceeding the esteem accorded any politician or public figure before his time, and unmatched by anyone since. FDR's promise of economic and social justice was consonant with the mainsprings of Jewish culture and with the ethos of the Old Testament and the prophets. And of course these themes were particularly resonant during the desperate days of the Great Depression.

Jewish confidence in Roosevelt was buttressed by the unprecedented number of Jews who came to Washington to work for the New Deal. Indeed, there were so many Jews that they became something of an embarrassment and nurtured anti-Semitic jibes. But American Jews should have been able to shrug off such slurs. They were the richest, most influential Jewish community in the world, leaders in government, commerce, and the arts.

Yet by the time Franklin Roosevelt died in office in 1945, six million European Jews had been murdered by the Nazis with neither FDR nor American Jews lifting much more than a finger to help them. How did Roosevelt, the country he led, and

American Jewry permit this to happen? That is the question this book attempts to answer.

Of course horrific social conditions must be taken into account. A nativist revival, made worse by the Great Depression, darkened the public's mood and heightened resistance to immigration. Anti-Semitism, which took root in the South and Midwest in the 1920s, spread like a plague in the 1930s. And the threat to national existence from the Axis powers made all else seem less consequential. Yet for all of that, the decisions to act or not to act that controlled the fate of European Jewry were made by human beings, and it is their judgments that need to be held accountable. To understand those judgments, this book examines the behavior of a handful of Jews, so close to Roosevelt and supposedly so influential they could be considered the "President's Jews." Their actions, and often inactions, illuminate the strengths and limits of interest-group politics, the electoral strategy fostered by FDR which dominated American politics for the remainder of the century. More broadly, the response of the President's Jews to the Nazi threat illustrates with heartbreaking intensity the perpetual dilemma of politics: the conflict between conscience and self-interest, between principle and expediency.

The discovery of the Holocaust filled the world with grief and guilt, touching off a bitter debate about responsibility and blame that continues today. It is not within the scope of this book, which focuses on a small group of influential participants in the tragedy, to rehearse that argument in detail. But some of its more important points deserve brief mention here to help clarify the perspective of this study.

It is true, as defenders of the Roosevelt administration point out, that the United States did more than any of its allies to rescue European Jews, mostly through the belated creation of the War Refugee Board. But those rescued amounted to only a pitiful fraction of the total. The United States came to this feeble rescue effort very late, and it is reasonable to assume that it could have accomplished much more had it begun earlier. Moreover, by responding sooner it seems plausible that the United States could have spurred other nations to greater action.

Another point offered in mitigation is that at first no one knew that Nazi Germany would actually seek to annihilate the Jewish population of Europe. Yet from early on it was clear that Hitler's persecution of the Jews was intended to drive them out of Germany. And that served notice on the world, including the United States, that it faced a refugee problem which demanded response, a demand that would grow more urgent with each new nation conquered by the Wermacht. It did not take much imagination to see that no pleasant fate awaited the Jews if they could not escape Germany or the other countries Hitler occupied.

Late in the war the United States rejected appeals to bomb the death camps and the rail lines leading to these installations where the Jews awaited their extermination. The reasoning was that it would divert airpower needed elsewhere. Yet during this same period numerous U.S. bombing raids were staged within fifty miles or so of Auschwitz, the largest of the hellholes that Hitler devised. It may be, as some scholars have proposed, that the bombing and other desperate schemes that were suggested would not have saved a single Jewish life. But we do not know, because they were never tried. What we do know is that it is impossible to imagine a more terrible result than the ultimate toll of the Holocaust. The brutal efficiency of the Nazis, pervasive anti-Semitism, and the military burden of defeating the Axis all stood in the way of helping the Jews. But there was another more subtle hindrance, and that was indifference. The U.S. government, the media, and the public had higher priorities than the lives of the Jews. As Edmund Burke put it two centuries ago, "All that is necessary for evil to triumph is for good men to do nothing."

PRELUDE TO CATASTROPHE

I

QUANDARY IN THE GOLDEN LAND

THE PARADE began assembling in Cooper Square in lower Manhattan, with four thousand ex-doughboys on hand. Many of them remembered an earlier march, nearly fourteen years in the past, when ticker tape had rained down on returning heroes and triumphant banners had stretched across the canyons of Manhattan. But that was 1919, and the taste of victory in the Great War was still fresh. This day's procession had a grimmer inspiration.

It was supposed to be spring, but the snow flurries drifting down on the shivering crowd made the calendar hard to believe and seemed appropriate to the bleak times. The date was March 23, 1933, four years into the worst economic collapse the modern world had endured. But those gathered at Cooper Square had on their minds a threat darker even than the Great Depression. It was a danger that emanated from an old U.S. foe across the sea, Germany.

As might be expected in such an assemblage, some carried the Stars and Stripes and many wore the insignia of the American

Legion or the Veterans of Foreign Wars. But what set this group of erstwhile fighting men apart were other banners with a difference device, the six-pointed Star of David. For most of the marchers were members of the Jewish War Veterans of America, who had done their bit to vanquish Kaiser Wilhelm's empire. Now they had come to protest the rebirth of that imperial regime known as the Third Reich, under a new leader, Adolf Hitler, who had made unrelenting anti-Semitism the cornerstone of his rule.

When all the marchers were assembled, a rabbi blessed their venture and prayed that "God might bring Germany to see the light of justice and humanity." In tribute to fallen comrades, a cantor chanted "El Mo Rachim," the Hebrew prayer for the dead. The Seventy-first Regiment band struck up the Star Spangled Banner, and then the parade moved out while 5,000 cheered them on, striving to maintain a column of fours along Lafayette Street and finally to City Hall. There J. George Freedman, commander of the National Jewish War Veterans, told New York mayor John L. O'Brien that he was speaking on behalf of the 250,000 Jews who had fought against Germany in the Great War. "We are going to spread our opposition to present conditions in Germany throughout the United States," Freedman vowed. He backed up his rhetoric by presenting the mayor with a set of resolutions demanding a boycott of German goods and services and an official protest to the Nazi regime by the U.S. government against the persecution of the Jews. For his part, the mayor promised to attend a protest meeting at Madison Square Garden the following Monday. "Any regime that has for its basis religious or racial persecution is bound to meet the moral opposition of the entire world," he declared. The veterans cheered.

A few days later some fifty thousand New Yorkers flocked to the protest rally at the Garden and to other mass meetings around the city. At the Garden gathering, along with Mayor O'Brien, former New York governor Al Smith and other Christians joined the protest. Echoing the demands of the Jewish war veterans, they called for an economic boycott of the Germany that the rabbi at Cooper Square had asked the Almighty to guide with the light of justice. Not many allowed much chance of that prayer being answered under Hitler's rule. For the Führer's main goal, aside from seeking revenge against the inequities of the Treaty of Versailles, seemed to be the persecution of Germany's once comfortable and respected Jewish minority.

Hitler had been in power only three weeks and already American Jews and their Christian allies were publicly challenging his various anti-Semitic schemes. Jewish hopes that their government would join in their protest depended greatly on the nation's freshly minted president, Franklin D. Roosevelt.

If Hitler represented the Jews' darkest nightmare, FDR seemed their brightest hope. Roosevelt was new to the Oval Office, but he was an old friend to Jews as governor of New York, where he had succeeded Al Smith, another Jewish ally. Although Roosevelt's Republican opponent in his first try for governor in 1928 was State Attorney General Albert Ottinger, himself a Jew and a formidable campaigner, Jewish voters by and large backed FDR. And Roosevelt bolstered their allegiance by promoting economic and social reforms embodying Jewish cultural and religious traditions. Now Jews were drawn to the chance to participate in the even grander reforms they envisaged that Roosevelt's New Deal would unleash.

This was an opportunity that Roosevelt had begun creating even before he took office, as he staffed his new administration. Among the many changes he was bringing to Washington as he launched the New Deal was the recruitment of an unprecedented influx of Jews into the federal government. Roosevelt's enthusiasm for Jewish recruits had been fostered by his experiences as governor of New York, where he filled a number of key positions from the state's large Jewish population. He was determined to extend and expand this practice on the national level.

"Dig me up some 15 or 20 youthful Abraham Lincolns from Manhattan and the Bronx to choose from," he instructed one of his recruiters, mentioning two New York boroughs with heavy Jewish populations. And he added: "They must know what life in a tenement means," a qualification that was bound to ensure a robust Jewish response.

It was not a difficult order to fill. In flocking to the New Deal, Jews would be motivated not just by their enthusiasm for its promise of economic and social justice but by the chance to overcome the discrimination and prejudice they had encountered almost everywhere during more than three centuries in the New World. Despite their material and cultural accomplishments and their contributions to their adopted homeland, most of the barriers against Jews remained in place in the twentieth century as in earlier times. Private enterprise—the great corporations, law firms, and universities—that employed the Gentile elite for the most part did not welcome Jewish applicants, regardless of their qualifications. The federal government had long followed much the same pattern. But under the Roosevelt administration that had already begun to change. "The Jews now have three *velten* [worlds]," a New York judge, Jonah Goldstein, would exult early in the New Deal. "*Die velt* [this world], *yenneh velt* [the world to come], and Roosevelt."

This third *velt* was in good measure part of the broader effort by the national Democratic party to rehabilitate itself from the discredit it suffered as a result of the Civil War, when its temporizing leadership brought it into disrepute. The party faced a long road back, as the election results testified. Of the sixteen presidential contests following the Civil War, from 1868 through 1928, Democratic candidates won only four times.

The partisan divide was defined vividly if somewhat hyperbolically by Massachusetts senator George Hoar, an eloquent foe of corruption and a champion of civil rights and civil liberties. Asked by a foreign visitor near the turn of the nineteenth century to explain the differences between the Democrats and his fellow Republicans, Hoar replied: "The men who do the work of piety and charity in our churches, the men who administer our school system, the men who own and till their own farms, the men who perform skilled labor in the shops, the soldiers, the men who went to war and stayed all through . . . find their places in the Republican Party. While the old slave owner and slave driver, the saloon keeper, the ballot box stuffer, the Ku Klux Klan, the criminal class of the great cities, the men who cannot read or write find their congenial places in the Democratic Party."

A path out of this abyss was provided the Democrats by two related trends that began in the late nineteenth century and continued into the twentieth: the flood tide of immigration and the mushrooming growth of urban America. Spearheading the Democratic renaissance was Al Smith of New York, Roosevelt's onetime ally and more recently his rival. Born in one of New York City's tenements, Smith's own family with its German and Italian as well as Irish bloodlines was almost as much a melting pot as his native city. Like his fellow Democrats, he reached out to the cities and the polyglot mass of immigrants who lived there in large part because, given the political environment described by Senator Hoar, the Democrats had nowhere else to turn.

Slowly but surely the Democratic return on these efforts became visible in the ballot box, particularly in Smith's rise to the governorship of what was then the nation's largest state. The greatest response came from the largest groups then in the late stages of immigration, Irish and Italian Catholics. Jews, for their part, had been attracted to the Republican banner beginning with the Civil War and the Lincoln presidency, and many, particularly the wealthier German Jews, stayed with the GOP well into the twentieth century. As late as 1912 President William Howard Taft told a meeting of the B'nai B'rith's Anti-Defamation League that Jews "make the best Republicans." But steadily the Jews followed other immigrant groups into the burgeoning Democratic tent. They were drawn particularly by Smith, with whom they felt a kinship as a fellow victim of bigotry, offsetting their resentment of the virulent anti-Semitism expressed by some Irish Catholics in the Democratic party. So Jews, most of whom had voted for the Republican Warren Harding in the 1920 presidential election, by 1928 gave an estimated 72 percent of their support to Smith for president. They would offer FDR an even greater margin, 82 percent, in 1932.

As governor of New York, Smith had not only pushed through legislative reforms that improved the living and working conditions of Jews and other urban immigrants, he had also appointed Jews to key offices. Belle Moskowitz, a striking-looking Jewish woman, became his most trusted political adviser. Thus in staffing the federal government with Jews, Roosevelt followed a path blazed by his predecessor as governor of New York and standard-bearer of the Democratic party. In the Roosevelt administration Jews, mostly lawyers but also economists and social welfare professionals, would be given substantial responsibilities not because they were Jewish but because they were talented. As the New Deal took root in the nation's capital, Jews by one rough reckoning comprised about 15 percent of the "most important intellectuals," in government and out, associated with the Roosevelt administration. Of particular note was the handful who, as the New Deal developed, would be seen as particularly close to Roosevelt and said to have special influence with him. They fell into a category dubbed the "President's Jews" by the Israeli scholar Gulie Néeman Arad, a term recalling the so-called Court Jews of eighteenth-century Europe.

Like the Court Jews, bankers and businessmen who had served Central European monarchs in the late Renaissance, FDR's Jews had no official mandate to speak for or to the Jewish community. Initially their religion was merely coincidental to their relationship with Roosevelt. But as the Nazi menace to

European Jews steadily mounted, their identity as Jews brought an added dimension to their relationship with the president and gave them in the eyes of many Jews outside Washington enlarged importance. The most prestigious was Louis D. Brandeis, whom Woodrow Wilson had named as the first Jewish Supreme Court justice, and who as a sitting justice of the high Court found occasion to advise the president and others in the executive branch—despite his professed devotion to the principles of judicial propriety. Next in prominence was Felix Frankfurter, Harvard law professor and early Roosevelt confidant, who would not join the federal government until six years into his presidency when Roosevelt appointed him to the Supreme Court. In somewhat similar circumstances was Sam Rosenman, officially a New York state judge, courtesy of an appointment by then Governor Roosevelt, whose true significance lay in his role as FDR's chief speechwriter and a leading general adviser. Next in importance, though often overlooked by outsider Jews, was the only cabinet member among the President's Jews, Treasury Secretary Henry Morgenthau. An old Dutchess County neighbor of Roosevelt's, in this group Morgenthau was probably closest to the president personally. Finally there was Benjamin V. Cohen, a relative newcomer to Roosevelt's inner circle, who would gain access to the Oval Office because of his skill as a legislative craftsman.

For all the speculation, some of it wishful, about their behind-the-scenes relationship with the president, it was hard to tell how much real weight these men carried with the president. Certainly none of them would discuss such matters publicly, and even among themselves their utterances were discreet to the extreme. Rarely did they refer to Roosevelt by his name or the title of his office, instead adopting various sobriquets, the most common being "the skipper," an allusion to Roosevelt's strong interest in things nautical.

This Jewish presence in the Roosevelt administration, symbolized by the President's Jews, would prove to be a mixed blessing for FDR and for American Jews. It would furnish ammunition to anti-Semitic critics of the New Deal, who coined the epithet "Jew Deal" to stigmatize Roosevelt's program and his Jewish advisers. At the same time the supposed influence of the President's Jews fostered the hopes of American Jews at a crucial historical moment when the rise of Adolf Hitler and the National Socialist movement he had founded posed the gravest threat to Jewry since the pogroms of the Russian tsars. Over the next dozen years the menace of Nazism would darken, creating a test of will and conscience that would indelibly stamp the record of the President's Jews, cast a long shadow over Roosevelt's own legacy, and lead to a tragedy surpassing all others in the star-crossed history of the Chosen People.

For the present moment in the early 1930s, this terrible new danger sharpened a quandary that American Jews had faced since they had begun arriving in the United States in substantial numbers, half a century earlier. On one hand, Jews urgently sought recognition as fully privileged Americans. On the other hand, they just as urgently wished to maintain their traditions, their faith, and their bonds to Jews in the lands they had left. Both drives were part of a quest for survival. Newly arrived Jews soon discovered that America, for all the wonders it promised, placed a high value on acceptance of its national standards and mores. The new homeland officially welcomed immigrants more or less freely. But unofficially America demanded from these strangers, first and foremost, allegiance to American values. The demand for assimilation seemed to threaten the Jewish commitment to their more than four thousand years of history and their sense of community. Some wondered about the benefits of surviving as Americans if they should lose their identity as Jews.

This was no easy question to answer, given their collective experience in the United States. Although Jews liked to think

of their adopted land as the *goldene medine*, the golden country, their sojourn had not always been bright and shiny. They
had been buffeted by storms from without and within, at times
chastened by the hostility of strangers and at other times undermined by bitter disagreements among themselves.

The first self-acknowledged Jews to come to America arrived
in New Amsterdam in 1654. There were twenty-three of them—
four couples, two widows, and thirteen children—refugees from
the city of Recife in Brazil. They had gone there when the Dutch
seized it from the Portuguese in 1630, but it had proven less
hospitable when Portugal took over. Their journey to America
prefigured the frustration that some coreligionists fleeing Nazi
persecution would suffer three centuries later. Sailing originally for the islands of the Caribbean, they first made port in
Cuba and Jamaica. Authorities there refused to allow them to
remain, roughly the same treatment notoriously rendered by
twentieth-century officialdom to the thousand refugees fleeing
Nazi Germany in the ship *St. Louis.*

The Jews' presence in New Amsterdam took on significance
chiefly because, after early difficulties, they won a sort of grudg-
ing acceptance, a pattern that was to become familiar for later
arrivals. Things did not begin well. Peter Stuyvesant, the cur-
mudgeonly Dutch governor whose ill-fitting peg leg was said
to worsen his disposition, wanted them gone. Stuyvesant was
no champion of religious freedom. He had cracked down on
Quakers and tortured one of their preachers. But the reasons
he gave for commanding an exodus of his Jewish visitors were
economic rather than theological. The cranky governor viewed
the Jewish immigrants as likely to become a financial burden on
the hard-pressed community of only one thousand. "Owing to
their present indigence they might become a charge in the coming winter," he warned the directors of the Dutch West Indies
Company, which had founded the colony. This same concern,
that Jewish immigrants would be unable to support themselves,
would be used to bar would-be refugees from Hitler's Europe

three hundred years later. But in seventeenth-century New Amsterdam it was brushed aside by the intervention of Jewish investors in the West Indies Company who forced Stuyvesant to suffer the presence of the refugees, however indigent.

Those Jews who followed in the footsteps of the New Amsterdam arrivals confronted similar problems wherever they went in the American colonies, whether among the Puritans of New England or the more traditional Protestants in the South. The Puritans, who considered themselves the true Jews and the ultimate beneficiaries of the promises God had made to his Chosen People, could not abide the presence in the New World of these "pretenders from the Old World." But the tenets of their faith presented the Puritans with a conundrum, for they believed that the Second Coming could not occur unless most Jews were converted, and that seemed impossible as long as most remained out of their reach in Europe. Thus the Puritans could not abandon their absorption with the Jews, whom they continued to view as linked to their hoped-for return of the Messiah. One of the foremost Puritan scholars, Cotton Mather, the progenitor of the Salem witch trials, took to wearing a skull cap and calling himself "rabbi," all the while pressing for the conversion of the Jews to Christianity.

Jewish acceptance in the New World was hindered not only by suspicion of their religion but by understandable doubts, first voiced by Peter Stuyvesant, about their ability to survive economically. The Jewish newcomers were mostly merchants, shopkeepers, and tradesmen in a land that needed farmers to till the soil. Most were Sephardim, from Spanish and Portuguese backgrounds, who ultimately would be outnumbered by the Ashkenazim Jews from Central and Eastern Europe.

For all their lack of agricultural aptitude, however, the merchants among them, along with Christians of the same calling, helped develop commerce in the early port cities of the colonies. The principal locations included New York but also Philadelphia, Boston, and Charleston. Indeed, in the early nineteenth century Charleston would become home to the largest Jewish community in the newly independent nation. By the time of the Revolution about two thousand Jews lived in the thirteen colonies, with synagogues in Charleston, New York, and Philadelphia. Their circumstances attracted little attention because their numbers were so small. But that situation began to change with the industrialization in Europe that marked the second third of the nineteenth century. In the Old World, discrimination against Jews mounted, limiting their freedom, threatening their welfare, and spurring greater migration to America. There industrialization was also under way, though on a far broader landscape that offered Jews more liberty and opportunity.

In the 1820s a great influx of population began that was to sweep over the United States and during the course of the next hundred years reshape the country. Part of this immigration included Jews whose arrival transformed Jewish life in America and changed the way Americans viewed the Jews among them. From 1820 to 1870 the Jewish population of the United States grew to more than 250,000, mostly Ashkenazim from Germany and neighboring parts of Central Europe. These newly arrived Germans did not fuse with their native brothers and sisters in the faith. Unlike earlier Jewish immigrants who had only tenuous ties to the lands they left, this new crop saw themselves as Germans at least as much as Jews. Eager to break away from the rigid limits that went with their identification as Jews in the old country, they promptly joined German-American institutions that gave them entry to the larger society of their adopted country.

The mobility of Jewish immigrants was fostered by the thrust toward social openness and economic development that were dominant features of the *zeitgeist* of pre–Civil War America. Its citizens were determined to fulfill what many regarded as their manifest destiny, and welcomed all the help they could get. It was a spirit epitomized by the new president John Tyler in 1841 when he invited people of other countries "to come and settle among us as members of our rapidly growing family, and for the blessings which we offer them we require of them to look upon our country as their country and to unite with us in the great task of preserving our institutions and thereby perpetuating our liberties."

With such rhetoric ringing in their ears, it was not hard to understand why German Jews came to believe they would be free from the prejudices and stereotypes of the past. Counting on being able to pursue their own destinies, they spread themselves around the country, with clusters in Wisconsin, Michigan, Pennsylvania, and Ohio. And they entered a great variety of occupations as retail merchants and ultimately as bankers and large-scale businessmen, with their dispersion abetting their assimilation and success.

But the speedy absorption of German Jews in the years before the Civil War created problems. Many Jews feared that assimilation fostered intermarriage and defection from the Jewish community. As members of the second generation of German Jews grew to maturity, some scholars worried that in their eagerness to be Americanized they would turn their backs completely on their immigrant heritage, including their religion. To stem this threat in the post–Civil War era, leaders of the German-Jewish community sought to hasten the adaptation of Jewish religious patterns to American conditions. These efforts culminated in 1885 when rabbis from a dozen congregations met in Pittsburgh and adopted a drastic revision of traditional Jewish teachings. The new approach reflected contemporary American idealism and Protestant liberalism, de-emphasizing the Talmud and stressing the American faith in progress. The dream of Zion, a Jewish homeland in Palestine, was all but forgotten.

This was the profile of Reform Judaism. But many congregations, while willing to accept the more practical procedural changes sponsored by the Reform movement, balked at theological innovations. The result was another schism in American Jewry. Just as the Reform movement broke away from old-school Orthodox Jewry, a new group of Jews unwilling to abandon traditional theology split from the Reform movement and called themselves Conservatives.

Meanwhile new tensions arose among American Jewry stemming from the mass migration of a new wave of Ashkenazim, these from Eastern Europe, beginning in 1881. For the next forty years, until Congress rejected the welcoming philosophy expressed by President Tyler and wrote the first exclusionary immigration laws, some 20 million immigrants entered the United States. About 2.5 million of these were Jewish. Their arrival challenged the existing Jewish population and once again greatly metamorphosed the American Jewish community.

It was not hard to understand why the immigrants fled Eastern Europe. There they had lived under what the writer Irving Howe called a condition "of permanent precariousness." The world outside the *shtetls*, the villages in which they dwelled, offered little but hostility and brute force, threatening their faith and their existence. "The Jew has no available means for improving his condition as long as he lives among alien peoples," wrote the Yiddish literary critic Ba'al Makhshoves. The Jews, Makhshoves noted, "regard themselves as a chosen people, and they live like dogs."

As bad as the Jewish plight was, it worsened measurably after the assassination of Tsar Alexander II in 1881. The chaos that followed ended the reforms that Alexander had promoted and left the Russian masses facing rising prices and soaring unemployment. They vented their rage against the easiest available target, the Jews. And on top of the pogroms which killed scores of Jews, the government of the slain tsar's successor, Alexander III, forced them out of the villages where they had eked out a living.

And so they abandoned their homeland and crossed the ocean. But when they sought to reorder their lives in a strange place, they found that the change they had so desperately sought in some ways imposed another kind of torment. "The alien who comes here from Europe brings with him a deep-rooted tradition, a system of cultures and tastes and habits," wrote Marcus Ravage in his chronicle of the experience. "And it is this thing, this entire Old World soul of his—that comes in conflict with America as soon as he has landed."

This sense of estrangement bordering on despair was not uncommon. "Curse you immigration!" cried the journalist Abraham Cahan in a letter written for a Russian newspaper in 1922. "Accursed are the conditions that have brought you forth. How many lives have you broken, how many brave and mighty have you rubbed in the dust?"

The circumstances under which the new immigrants lived made such anguish inevitable. On New York's lower East Side, where many huddled, peril was ubiquitous and constant. Gangs of German youth struck at them from the north, Irish from the south. In between such forays they were left to fend off the congestion of their own *landsmen* and the consequent assault of a concatenation of disturbing sights, smells, and noises. The social and religious norms that had once governed their lives were shattered by the tumult and tension of urban America.

It was all very well for Americans to boast of the material benefits of rigorous striving. But these putative rewards had little meaning for immigrants trapped in sweatshops and isolated from the language and mores of the bustling New World. In the New York of those days, the sweatshops of the clothing trades were jammed together in the streets near their homes, making it easy for Jews to find their way to work in a strange city. And their bosses were often willing to allow the Jews to work on Sunday so they could take Saturday off, a concession that the Jews were forced to pay for in many other ways. Many of their bosses were Jews too, usually German Jews, and eager to exploit the greenhorn workers. This natural conflict between worker and boss contributed to the pervasive cultural tensions between East European and German Jews.

But there were plenty of other reasons for the hostility that greeted the East Europeans, not only from German Jews but from Gentile Americans. Indeed, the overall response to this new wave of immigrants, which would amount to the greatest movement of Jews since their expulsion by the Spanish Inquisition in the fifteenth century, was complex and ambivalent. It reflected competing strands of self-interest. The new economic barons who emerged in the post–Civil War economic expansion welcomed the latest influx of Jews, along with other immigrants, as a source of cheap and readily exploitable labor. But the fading economic elite of New England and the populists of the South and West resented and feared them because they were part of the threat posed by the new economic order to their own survival.

Caught in this maelstrom of social and economic tensions were the German Jews. They viewed the anti-Semitism and nativism generated by the flood of newcomers as imperiling their own shaky status as Americans, and so they sought to separate themselves from the East Europeans. The resentment against Jews, particularly the most recent arrivals from Eastern Europe, intensified and took on greater potency amid the economic turmoil of the 1890s. The Jews then became perceived not only as believers in an alien faith and competitors for employment but also as threats to dominate the economy. Early in history, anti-Semitism had been linked to issues of money and credit. In America, as far back as the Panic of 1837, when foreign bankers foreclosed on the obligations of many destitute state governments, Mississippi's chief executive Alexander McNutt, in condemning Baron Rothschild, head of the powerful banking family, declared: "The blood of Judas and Shylock flows in his veins, and he unites the qualities of both his countrymen."

As the century advanced and immigrants, including many Jews, poured in, the anti-Semitic chorus swelled. New England Brahmins, notably Henry Adams, picked up the refrain. "With communism I would exist tolerably well," he wrote a friend. "But in a society made up for Jews and brokers, with maniacs wild for gold, I could not exist."

But it was the prophets of populism, the writers and politicians of the era who sounded these themes most blatantly. The advocates of a silver-based currency to remedy the supposed tyranny of gold viewed Jews as the key element of a conspiracy that imposed gold-based commerce on the world, to the detriment of mankind. This attitude was implicitly expressed in the speech with which William Jennings Bryan electrified the 1896 Democratic National Convention and made himself its nominee. The linchpin of Bryan's candidacy was his plea to ease the plight of debtor farmers by adopting silver as at least a partial substitute for gold as the basis of U.S. commerce. Although at times he inveighed against prejudice, in his most memorable address Bryan not only railed against the gold standard, to which Jews were supposedly linked, but also alluded to the execution of Christ, the most infamous Jewish crime of all in the minds of anti-Semites. "You shall not crucify mankind upon a cross of gold," he warned supporters of the gold standard. "You shall not press down a crown of thorns on the brow of labor." The anti-Semitism evoked by this metaphor, as the Judaic scholar Leonard Dinnerstein points out, appealed powerfully to rural Protestants.

The dangers raised by rising anti-Semitism in their adopted land helped focus the energies of American Jews to do what they could in stemming the Eastern European tide. In 1891 the Jewish financier Joseph Seligman, who had helped fund the Union effort against the Confederacy, led a group of other prominent

Jews to seek the help of President Benjamin Harrison in easing the persecution of Jews in Russia and Rumania. Wary of appearing too "international" and thus not sufficiently "American," they did not build their case on the welfare of these alien Jews. Rather, they stressed the urgency of avoiding the problems that would plague the United States (and, though they didn't mention it, resident American Jews) if brutal treatment compelled Eastern European Jews to cross the ocean.

Out of respect for the standing of his visitors, Harrison agreed to appoint a commission to investigate. But the commission did nothing to reverse the momentum of the exodus from Europe. The episode was less significant for what it accomplished than for what it revealed about the cautious mind-set of established Jewish leadership in America.

More than a decade later, following a particularly horrific pogrom in Kishinev, the capital of the then Russian province of Bessarabia, American Jews once again appealed to their government on behalf of persecuted foreign Jews. The Kishinev outrage was triggered by the murder of a boy in a nearby town, which anti-Semitic newspapers blamed on the Jews. During three days of rioting nearly fifty Jews were killed, several hundred wounded, and seven hundred houses looted and destroyed. "The Jews were taken wholly unaware and were slaughtered like sheep," the *New York Times* reported.

Once again a delegation of Jewish leaders called on an American president, this time Theodore Roosevelt, who responded with a high-level brush-off. The United States could not protest, he explained, because "unless we mean to do something further it would seem like an effort to gain votes." Unpersuaded by this somewhat elliptical reasoning, the Jewish leaders presented Roosevelt with a petition, which they asked him to forward to the Russian government. As Roosevelt's secretary of state John Hay had predicted, the Russian ambassador would not even accept the petition. The document, suitably bound, was placed in the

State Department's archives, representing what Hay called "a consolation prize." With notable condescension, Hayes praised the petition for its "language so earnest and eloquent and yet so dignified, so moderate and decorous." It would be "a valuable addition to public literature," he added, and would be "sacredly cherished among the treasures of this department."

Meanwhile oppression and immigration continued. In October 1905, two years after the first pogrom in Kishinev, a second erupted in the same city. Beginning as a protest against the tsar, the riots turned into a wholesale attack on Jews; nineteen were killed and three score injured. Spurred by this continued persecution, half a million Russian Jews arrived in the United States between 1903 and 1908. Leading German-American Jews, notably Oscar Strauss, Theodore Roosevelt's commerce secretary, and Benjamin Schiff, banker and financier, organized a relief committee.

This sort of humanitarianism bolstered the effort by German Jews to confirm their leadership of American Jewry. It was crowned in 1906 by the creation of an organization to defend and advocate Jewish interests. The new group, the American Jewish Committee, was the first such American organization created to defend the rights of an ethnic-religious group.

The Committee's strategy and thinking were greatly shaped by one of its prime organizers and its second president, a renowned attorney named Louis Marshall. Fifty years old at the time of the Committee's founding, Marshall grew up in Syracuse, New York, the son of Bavarian immigrants whose struggle to make ends meet marked his early life. At the age of eight he began helping his father in his small fur business, keeping books and cleaning the floors. His mother never learned to speak English but knew three other languages, which she taught her son. Ultimately Louis would speak all the major modern languages in addition to a grasp of Latin, Greek, Hebrew, and Yiddish.

A bookish youngster, he joined a debate club at twelve. There arguments about constitutional principles and the role of government kindled his ambition to study law. Two years after he graduated from high school, Marshall entered Columbia University Law School and finished the two-year course in one year. He was admitted to the New York Bar at age twenty-one, joined a leading Syracuse law firm, and soon became a partner. In eighteen years of practice in Syracuse he set a record by arguing no fewer than 150 cases in the New York Court of Appeals, involving every branch of jurisprudence. It was also said of Marshall—who ultimately became a partner in a major New York City law firm—that he appeared in more cases before the United States Supreme Court than anyone at the time, except for lawyers representing the government itself. Cyrus Adler, a close associate and scholar of Semitics, described Marshall as "an American, a Republican, a law-abiding lawyer, a citizen of the Old School."

It was largely because of Marshall that the American Jewish Committee set itself up as the defender of Jewish liberties, with its charter proclaiming its mission to protect the civil and religious rights of Jews "in any part of the world." If the German Jews did not take this step, Marshall warned, other "objectionable" elements would. The underlying elitism of this approach was reflected in the Committee's organizational statement, which emphasized that its strength stemmed not from numbers but from the quality and status of its carefully selected membership.

The first test of the Committee's charter came a few years after its birth when it launched a protest campaign against the U.S. commercial treaty with Russia, which dated to 1832. The attack on the treaty was prompted by the Russian persecution of Jews and more specifically by the tsarist government's refusal to honor the passports of Jewish Americans. The Committee contended that by going along with the Russian edict, Washington was enforcing a test of religious discrimination against a million or more of its citizens. At first the Committee tried to persuade President Theodore Roosevelt and Democratic party leaders to use diplomatic pressure on the Russians to halt the offensive policy. But when this led nowhere the Committee shifted its objective from diplomatic protest to abrogation of the old treaty. A key to the Committee's strategy was to frame its demand as a plea to protect American interests in general, not just the rights of Jews. Underlying the approach was the argument that the U.S. threat to void the treaty would force the Russians to lessen persecution of Jews, which would diminish the flow of Jewish immigrants to America from Russia. This point was made directly to the Republican presidential candidate, William Howard Taft, who won the White House in 1908.

When President Taft promised only to study the matter, the Committee stepped up its lobbying as the 1912 election approached. The Democrats set out to make what political hay they could. In December 1911 the Democratic-controlled House of Representatives passed a resolution denouncing the treaty by a 300-to-1 margin. Although the Republican Senate followed suit, and Taft agreed to go along, the Democrats claimed credit for pushing Taft to the brink and over.

A year later, thanks in good measure to Democratic agitation, the treaty was a dead letter. For their part, the Russians were stunned by this repudiation of commercial interests by the strange republic across the sea. "Astonishment that the American government has responded so readily to the Jewish outcry," was the prevalent sentiment in the Duma, the Russian parliament, the *Los Angeles Times* reported. "The opinion is expressed by members of the Duma that in all probability the Jews will attempt to force matters further."

Actually the architects of this success that so amazed the Russians had no such ambitious program in mind. Despite the Russian view of the U.S. government as obeisant to the Jews, American Jewish Committee leaders well knew they had spent the better part of a decade getting the job done. Their future goals were limited by their understanding of the realities that had made their success possible. Their key argument against the treaty was that it should be abrogated not for the sake of the Jews but for the benefit of all American citizens. And probably the most potent if unspoken argument for this claim was that easing the plight of the Russian Jews would help spare the United States the burden that came with further Jewish migration—and not incidentally, though left to be inferred, thus protect the still-emerging role of German Jews in American society.

Despite their success in the battle over the treaty, American Jews still faced two fundamental problems that far overshadowed the hard-gained victory. One was the continuing flood of immigration, especially from Eastern Europe, which was bound to stir intense feelings against foreigners in general and Jews in particular. A second problem, resulting from the first, was the bitter conflict over the future role of Jews in America between German Jews, led by Louis Marshall, and Eastern European Jews, whose champion, a relative newcomer on the Jewish national scene, was Rabbi Stephen Wise of New York.

Himself an Eastern European Jew, almost twenty years younger than Marshall, gifted not only with eloquence but with a flair for self-promotion, Wise had made himself the most prominent rabbi in the country and in the eyes of many Jews their new prophet. He viewed as "stupid" and self-defeating the tendency of German Jews to blame the newer immigrants for the upsurge in feelings against them and to press for their assimilation. This was a mistake, Wise claimed, because to a large degree the *goyim* did not bother to distinguish one Jew from another. The Gentile world, he contended, "sees a minimum of difference between Jew and Jew and lumps all together with very much more justice than we Jews separate ourselves from one another."

To better serve the Eastern European Jews, Wise organized the American Jewish Congress, which by reaching out to the newer immigrants sought a broader base of support than the American Jewish Committee. This stirred alarms and protest among the German Jews leading the Committee. They argued that the Congress, by its very existence, would reinforce the always-present suspicions of the Gentiles that the American Jewish community was tantamount to a state within a state. "We will become Jews first and Americans second," warned Jacob Schiff, one of the old-line leaders. Perhaps so. But underlying the objections of Schiff and Louis Marshall was their fear that Wise's Congress would supplant the established leadership of their Committee.

Wise wanted to be a unifying figure for American Jewry. This meant overcoming the opposition of German Jewish leaders while stirring the interest of Eastern European Jews—a challenge that required a source of intellectual and emotional energy more powerful even than his own compelling personality and rhetoric. And for this he turned, in the fateful summer of 1914, as Europe was being engulfed by the cataclysm of world war, to the rising cause of Zionism. It was a decision that would bring great benefits both for the growth of Wise's Congress and for the spread of Zionism. The luminous goal of a national homeland in the Land of Israel provided much of the inspiration for Jews to enlist in the Congress, just as the Congress provided an organizational framework for their pursuit of Zionism.

Not that Wise was a newcomer to the Zionist cause. He had been caught up with the idea soon after the birth of modern Zionism in 1897 with the first Zionist congress in Basel, Switzerland. Its chief progenitor, the Viennese journalist Theodor Herzl, had been stirred to action by the Dreyfus Case. In the wake of the French army's wrongful conviction of Captain Alfred Dreyfus on charges of treason and the subsequent surge of anti-Semitism in France and elsewhere, Herzl became convinced that the Jewish hope for acceptance in the Western democracies was a delusion. The only solution, he felt, was a Jewish national homeland, ideally in Palestine.

But for all of Herzl's passion, many American Jews turned a deaf ear to his trumpet. In Western Europe, despite the Dreyfus case, many Jews refused to abandon their efforts of more than a century to win acceptance as citizens of their adopted lands, whether England, France, or Germany. American Jews by and large were even more resistant. Many chose to believe that they did not need a national homeland; America itself was the promised land. This was particularly true for Reform Jews, of whom Wise was a principal leader, who viewed the mission of Judaism as universal, not to be limited by a nationalist objective. But Wise, who despite his Eastern European roots had been drawn to Reform Judaism by its emphasis on social action, was also inspired by the passion of Herzl. And so he became a notable exception to the Reform movement's rejection of Zionism. Even so, frustrated by a failure to win wider support and by infighting among the leaders of various Zionist groups, Wise had turned his energies elsewhere.

The revival of Wise's interest in Zionism and of the vitality of the movement in general was due largely to the efforts of one man, Louis Dembitz Brandeis. Widely regarded as the most gifted lawyer in the country, by the time of World War I Brandeis had also become the preeminent American voice for the Zionist cause. Wise recognized in Brandeis, with his intellectual brilliance and pragmatic grasp of politics, a star to whom he could hitch his wagon. He joined with him in promoting the Zionist cause. But just as Brandeis and Wise launched a push for Zionism, their efforts were disrupted by the outbreak of the Great War. Forced to move its headquarters to the United States, the World Zionist Organization chose Brandeis to head its operating committee.

As it turned out, the war would bring benefits to the Zionist cause in part because of Brandeis's role as a trusted adviser to President Woodrow Wilson. Shrewd advocate that he was, Brandeis did not find it hard to convince Wilson that the Zionist goal of a national homeland for Jews was congruent with the principle of national self-determination embedded in Wilson's war aims. Even before Wilson spelled out his Fourteen Points in 1918, Brandeis had gained Wilson's support for Great Britain's Balfour Declaration of 1917, pledging the creation of a national homeland for the Jewish people in Palestine.

By war's end Louis Marshall and other leaders of the American Jewish Committee softened their opposition to the upstart American Jewish Congress. When the Congress held its first meeting in December 1919 in Philadelphia, Wise was in Paris, on assignment from President Wilson to head the Zionist delegation to the peace talks. But his old adversary Louis Marshall was on hand in Philadelphia to address the Congress's opening session. "We here in America sympathize with every Jewish aspiration," Marshall declared. And he won cheers when he declared that "it would be a privilege to assist in the rehabilitation of the land of our fathers." For American Jews, marching under the banner of unity, the future never seemed brighter.

This euphoria barely lasted into the first postwar decade. The idealism generated by Wilson's "world safe for democracy" rhetoric collapsed, just as did his hopes for U.S. participation in the League of Nations. America's new mission became not to save the world but to preserve and promote the benefits of Americanism, a crusade dominated by untrammeled individualism, grasping materialism, and pervasive mistrust of the foreign-born. Feeding the xenophobia were two postwar traumas: economic hard times created by the difficulties of converting a wartime economy to peacetime needs, and the great Red Scare. This paranoid anti-radical crusade was triggered by Wilson's attorney general A. Mitchell Palmer, who saw an unmistakable link between subversives and the foreign-born, and viewed the connection as a way to boost his political ambitions. Describing those caught in his effort to preserve the republic, Palmer resorted to phrenology. "Out of the sly and crafty eyes of many of them leap cupidity, cruelty, insanity and crime," he declared. "From their lopsided faces, sloping brows and misshapen features they may be recognized as the unmistakable criminal type."

Egged on by such rhetoric, Congress quickly pushed through the Emergency Restriction Act of 1921. Although the nature of the emergency was unclear, the purposes of the act were: to stop the incursion of the foreign-born and to freeze the ethnic makeup of the United States as it had been in 1910. Quotas based on national origins were instituted in 1921 as a temporary measure, and total immigration was limited to approximately 350,000 per year, with immigration from each country in any given year limited to 3 percent of all nationals from the country who were living in the United States during the 1910 census. By 1924 Congress tightened the screws on Eastern Europeans and particularly Jews even further. The base year was shifted to 1890, when the massive influx of Jews and other Eastern Europeans was just beginning. And the quota formulas were cut from 3 percent to 2 percent.

The Jews cried out in pain. "Chauvinistic nationalism is rampant," complained Louis Marshall. But the Protestant majority was driven by its own agenda, based on a racism it was frank to acknowledge. Calvin Coolidge, about to be sworn in as vice president and only three years away from the White House, declared that "biological laws show us that Nordics deteriorate when mixed up with other races." And a chilling warning to those who had recently passed through the Golden Door came from Herbert Hoover, secretary of commerce in 1924 when the new national origins law passed, who in four years would be elected president. "Immigrants now live in the United States on sufferance," he said, "and would be tolerated only if they behaved."

Jewish anxieties aroused by the rhetoric and actions of the nation's political leaders were exacerbated by the fuel poured on the flames of anti-Semitism by the country's leading industrialist, Henry Ford. His path to anti-Semitism illuminates the roots of this obsession and the broader xenophobia that seized many of his countrymen in the years just after the Great War. Ford's campaign was all the more pernicious because he was regarded as an American icon, embodying the values that the nation had learned to cherish.

A self-made success in business, upright and unpretentious, Ford had been born in 1863 in Michigan, which was still a rural land when he grew to manhood. There people resented the burgeoning new cities and clung to those ideals cherished by folks who lived in the countryside, as preached by McGuffey's *Readers*: hard work, conformity, and success, all based on an unquestioning belief in the truth of the Bible and an omnipresent God. The *Readers* used stories from the Scripture to inculcate these values. They also condemned Jews for not accepting Christianity, depicting them as greedy moneylenders who were somehow different and dirtier than the rest of humanity.

Emerging from this background, Ford saw American life and values threatened by dark forces, principally Jews and Communists. To get this message across, the auto tycoon bought a newspaper published in a Detroit suburb, the *Dearborn Independent*, which blamed the Jews for starting the war and trying to manipulate the economy to advance their own interests. In 1920 the *Independent* began publishing a series of articles under the title "The International Jew," which portrayed Jews as monolithic, malicious schemers plotting to control the planet. The articles were based in part on *The Protocols of the Learned Elders of Zion*, supposedly the record of a secret Zionist meeting in Switzerland, where Jews had plotted to take control of the world. The *Protocols* were in fact well known to be a forgery created by the tsar's secret police, but that did not alter the effect they had on people already suspicious of Jews and other immigrants.

Jews complained bitterly about Ford's handiwork, as did some prominent Gentiles, including former presidents Taft and Roosevelt, the black intellectual W. E. B. DuBois, and the renowned attorney Clarence Darrow. In response to the public outcry, Ford suspended printing the articles in 1922. But, missing the public spotlight, he resumed the onslaught in 1924, leading to a $1 million federal libel suit against him by Aaron Sapiro, leader of the farm cooperative movement. The legal battle raged until Louis Marshall entered the case. Fearful that the litigation would appear to be an attack on free speech and boomerang against the Jews, Marshall mediated an end to the suit. He dictated an apology by Ford, addressed not to Sapiro but to American Jewry in general.

Jews were so preoccupied with the new threats in what they had once thought to be their *goldene medine* that few paid much attention to signs of more serious trouble brewing in Germany. There resentment born out of the harshness of peace terms at Versailles, overwhelming inflation, and pervasive unemployment predictably found an outlet in anti-Semitism and helped launch Adolf Hitler and National Socialism. In 1923, coincident with Hitler's abortive *putsch* against the Weimar Republic, mobs in the tens of thousands attacked Jews and looted Jewish-owned stores.

While most American Jews looked the other way, Rabbi Wise vociferously expressed his concern. Secretary of State Charles Evans Hughes promised the matter would get his "careful attention." But no further statement or action was forthcoming, a response that would set a pattern for the State Department's stance on such episodes for years to come.

As anti-Semitism burgeoned and Nazism flourished, most Americans, Jew and Gentile alike, seemed impervious to the danger. When in September 1930 the Nazis emerged from the Reichstag elections as Germany's second-largest party, America's leading newspaper, the *New York Times,* somehow concluded that "the menace of Adolf Hitler has been greatly exaggerated." But in Germany events moved in Hitler's favor, far more swiftly and ominously than the *Times* had imagined. Fewer than two years after the *Times* had shrugged off the Nazi threat, in the July 1932 elections to the Reichstag the Nazis gained important headway.

When a few months later they lost ground in another vote, the most fervent Nazis urged Hitler to stage another *putsch*. But the future leader of the Third Reich shrewdly planned on coming to power legally and insisted he would accept nothing less than the chancellorship. Meanwhile, in that worst winter of the Great Depression, economic chaos spread throughout Germany as everywhere else in the world, including the United States. Nazi storm troopers roamed the streets beating Jews and establishing mob rule. A group of frightened industrialists persuaded the country's eighty-four-year-old president and war hero, Paul Hindenburg, to make Hitler chancellor. On January 30, 1933, during the long U.S. interregnum, while President-elect Franklin Roosevelt was drafting his inaugural address, Hitler got just what he wanted, the chancellorship of Germany by legal means. He immediately decreed an end to political opposition parties. And after a fire gutted the Reichstag building a month later, he convinced a frightened Hindenburg to suspend all civil rights of the citizenry, an edict that was never lifted during the years of Nazi rule.

With new elections called, Hitler staged mass arrests while truckloads of storm troopers rampaged through the streets, broke into homes, rounded up victims, including many Jews, and took them to the storm troopers' barracks where they were beaten and tortured. In the Reichstag elections that followed, the Nazis received 44 percent of the vote and emerged as Germany's unchallenged rulers. In one of history's bizarre coincidences the date was March 5, 1933, only twenty-four hours after Franklin Roosevelt was sworn in as the thirty-second President of the United States.

Not surprisingly, it was to this new leader of their adopted country that the thoughts and hopes of American Jews turned as their anxiety increased in the face of the alarming news from the Third Reich. But for all the positive impression that Roosevelt had made, experience had taught Jews to be cautious when asking American presidents to intervene on behalf of Jews abroad. Those with long memories could recall that thirty years earlier Jews had sought the help of another president named Roosevelt in the wake of the Kishinev pogrom and had been fobbed off with the "consolation prize" of having their petition preserved in the State Department archives. Their hopes now for a more constructive response rested in part on what they could ask from the inner circle of Roosevelt's Jewish advisers, the President's Jews—principally Justice Brandeis, Felix Frankfurter, Sam Rosenman, Morgenthau, and Ben Cohen.

In the end, of course, as the Jewish outsiders came to realize, what the President's Jews could do would depend on Roosevelt himself and how he chose to deal with the conflicting demands upon him. The outsiders saw Roosevelt as they wanted to see him, a man driven by deep-rooted humanitarianism and dedicated to the triumph of good over evil. But the Jewish insiders knew that the president, like most politicians, would be more inclined to act not to advance some lofty belief but to promote his own political interests. If they wanted to persuade him to do one thing or another, they needed to remember this was a man who considered himself to be far and away the best judge of his own interests, an appraisal amply supported by the evidence of his already remarkable career.

II

THE HIDDEN-HAND
SKIPPER

ROOSEVELT was as close to Henry Morgenthau, who would be his treasury secretary and had long been his Dutchess County neighbor, as to any man. Still there were limits to their friendship, as FDR himself made plain. "Never let your left hand know what your right is doing," he once told Morgenthau. "What hand am I?" Morgenthau wanted to know.

"My right hand," FDR replied, adding, "but I keep my left hand under the table."

The president's relationships with Morgenthau and his other Jewish friends and advisers suggest that he was largely free of the more rancid strains of anti-Semitism that infected many of his fellow Americans in that time. Still, he harbored some of the stereotypical views of minorities that stamped his social class. As one analysis of Roosevelt's immigration policies notes: "Some of FDR's best friends were anti-Semites," and some relatives too. More important in terms of public policy, whatever Roosevelt's own sentiments were he was well aware that millions of his constituents resented and disliked Jews to varying degrees. And this knowledge, along with other political realities, influenced his response to the growing danger enveloping European Jewry.

Perhaps just as serious an obstacle for American Jewish leaders who sought Roosevelt's intervention on behalf of the targets of Nazism was the president's resolute elusiveness, suggested by his insistence on keeping at least one hand hidden from view. This trait helped him navigate treacherous political shoals by keeping both friends and allies off guard while shielding himself from accountability.

"You know I am a juggler," Roosevelt said of himself, and indeed he liked to keep many balls in the air at once. That was the nub of the problem for advocates—in government and outside it—of the cause of Jewish refugees: the Skipper's sinuous decision-making. Despite the straightforward and lofty public image he projected, the nation's new chief executive proved to be a master of indirection and misdirection, a gift that helped him escape the normal penalties for inconsistency and self-contradiction.

As his tenure in the White House lengthened, this characteristic would become increasingly evident to those who worked closely with him. "His mind does not follow easily a consecutive chain of thought," his secretary of war, Henry Stimson, once noted in his diary, "but he is full of stories and incidents and hops about in his discussions from suggestion to suggestion and it is very much like chasing a vagrant beam of sunshine around a vacant room."

After vainly trying to get a straight answer out of the president on a key appointment, his interior secretary, Harold Ickes, exploded. "You won't talk frankly even with people who are loyal to you and of whose loyalty your are fully convinced," Ickes told Roosevelt. "Your keep your cards close up against your belly. You never put them on the table."

Roosevelt cloaked his guile with a personal charm reputed to be so overpowering that some political foes were said to shrink from private encounters with him lest they succumb to his wiles. At Harvard, editor Roosevelt got along so well with other *Crimson* staffers that his co-editor recalled, "in his geniality was a kind of frictionless command." His distant cousin, Anna Eleanor, who happened to be the favorite niece of then-president Theodore Roosevelt, was so captivated by his gaiety and natural ease that she married him in 1905, soon after his graduation from Harvard.

But after a while some found his personal appeal wearing thin. Rexford Tugwell, an early architect of the New Deal, thought Roosevelt's charm ultimately became "part of a whole apparatus of defense" designed to conceal his true beliefs. "He had a trick of seeming to listen, and to agree or to differ partly and pleasantly, which was flattering," he recalled. "This was more highly developed as he progressed in his career, and it was responsible for some misunderstanding. Finally no one could tell what he was *thinking*, to say nothing of what he was *feeling*." Among those he shut out of his life was his wife, who discovered that while Franklin was serving as assistant secretary of the navy during the Great War he had been conducting a romance with her part-time secretary, a graceful twentyish belle named Lucy Mercer. In 1918, with the war ending, Eleanor confronted her husband and threatened him with divorce. He tried to make little of the problem. "Don't be a goose," Roosevelt told his wife.

"I *was* a goose," the newly awakened Eleanor retorted, and refused to back down.

Roosevelt's mother, Sara, backed her daughter-in-law, warning she would cut Franklin off financially if he left his wife and children. Then, too, there was the question of how Theodore Roosevelt might feel toward cousin Franklin if he turned away from the niece of whom he was particularly fond. Roosevelt broke off the relationship with Lucy, preserving his marriage and his political future.*

Contributing to Roosevelt's tendency to deceive was his disability produced by polio, the extent of which he managed to keep from the public. Before his inauguration his longtime political operative, Louis Howe, inspected the hallways and doorways of the White House with an eye for locations where the president in his wheelchair might be exposed to view and to photographs by visitors. He sent Roosevelt's press secretary, Steve Early, to consult with the chief of the Secret Service, Colonel Ed Starling, a veteran of the last months of Woodrow Wilson's presidency when he too had been in a wheelchair. Howe's arrangements and later procedures helped ensure that most Americans had no more than a dim idea of the severity of the president's condition—that he actually spent most of his life in a wheelchair, that despite the help of his braces he could not stand erect without support, and that even with assistance he could walk only a few yards at most, usually along a well-planned route.

"We have nothing to fear but fear itself," FDR had declared with typical aplomb on taking the oath of office. It gave the nation a burst of hope. But that would not long sustain itself without strong and effective action by the new president. He was taking office in 1933 with the nation's economy in ruins, its social and civic institutions undermined, its populace demoralized, and its government seemingly helpless. Along with the other harm it had wrought, the depression had inflamed nativism and heightened anti-Semitism and resistance to immigration. And America's Jews, who read of the growing threat to Germany's Jews, worried how the fate of their brethren would

---

*Decades later, after Roosevelt had become president, his old flame, since married and widowed and now known as Lucy Mercer Rutherfurd, came back into his life. The two began seeing each other again in 1941, without Eleanor Roosevelt's knowledge. Lucy Rutherford was with FDR in Warm Springs, Georgia, when he died on April 12, 1945.

play out against these mounting tensions at home. Among themselves, the country's leaders and ordinary citizens, Jew and Gentile alike, asked the same question: Was Roosevelt up to the job?

The answer was by no means clear. But those searching for clues at the moment found it less rewarding to analyze his evanescent positions on issues and policies than to examine the profile of his personality and biography.

Certainly he had a fine pedigree as the cousin, however distant, of one of the nation's most vigorous chief executives. And he had shown remarkable fortitude in overcoming a crippling disease to become governor of the nation's largest state and then capture its highest office. But his campaign for the White House against the doomed incumbent, Herbert Hoover, offered few clues. FDR clearly enjoyed stumping more than propounding positions. "To Roosevelt a good cause does not justify any trip, a good trip justifies any cause," wrote Raymond Moley, one of the mainstays of the early New Deal's brain trust who wrote many of FDR's 1932 campaign speeches. "Campaigning for him was unadulterated joy. It was hands extended in welcome, voices warm with greeting, faces reflecting his smile along the interminable wayside."

Issues were another matter. Roosevelt brushed them aside unless they offered no risk. For the most part he sought to preserve his base of popular support while keeping his finger to the political winds. "No one who voted for him did it because he presented himself as learned or competent in all the matters he talked about," Rex Tugwell later pointed out. "They voted for the big easy smiling man who had no fear of failing at anything, who seemed capable even of saving sinners from themselves." In view of his healthy margin of victory—he won 57 percent of the popular vote and all but six states—Tugwell thought it a waste that Roosevelt had not been bolder and more explicit as a candidate. "The fact was that Franklin was continually accused by Hoover and others on the Republican side of intentions that were precisely those he should have proclaimed," he wrote. "He denied the accusations, only to reverse himself embarrassingly later on."

But for Roosevelt it was more important that he preserve the utmost flexibility. "It is a little bit like a football team that has a general plan of game against the other side," Roosevelt said early in his presidency, explaining his approach to economic policy to a group of White House reporters. "Now the captain and the quarterback of the team know pretty well what the next play is going to be and they know the general strategy of the team, but they cannot tell you what the play after the next play is going to be until the next play is run off. If the play makes ten yards, the succeeding play will be different from what it would have been if they had been thrown for a loss. I think that is the easiest way to explain it."

"A second-class intellect but a first-class temperament" was the famous judgment rendered by Oliver Wendell Holmes when he first encountered FDR as president-elect in 1933. It was Roosevelt's personality that came to define his presidency.

His most prominent trait was his supreme confidence in himself and his judgment. Just turned fifty when he took office, his handsome, patrician features, regal bearing, and strong, resonant voice all reflected his invincible self-assurance. "He must have been psychoanalyzed by God," a spellbound aide once remarked.

This self-confidence stemmed not from therapy but from breeding. It was rooted in a privileged upbringing as the only child of an indulgent father and a doting and domineering mother. His father, James, who was fifty-three when Franklin was born in 1882, rode to hounds and hosted afternoon teas and formal dinner parties at Springwood, his Hyde Park estate. Franklin's mother, Sara, a tall and stately beauty, was proud of her Huguenot Delano forebears who had set foot in the New

World even before the Dutch Roosevelts. "In the past—on both sides of your ancestry—they have a good record and have borne a good name," Franklin was reminded by his father.

James Roosevelt was worth about $300,000, hardly more than petty cash when compared to the holdings of some of his Hyde Park neighbors. Among them was Frederick W. Vanderbilt, who had inherited from his grandfather Commodore Vanderbilt, the shipping and rail tycoon, an estate of more than $70 million, including a lavish Italian Renaissance mansion which dwarfed the seventeen-room home of the Roosevelts. With the exquisite snobbery that comes with old money, the Roosevelts looked down on such *nouveau* ostentation. When he turned down an invitation to the Vanderbilts, James had only to tell Sara: "If we accept we shall have to have them at our house."

Still, the family's own way of life was scarcely plebeian. Franklin had governesses and tutors to polish his manners and drill him on his lessons, and yachts and ponies to enliven the free hours at Springwood. By the time he was fifteen he had been to Europe eight times and had been introduced to the likes of Mark Twain and President Grover Cleveland, not to mention his frequent visits with his fifth cousin, Theodore.

Another man blessed with such comforts from childhood might have been content to coast the rest of the way in privileged ease. But Roosevelt burned with an ambition that matched the fire of any son of the underprivileged. This drive was given focus and encouragement by the example of his eminent cousin. By his startling swift ascent of the political heights, TR, who was twenty-four the year Franklin was born and had already won a seat in the New York legislature, convinced the younger man that for a Roosevelt no political goal was unattainable.

In 1907, at twenty-five, having completed Columbia Law and passed the New York Bar, FDR was clerking for a distinguished Wall Street law firm while his cousin was finishing his second term in the White House. Franklin confided to his colleagues that he did not intend to pursue the law as a career but instead had his eye on the presidency. "Any one who is Governor of New York has a good chance to be President with any luck," he remarked.

Fortune often smiled on Roosevelt. But early on, despite his privileged upbringing, he displayed an imagination and determination to succeed even when the cards turned against him. In 1910 Democratic leaders in Dutchess County, Roosevelt's longtime home and one of the party's few strongholds in the state outside New York City, sought him out to run for a seat in the state assembly in a district where the incumbent was said to be planning retirement. The seat itself was safe, but party leaders figured that the Roosevelt name would help the ticket elsewhere in the state. Not incidentally, they thought the wealthy young recruit could make a generous contribution to campaign funds.

Having secured clearance from Republican cousin Ted, whose only demurrer was that he wished the young man was a member of the GOP, Franklin plunged into the race. But he suffered what seemed like a bad break: the "retiring" incumbent decided not to retire after all. There was nothing left for the young man to do but run for the state senate, a much higher and more difficult goal.

The seat he sought was held by a formidable incumbent, and young Roosevelt was very much a long shot. But he demonstrated a flair for innovation that would be one of the hallmarks of his presidency and pioneered a new approach to politics. In an era when political parties dominated the scene, Roosevelt's campaign was based on his own personality and fueled by his own ambitions. Later in the twentieth century this sort of entrepreneurial politics would become the rule, not the exception. Roosevelt's campaign and his subsequent career helped establish the trend, often to the discomfort of party elders. Hitting on the idea of campaigning by automobile, a tactic then so novel it won him badly needed attention, Roosevelt was able to cover the district as no previous candidate had done. The tyro politician's ingenuity, energy, and money—he outspent his foe five to one—helped carry him to a stunning upset victory.

Remembering the rambunctiousness of the last Roosevelt to serve in Albany, Democratic elders feared that this newest member of the clan might trigger divisiveness in their ranks. They were right to be concerned. In office FDR carried forward the personalized approach that had marked his campaign. Not content to spend his time on the mundane affairs of the good folk of Dutchess County, he looked for a cause that would dramatize his career. He found it in Tammany Hall, the well-established dragon of corruption in New York state politics. Roosevelt had scarcely taken his seat in January 1911 when he picked a fight with Tammany, the machine that ran Democratic politics in New York City and exercised formidable clout throughout the Empire State.

The very name "Tammany," after years of scandal, had become an epithet in many parts of the state and a popular target for would be reformers. The particular issue on which Roosevelt chose to challenge the Tammany Tiger was the selection of a candidate for the United States Senate, a responsibility then left to state legislatures.

Tammany's choice, an old-line former county boss, was opposed by upstate Democrats who resented the big-city machine. Looking for a fight, Roosevelt joined the opposition and soon became their chief spokesman. The rebels succeeded in blocking the Tammany candidate, though they could not get a majority for their own favorite. The battle raged for three months, all but stalemating the state government and finally ending when Tammany put forward a so-called compromise candidate who gained enough insurgent backing to become the nominee. Since the eventual winner had even closer ties to the machine than its original choice, the outcome amounted to a Tammany victory.

But to hear FDR tell it; he hailed the outcome as a triumph. In a way he was right, at least as far as he was concerned. It made the young politico a national symbol of reform and attracted the attention of significant party leaders.

Otherwise Roosevelt's record was nothing to make reformers' hearts beat faster, at least when it came to social welfare legislation. In 1911, his first year as state senator, the fire at the Triangle Shirtwaist factory in lower Manhattan killed more than a hundred young women and stunned the nation. The New York state legislature, spearheaded by thirty-seven-year-old Democratic assembly leader Al Smith, launched a full-scale investigation. A flood of proposals for remedial legislation followed, most important among them a fifty-four-hour limit on the workweek for women. A dedicated young reformer, Frances Perkins, the chief investigator for the probe into the disastrous blaze, had to beg for support for the bill. But Franklin Roosevelt turned a deaf ear; the votes of two Tammany Hall loyalists actually provided the winning margin. Perkins was "considerably disappointed" that "a young man who had so much spirit did not do so well in this." Later Roosevelt, without even blushing, took credit for helping push the bill through, confident that no one would remember the truth except for Perkins, who was by then in his cabinet as labor secretary, and that no one would bother to look back on the issue.

More important to Roosevelt at the time was that among those who noticed his much ballyhooed battle with Tammany over the Senate nomination was Woodrow Wilson. Elected governor of neighboring New Jersey on a reformist platform in his first try for elective office, the scholarly former Princeton president turned out to be a fast learner as he built support for the 1912 Democratic presidential nomination.

FDR worked desperately hard to win backing for Wilson in New York before and during the 1912 Democratic convention, particularly because Tammany, which controlled the state's convention delegation, wanted no part of the reformer Wilson. In the fall campaign, with Tammany still resentful of Wilson, Roosevelt created a separate organization to support the Democratic candidate. Aided by a split in the Republican party between the William Howard Taft regulars and the Theodore Roosevelt Bull Moosers, Wilson captured the presidency, boosted by New York's forty-five electoral votes.

Roosevelt meanwhile regained his state senate seat with the substantial help of a reprobate political reporter, Louis McHenry Howe. His new aide's most conspicuous characteristics, an ugly temper and a slovenly appearance, were more than made up for in FDR's view by his political astuteness—and even more important, over the long run, his total devotion to the advancement of Franklin D. Roosevelt. Howe would become FDR's chief political strategist and the principal driving force in his effort to reach his ultimate goal of the White House.

These hopes were nourished when newly elected President Wilson, though he had built his reputation as an academician and a reformer, adopted swiftly to the first rule of old-fashioned politics: reward your friends. He chose Josephus Daniels, a North Carolina newspaper editor who had done yeoman work as a publicist for Wilson's candidacy, as navy secretary, though Daniels had never been to sea. And it was only natural that Daniels, who had become fast friends with FDR at the Democratic convention, should ask the younger man to be assistant secretary of the navy. It was the same post cousin Ted had held and exactly the job Roosevelt wanted." All my life I have loved the sea," he told Daniels.

In childhood Franklin had been enthralled by his mother's stories of the seafaring Delano family. He sailed toy boats and carved and collected miniature ships. As he grew older he read naval history and took his turn at the tiller of the *Half Moon*, his father's fifty-one-foot sailing yacht, named after the ship on which Henry Hudson explored the river that bears his name. At sixteen Franklin got his own boat, a smaller version of the *Half Moon*, and learned to navigate the rocks and tides of the Bay of Fundy, surrounding his family's summer place at Campobello. This youthful nautical interest and know-how would stand both FDR and Daniels, his landlubber boss, in good stead.

The news of Roosevelt's appointment was greeted with many a dry eye in Albany, where fellow Democrats were relieved to be free from the complications caused by the headstrong young man. "Go, Franklin, go," state senate leader and future U.S. senator Robert Wagner counseled him. "I'm sure you'll be a big success down there."

In Washington the reputation of the eminent cousin, whom Franklin worshiped, preceded him and stirred premonitory frissons. "You know the Roosevelts, don't you?" veteran Republican Senator Elihu Root, former secretary of state to the first President Roosevelt, remarked to Daniels when informed of FDR's appointment. "Whenever a Roosevelt rides, he likes to ride up front."

The new position suited FDR perfectly because his duties were not strictly circumscribed by statute. "I get my fingers in everything and there's no law against it," he wrote Eleanor. Still, in a position where he could not exercise any real influence on policy or gain much public attention, he was restless. When on August 14, 1914, war broke out in Europe, FDR could hardly contain his enthusiasm. "It will be the greatest war in the world's history," he exulted to Eleanor. "Mr. D. totally fails to grasp the situation," he added uncharitably about his boss. In his zeal Roosevelt, disregarding caution and the chain of command, leaked a memo from disgruntled admirals complaining that the navy badly needed more men and ships. This was intended to light a fire under Congress. Instead it ignited Navy Secretary Daniels, who gave his bumptious assistant a taste of his Tarheel temper. The very next day FDR repudiated every assertion the leaked memo had made and for the most part did not again stray from the reservation.

Wilson fought against odds to win a second term in 1916, under the banner of "He Kept Us Out of War." Meanwhile, though, he deployed the war hawk Roosevelt on the campaign trail to meet criticisms of Wilson as a weak sister in the world crisis. When Wilson did lead the United States into war, Roosevelt, with visions of TR's wild charge up San Juan Hill embedded in his memory, sought active duty. But Wilson was unwilling to sacrifice the experience of his assistant secretary and ordered him to stay on the job until victory was won.

The postwar era brought Roosevelt a shiny new political opportunity, the 1920 Democratic vice-presidential nomination on a ticket with Governor James M. Cox of Ohio. Roosevelt saw that slot, though often shunned by more senior politicians, as another step toward the top, offering an opportunity to meet Democrats in every corner of the nation. Then too, the vice presidency was another of the elective offices that cousin Ted had held. At the 1920 Democratic convention, delegates viewed young FDR as an attractive, energetic figure and, most important, as the possessor of a magic political name, particularly in his home state of New York.

Roosevelt's campaign role was tailor-made for his ambitions. He crisscrossed the country twice, delivering nearly a thousand speeches, not to mention numerous off-the-cuff pep talks. Not surprisingly, he sought to mimic TR both in style and substance, not always with great success. Many viewed the thirty-eight-year-old FDR as merely a jejune facsimile of his recently departed distinguished relative.

"Franklin is as much like Theodore as a clam is like a bear cat," jeered the *Chicago Tribune*, which vigorously supported the Republican ticket of Harding and Coolidge. "If he is Theodore Roosevelt, Elihu Root is Gene Debs and Bryan is a brewer."

FDR also ran into difficulty when he once again exhibited the tendency to inflate his accomplishments, as he had done in claiming that his early struggle with Tammany over New York's Senate seat had been a great personal victory. This time he was caught red-handed. Attempting to promote U.S. entry into the League of Nations so dear to Woodrow Wilson, Roosevelt argued that if the United States joined, it would be able to count on the support of its smaller neighbors in the Caribbean. In a clumsy effort to emphasize his point, he bragged of the influence he had wielded as assistant secretary of the navy. "You know I have had something to do with the running of a couple of little Republics," he asserted. "The facts are that I wrote Haiti's constitution myself and, if I do say it, I think it's a pretty good constitution."

Aside from its heavy-handedness, Roosevelt's boast was considerably off the mark. Assistant Navy Secretary Roosevelt's involvement in Haiti had been limited to a brief visit there during the U.S. occupation in 1917. And he had never contributed as much as a comma to the Haitian national charter.

Republican standard-bearer Warren Harding called Roosevelt's statement "shocking," and in his discomfort Roosevelt could think of no better response than to claim he had been misquoted by the Associated Press. This only worsened matters when supporters of both parties who had heard Roosevelt's remarks signed a statement backing the AP's story.

The Cox-Roosevelt campaign was doomed from the start. The Democrats were linked to Wilson and to the League, and voters wanted no part of either. Republican Harding won more than 60 percent of the popular vote, and the Democrats did not carry a single state outside the Solid South. Among the casualties of the Republican tide was Al Smith, who lost his bid for a second term as New York's governor.

Yet Roosevelt came out ahead. He gained the experience of a national campaign and thousands of new allies around the country. Although his service in Washington had ended for the time being, his future looked bright. To help restore his depleted bank account, he accepted the offer of a Democratic contributor to be vice president of a leading bonding company. FDR would be based on Wall Street, would earn five times what he had been paid at the Navy Department, and would be free to roam the state of New York to lay the groundwork for his next campaign.

But then, as at the start of his political career, his luck took a bad turn. Polio assaulted his body and tested his character as never before in his life. The onslaught began within a few days of his arrival with his family for their annual summer vacation on Campobello Island off the Maine coast. There began a long struggle first to identify the scourge and then to combat it. Progress was slow and hard. But Roosevelt's spirits did not flag, as those near him could testify, nor did he ever seem to consider that the disease would deprive him of the ultimate goal of his life. In this he was greatly aided by his wife and by the ever-present, ever-scheming Howe. Asked by Eleanor whether he thought FDR still had a political future, without blinking an eye Howe replied, "I believe someday Franklin will be president."

In the years that followed, some friends suggested that the ordeal had transformed the thirty-nine-year-old Roosevelt by opening the gates to his accomplishments. But the struggle for physical recovery did not so much change the man as bring out and reinforce qualities he already possessed: an iron will and a fierce determination. The insult to his physical well-being, together with the crisis of his confrontation three years earlier with Eleanor over his dalliance with Lucy Mercer, forced Roosevelt to come to terms with realities that those less privileged had always accepted. Now he was compelled to recognize limits to life; if he were to achieve his deepest ambition, he could no longer afford dilettantism or self-indulgence. He would have to set priorities, concentrate his energies, and husband his resources.

His first step was to accept and encourage Eleanor to play a new role in his life as political partner. In 1922, alongside Louis

Howe, she campaigned for Al Smith, who sought the New York governorship that fall. Smith's victory returned him to the office he had lost two years before, and FDR was back in the political swim.

Two years later, in 1924, Smith saw a chance for the presidency. Once again he asked for Roosevelt's help, this time to chair his campaign and then to place his name in nomination for the presidency. As a Protestant with a national reputation, FDR would provide balance to Smith's candidacy in a nation rife with anti-Catholicism and badly torn by prohibition and the Ku Klux Klan. Or so Smith and his strategists believed.

Roosevelt now faced a tough decision. If he accepted Smith's invitation to nominate him, Roosevelt ran the risk of having his speech and indeed his political future submerged by the bitterness surrounding Smith. But ambition and self-confidence overrode caution, and FDR took the gamble.

At first, circumstances made it seem a mistake. The Democrats' internal divisions erupted during their nominating convention at New York's Madison Square Garden, overshadowing the contest for the presidency. By the third day, when Roosevelt was scheduled to deliver his nominating speech for Smith, the convention chairman had to summon a minister to deliver the invocation to get the unruly delegates to come to order. Meanwhile Roosevelt, on one crutch, had slowly made his way down the aisle in Madison Square Garden, leaning on his eldest son, James, until he reached the speaker's platform and took a seat in the rear. When the time came for FDR's introduction, James handed his father the other crutch, and he started for the podium. Roosevelt struggled step by step, his eyes riveted on the floor, sweat running down his forehead. The delegates and galleries watched in silence, remembering the dashing figure FDR had cut four years earlier when he had been the party's vice-presidential candidate. At last he reached the lectern, set down the crutches, threw back his leonine head, and flashed a smile of triumph. Electrified, the crowd gave him a thunderous salute.

Roosevelt took advantage of the crowd's warmth to gently scold Smith's supporters on the convention floor and in the galleries for their unruliness. "We expect that the guests of this convention will render the same fair play to all candidates and their friends that we would expect in any other city," he said. The gesture of good sportsmanship won applause even from the superheated galleries.

Roosevelt's thirty-minute address, most of which had been drafted by Smith's advisers, was standard campaign boilerplate except for a passage near the end in which FDR dubbed Smith "the happy warrior of the political battlefield." Roosevelt had been reluctant to use that expression, thinking it might be too high-flown for the convention crowd. But the phrase sent the Garden into a new height of pandemonium and, along with FDR's struggle to reach the podium, became one of the most memorable aspects of the occasion.

In the long run Roosevelt benefited more from the moment than did Smith. FDR's rhetoric, and the physical feat of his getting to the podium, placed him where he wanted to be, in the front rank of his party. As for Smith, even the enthusiasm of his supporters or FDR's dramatic oratory could not save his candidacy, so deeply divided were the delegates. The convention dragged on for a record 14 days and 103 ballots, finally nominating John W. Davis, a Wall Street lawyer whose handsome looks could not offset his modest talents. In the election he was swamped by President Calvin Coolidge.

In the wake of the party's defeat, Roosevelt, while keeping his political lines open in New York, devoted most of his time to regaining his ability to walk. He pursued this goal mostly in the little town of Warm Springs, Georgia, where he found the warm mineral waters particularly therapeutic. He was so impressed with the treatment there that eventually he established a rehabilitation center in Warm Springs not only for himself but for polio victims around the country, bringing in skilled medical staff and raising a small fortune to finance the project, which became the nucleus of the celebrated March of Dimes campaign against the disease.

But it was hard for him to stay out of politics. Smith, having twice won reelection as governor, aimed again for the presidency in 1928 and persuaded Roosevelt to renominate him. Roosevelt must have sensed what was coming next. With the country enjoying an economic boom, and with the well-respected Herbert Hoover as the Republican nominee, Smith concluded that if he was to have any chance at all to carry his own state and win the presidency, he needed FDR to head the Democratic ticket in New York.

On the eve of the state Democratic convention, Roosevelt wired Smith his refusal, pleading that he needed more time in Warm Springs to regain his health. But Smith was adamant, and Roosevelt once again faced a difficult decision. To yield to Smith would very likely mean giving up his chances to walk again unaided. But his recently developed sense of realism helped him recognize that to achieve his political goals he would have to yield in other areas. As he told a friend, "When you're in politics, you've got to play the game."

Once in the game, as usual Roosevelt played to win. He laughed off criticism from editorial writers questioning whether he was physically up to the task. The *New York Post* called his nomination "pathetic and pitiless." The *Herald Tribune* said his selection was "unfair" to Roosevelt himself and to the citizens of New York.

FDR responded with a quip. Although most people *ran* for office, he said, "I am counting on my friends all over the state to make it possible for me to walk in."

Jokes aside, FDR knew he faced a Republican tide running across the country and a formidable opponent in the longtime

Republican attorney general Albert Ottinger, who happened to be Jewish. But Roosevelt had assets on this score. One was the recent trend toward the Democrats by Jewish voters in urban states like New York. Another was Herbert Lehman, of the prominent Jewish banking family, whom Democrats had selected as FDR's running mate and their candidate for lieutenant governor.

The Lehman-Ottinger juxtaposition was enough to set some Jews to worrying about how the *goyim* might react to a display of ethnic solidarity at the polls. The *American Hebrew*, perhaps the most consequential national journal of Jewish affairs, cautioned New York Jews against ticket splitting along ethnic lines, which might result in the election of both Ottinger and Lehman.

If Roosevelt had any thoughts on the matter, like most such sentiments he kept them to himself. Given his background, he could not escape some trace of anti-Semitism. His father's first wife, Rebecca, who died in 1876, six years before Franklin was born, complained about "the greatest number of Jews" among the passengers on a transatlantic voyage she took with her husband. And her son and only child, FDR's half-brother James Roosevelt, known as "Rosy," was an obsessive anti-Semite. "The place is packed," he wrote to Franklin from Bermuda in 1926. "Mostly an awful class of Jews, objectionable when sober and worse when drunk."

Eleanor Roosevelt too was not immune from such prejudice, though her biographer describes it as "casual, a frayed raiment of her generation, class, and culture." When Franklin entered Columbia Law School in 1904, she wrote to him: "I am anxious to hear about your first day, and whether you found any old acquaintances or had only Jew Gentlemen to work with." In writing about a celebration she attended in honor of the financier Bernard Baruch, an adviser to Wilson and later to her husband, Eleanor noted that "the Jew party was appalling." On first meeting with Felix Frankfurter she judged Frankfurter to be an "interesting little man, but very Jew." She also described Henry Morgenthau's wife Elinor, when introduced to her as "very Jewish but appeared very well." Ultimately she got along well with both Morgenthau and his wife.

FDR himself was not above using ethnic slurs in private conversation and communications, often in the guise of clumsy humor. Writing to a family friend on the birth of Franklin D. Roosevelt, Jr., in 1914, he mentioned that he had considered naming his new son Isaac, after his grandfather and great grandfather. "But this is not met with enthusiasm," he wrote, "especially as the baby's nose is slightly Hebraic & the family have visions of Ikey Rosenfelt though I insist it is very good New Amsterdam Dutch."

Such anti-Semitic gibes were common among well-to-do Protestants of the time, often reflecting upper-class arrogance as much as ethnic bigotry. One of Roosevelt's grandsons remembers the president telling relatively bland anti-Semitic stories in a heavy mock Jewish accent in the White House, with Henry Morgenthau joining in the laughter. The butt of these stories were usually recent Jewish immigrants from New York's lower East Side, whose lives were far removed from the circle of either FDR or Morgenthau.

None of this kept FDR from reaching out to Jews for advice or from working with them in politics or government. And Jews certainly supported him for office. In the 1928 gubernatorial election, New York's Jewish voters stayed with their recently forged allegiance for the Democrats and voted in the main for Roosevelt and Lehman. As it turned out, Roosevelt needed all their backing. He won by less than 1 percent of the vote.

Still, in an election in which Smith lost his own state by 100,000 votes and Democratic candidates almost everywhere were swamped by their GOP opponents, boosted by a tide of seemingly endless prosperity, Roosevelt's was an impressive performance. On the morning after the election, FDR awoke to find himself not only governor of the nation's largest state, with the greatest number of electoral votes, but also in the front rank of contenders for the next Democratic presidential nomination.

His first move was to get out from under Smith's shadow. Like many other politicians, Smith did not take Roosevelt seriously because of his illness and seeming superficiality. Assuming that Roosevelt would be dead in a year or so anyway, Smith reserved a suite in Albany's leading hotel to help run the state behind the scenes.

But Roosevelt was busy being his own man, establishing patterns for leadership he would follow in Washington. Although retaining some of Smith's advisers, for sensitive posts he chose new faces whose loyalty would be primarily to him and who would not rebel if the juggler's orders were sometimes inconsistent and ambiguous. Some of these aides would serve him for four years in Albany and then go on to Washington, notably Henry Morgenthau, Harry Hopkins, and Sam Rosenman.

Rather than follow Smith's trails, Roosevelt dabbled in new paths for state government, such as public power development and conservation. But his first term was memorable not so much for policy breakthroughs as for innovations in public relations. Just as Roosevelt had introduced the politics of personality in his run for the state legislature, now as governor he broke new ground in getting himself across to the voters, which he seemed to regard as at least as important as what he actually accomplished. Twice a day he held regular press conferences and made sure to be available to reporters in between times. Belying bleak assessments of the impact of his disease, the governor seemed to show up almost everywhere in the state. And then, of course, there was the radio. Other politicians had taken to the airways. But Roosevelt developed his own special style, engaging for its combination of informality with authority, and his mellifluous voice, a formula that would ultimately command the attention and support of millions of Americans when he deployed it from the White House in his celebrated "fireside chats."

Roosevelt's first serious challenge as governor, after evading Smith's attempts to control him, was the stock market crash and economic calamity that befell the nation in his first year in office. His initial response demonstrated the limitations of his impatient approach to governing, with its emphasis on short-term fixes for conditions rather than responses that required deeper understanding. Of course he was not the only national leader who failed to grasp the significance of the Wall Street crash of October 1929. But as governor of New York, with ready access to the heart of the financial crisis, he had less excuse than most. Initially he referred to "Black Tuesday" privately as "the recent little flurry downtown." And he seemed mainly interested in the possibility that the plunge in securities might allow him to find bargains in an estate sale at the Anderson Galleries in New York that he had been tracking.

More important, he shrugged off proposals for reforming the state's banking system despite abundant indications of unsound practices. Those portents took on ominous significance when in December 1930 one of the state's largest banks collapsed, imperiling nearly half a million depositors. Roosevelt then once again displayed his tendency to adjust history to his own advantage. He blamed the legislature for not taking remedial measures and cast himself as a champion of the same reforms he had earlier rejected.

But if his initial response illustrated one of his flaws, as the economy steadily worsened, reaching lows unimagined by FDR or most other politicians, Roosevelt demonstrated one of his strengths: the ability to acknowledge change and move himself front and center in public debate. To hard-pressed New Yorkers he offered unemployment relief and other emergency measures. Typically, as critics pointed out, his ideas lacked consistency and cohesion. But in one way he made a unique contribution in the national response to the crisis by articulating more cogently than anyone else a rationale for government going beyond the limited role it had played in America. "I assert that modern society, acting through its government, owes the definite obligation to prevent the starvation or dire want of any of its fellow men and women," he declared in August 1931, in a groundbreaking speech to the New York legislature. Aid must be extended, the governor declared, "not as a matter of charity but as a matter of social duty." It was a credo that rallied New Yorkers and that a few years later would form the philosophical undergirding of the New Deal. Not incidentally, it also helped account for FDR's strong appeal to Jewish Americans, for whom the idea of a benevolent and vigorous government matched their notion of Americanism.

By the time Roosevelt uttered those prophetic words, in the depression's third year, he was well on his way to becoming a White House candidate. Not that other party leaders were ready to concede. With Democratic hopes brightening as the economic outlook darkened, potential rivals for the Democratic presidential nomination had no difficulty finding flaws in his candidacy.

Roosevelt quickly rebutted the problem most often cited—his health—by having himself examined by a panel of eminent physicians who pronounced him able "to meet any demands of private and public life." But critics found other, less tangible shortcomings. One complaint was that he was insufficiently meticulous about ethical standards in politics. This charge, paradoxically enough considering Roosevelt's early battles with Tammany Hall, stemmed from his failure to respond more forthrightly to revelations of corruption within that scandal-tainted organization. At the center of the controversy was New York's flamboyant playboy mayor, James Walker, fondly referred to by some as "Beau James." Under pressure to punish Walker for the corruption of his city government but unwilling to antagonize Tammany in the midst of his drive for the nomination, Roosevelt demonstrated his tendency to delay unpleasant decisions even when the outcome was inevitable. Dealing with demands that he oust Walker, FDR hemmed and hawed until Walker—blessedly for Roosevelt—resigned.

Another reproach was that Roosevelt lacked gravitas and tended to glide around deeply rooted conflicts in public affairs rather than grapple with them. This critique was summed up memorably by Walter Lippmann, the most influential journalist of his day. "Sooner or later some of Governor Roosevelt's supporters are going to feel badly let down," Lippmann warned in one devastating column. "For it is impossible that he can continue to be such different things to such different men. He is an amiable man with many philanthropic impulses, but he is not the dangerous enemy of anything. A pleasant man who without any important qualifications for the office would very much like to be president."

For others an even more disturbing charge against Roosevelt was the suspicion that he was a dyed-in-the-wool internationalist. As president, his critics charged, he would be eager to involve America in other nations' problems around the globe, a complaint grounded in FDR's championship of the League of Nations as the 1920 Democratic vice-presidential candidate. This line of attack, spearheaded by William Randolph Hearst, the nation's leading publisher, was particularly threatening to Roosevelt because it undermined his efforts to build support in America's isolationist heartland, the Midwest, which along with the South was emerging as a Democratic political base.

At first Roosevelt tried to placate Hearst privately, but the publisher would not settle for such fragile assurances. He insisted on a public statement, and Roosevelt finally agreed to disavow the League, explaining in a speech in New York that "the League of Nations today is not the League conceived by Woodrow Wilson." In his peroration, calculated to cause the heart of every jingoist to beat faster, he declared, "Europe owes us. We do not owe her."

His statement appeared to give Hearst exactly what he wanted, as skeptical journalists quickly noticed. The liberal commentator Elmer Davis called Roosevelt "a man who thinks that the shortest distance between two points is not a straight line but a corkscrew."

Never mind the critics. Roosevelt's bargain with Hearst paid off richly. In the first place, the publisher ceased his relentless attacks on the New York governor. Then at the Democratic convention, in return for a promise by Roosevelt that once elected he would not meddle in European affairs, Hearst was persuaded to switch a sufficient number of the delegates he controlled to give Roosevelt the two-thirds majority he needed for the nomination.

The rest was easy. Facing the incumbent president, Herbert Hoover, whom the Republicans had renominated out of desperation, FDR marched to an easy victory. But the deal he had made with Hearst would resonate throughout the first years of his presidency.

Roosevelt's shift on the League of Nations drummed up support from many isolationists—not only from his own party, such as Montana's Senator Burton K. Wheeler and Tennessee's Senator Kenneth McKellar, but also from Republican ranks. Weary of President Hoover's stubborn passivity in the face of the depression, Republican senators Robert La Follette of Wisconsin, Hiram Johnson of California, and George Norris of Nebraska, all with strong ties to the old Progressive party, backed Roosevelt outright. Others such as the redoubtable William Borah of Idaho, who had mocked Roosevelt's reversal on the League earlier in the year, and Gerald P. Nye, a combative Senate newcomer from North Dakota, indirectly boosted Roosevelt's candidacy by refusing to endorse Hoover.

Although campaign-year pressures forged this alliance between Roosevelt and the isolationists in both parties, the marriage of political convenience would endure well beyond election day 1932. For most of his first term, no group would back the New Deal president more dependably, and to no group would he be more responsive, than to the coalition dedicated to America's keeping its distance from the rest of the world.

Another way to measure the impact of Roosevelt's shift on the League is to consider the potential benefits lost by giving in to Hearst. If he had stood his ground on the League, FDR could have rebutted the growing suspicion voiced by Lippmann and others that he was too willing to sacrifice principle on the altar of expediency. Doing so probably would have helped him gain support for his domestic policies. Moreover, had he been willing to risk Hearst's ire, Roosevelt could also have used his candidacy to argue that American self-interest depended on the security of other nations, particularly its longtime friends in Western Europe. This assertion would have stood him in good stead throughout the late 1930s as the menace of Nazism grew. And it would have better positioned him to respond affirmatively to the pleas of the President's Jews and other Jewish leaders to confront Hitler on behalf of the persecuted Jews in Europe, and to make a stronger case with the American public for easing immigration laws.

As it was, Roosevelt's serpentine approach to shaping policy deepened the dilemmas faced by the President's Jews in advocating the cause of the Jews of Germany. Each of them, of course, had to protect his own interests. And each also needed to be always aware that if he pushed the president too hard in a direction he did not wish to go, it would risk influencing him at all. It was a bumpy road to travel, and each of the men trod it in a different way, guided by his own inclinations and by his own path to prominence among Jews in a Christian country.

III

THE PASSIVE PROPHET

In April 1933, within a month of Roosevelt's inauguration as the nation's thirty-second president, Adolf Hitler, now fully empowered to rule Germany, escalated the persecution of Germany's half a million Jews. His first blow was aimed right at their wallets. Hitler ordered Julius Streicher, editor of the vehemently anti-Semitic newspaper *Der Stürmer,* to compile target lists of Jews and Jewish businesses. On April 1, Nazi pickets massed in front of Jewish stores and factories and Jewish professional offices, barring anyone from entering. Hermann Göring, the new regime's minister of the interior, meanwhile had ordered German Jewish leaders to deny reports of Nazi atrocities committed against Jews, warning that to disobey would mean even more stringent punishment. Germans who tried to buy from Jews were shamed and exposed publicly. The boycott lasted only three days, but it revealed how readily the Nazis could smother Jewish economic life. As such it established a template for more drastic measures that were to torment German Jews for the next decade.

Amid the protests that swelled in New York and elsewhere around the United States, Jews looked to the new president for a response, an official protest of some sort. And many counted on Justice Louis Brandeis to help persuade FDR to speak out. As it turned out, Brandeis was reluctant to act. On occasion he used his influence not on Roosevelt but on Jews, urging them to let the president be—as he did in April 1933 in the midst of the Nazi economic boycott. Two prominent Jewish leaders, Rabbi Stephen Wise and Irving Lehman, a New York judge and brother of New York's newly elected governor Herbert Lehman, made plans to visit Roosevelt to ask for action on his part. But then they were advised by Felix Frankfurter that "Florence Court," Brandeis's residence, which was used by insiders as a sort of cognomen for Brandeis himself, counseled against the idea. The visit was scrapped.

Only a few weeks before, Brandeis had encouraged Rabbi Wise as he labored to organize the massive protest rallies at Madison Square Garden and elsewhere in New York. But Roosevelt had signaled his disinterest in that issue by totally ignoring the rallies. Brandeis had no wish to be associated, however indirectly, with a visit that might antagonize a president who had dominion over an array of other fields in which the justice had interests.

Brandeis's apparent reversal should not have been surprising to anyone who understood this highly complex personage, the forces that shaped him, and his social and political priorities. If Louis Dembitz Brandeis was reckoned the most potent of the Jews in Roosevelt's presidential orbit, it was not because of his intimacy with the president. His contacts with FDR had been ephemeral at best until Roosevelt's election as governor of New York in 1928 made him a prime presidential prospect for 1932. By comparison, Henry Morgenthau, Sam Rosenman, and Felix Frankfurter all had worked with Roosevelt in one way or another for a number of years. Brandeis owed the high regard in which he was held as an influence on Roosevelt to his reputation, carefully burnished by himself and his allies and acolytes.

Not that the accomplishments underlying his prestige were lacking in substance. Brandeis's experience in manipulating the levers of statecraft, in Washington and in other world capitals, had been gained during the course of four presidencies in both parties and one world war, beginning with FDR's own erstwhile boss, Woodrow Wilson. Brandeis was commonly regarded as a liberal and a reformer. But such labels did not do him justice. For he had developed his own theories of governance and the ordering of society, which transcended what most people conceived of as liberalism or reform. And he had fought for these principles, even as they evolved, achieving what the world generally regarded as considerable success.

But however much his accomplishments had impressed others, Brandeis himself was not nearly satisfied. Over the years—he was seventy-six when Roosevelt took office—his ambitions had expanded even as his certitude in the correctness of his convictions had hardened. In Brandeis's view, much remained to be done. Moreover as Roosevelt took office Brandeis saw himself granted the chance of a lifetime now entering its twilight. For one thing, there was the unprecedented economic upheaval that created a hitherto undreamed-of opening for at last imposing on the polity the ideas and structure in which Brandeis believed. Just as important, the nation's new leader, charged with confronting this momentous challenge, was personally congenial and intellectually open, perhaps to a fault. If there was one flaw Franklin Roosevelt did not have, as both his admirers and detractors agreed, it was ideological rigidity. Many who knew him wondered whether he possessed any ideology at all.

But where some saw an intellectual vacuum, Brandeis saw a flexible mind, receptive to his own proposals. His greatest anxiety was whether there was time enough for him to take advantage of it. Of course Brandeis was not so naive as to imagine that it would be left to him alone to till this fallow field. He was sure there would be plenty of competition. But competition was the bedrock of Brandeis's convictions. And in a lifetime of striving he had rarely come off second best.

Born in Louisville in 1856 to Jewish parents who had fled their prosperous life in Prague in the wake of the revolutions of 1848, Louis entered Harvard Law at age eighteen, without benefit of an undergraduate degree. Almost destitute because of the collapse of his father's once prosperous grain business, Brandeis managed to get through Harvard, helped by a loan from his brother and by fees earned from proctoring and tutoring. By the time he finished his schooling he had repaid his brother and had saved more than $1,000, with enough left over to buy a railroad bond, the start of a lifelong sideline as an investor which made him a millionaire several times over. Meanwhile Harvard had to make a special exception to give him the law degree he earned because he had not yet reached twenty-one.

Soon after law school Brandeis joined a former classmate, Samuel D. Warren, in a partnership in Boston. It was a match the gods smiled on. Warren, no mean intellect himself, brought his partner into contact with the Brahmins who ruled Boston society. This helped both young lawyers recruit clients among the city's small and medium-sized firms that were taking advantage of the Gilded Age's economic boom. Warren also wangled membership for his partner in some of Boston's various social clubs, introduced him to Oliver Wendell Holmes, and arranged for his mention in the Boston Blue Book.

To be sure, given the anti-Semitism of the day, a number of other clubs turned Brandeis down. But he refused to be discouraged. Eager to keep pace with Warren, Brandeis turned his religion into an advantage by ingratiating himself with Boston's prosperous German-Jewish community, who rewarded his friendship by giving him their legal work. As a measure of his financial success, he was able to buy a country home in the fashionable suburb of Dedham. True, he was by and large socially isolated because of his religion. But his life experience drew him to the rugged individualism and tough-minded pragmatism of the New England ethic, and he became, according to his partner, "a better example of New England virtues than the natives." To cut costs, Brandeis kept the overhead low in his offices. To stay alert and vigorous, he avoided liquor, dancing, and other pleasures. And he labored to purify the lives of the downtrodden so they too might achieve the proper levels of morality. In short, this Southern Jew made himself over into the very model of a modern Boston Puritan. And a very successful one at that. By age thirty-four he was earning $50,000 a year, ten times as much as the average lawyer. At fifty-one he was a millionaire.

Brandeis, however, had much more on his mind than making money. Assured of financial security, he expanded his ambitions to encompass a broad range of intellectual goals. He was only thirty-four in 1890 when he and Warren published the "Right to Privacy," one of the most celebrated law review articles in the annals of American legal scholarship. Anticipating the U.S. Supreme Court by the better part of a century, the two young lawyers asserted that the Constitution gave Americans "the right to be let alone" by their government. This, they contended, was "the most comprehensive of rights and the right most valued by civilized men."

Even as Brandeis's private practice thrived by advising the nation's biggest corporations, he emerged as the preeminent legal champion of individual rights and human welfare, often arguing against the interests of the same business giants he served. Since he saw his own success as stemming from these values and morals, he became a determined advocate of a society that encouraged competition and individual efforts as opposed to "bigness." This he famously labeled "badness" in government or in corporate life. He viewed the federal system as a means for the sharing of power and responsibility, and so was inclined to sustain the authority of the states until Congress unmistakably preempted the field. Working pro bono, Brandeis battled the encroachments of governmental ukase and the selfish arrogance of great corporations. When a greedy monopoly threatened to take over the Boston subway system, he saved it from extinction by forming the Public Franchise League to mobilize opposition to the move. Joining forces with progressives in the Boston Jewish community, he exposed the inequities of private insurance companies, pressuring Massachusetts into adopting a state-run savings-bank life insurance system, which served as a model for other states. As part of his effort to place the law on the side of industrial workers, in 1908 he won a landmark victory by persuading the Supreme Court to uphold an Oregon law establishing minimum wages and maximum hours, relying on sociological data as well as legal theory. The concept underlying his argument, known as the Brandeis Brief, became the paradigm for a generation of lawyers arguing for social reform.

Brandeis's growing reputation brought increased demands for his services. One such assignment would have consequences for his life far beyond the boundaries of the legal profession. Called upon by both sides to mediate a strike in the New York garment industry in 1910, he secured an agreement under which continuing joint boards would fix working conditions and settle grievances, following union standards and giving union members preference in hiring. After a few years the agreement fell apart under the strain of increasing labor-management hostility. But the experience helped lead Brandeis down a path into a deeper sense of his personal roots in Judaism and the new movement of Zionism. Until then, Brandeis by his own account had not been much of a Jew. "Throughout long years which represent my own life I have been to a great extent separated from Jews," he would say later. "I am very ignorant of things Jewish." But as a result of the garment industry mediation and other contacts with Jewish political activists, Brandeis altered his outlook on Jewish culture and values. "I find Jews possessed of those very qualities which we of the twentieth century seek to develop in our struggle for justice and democracy," he said, "a deep sense of the brotherhood of man and a high intelligence, the fruit of three thousand years of civilization."

This increased appreciation of his own origins was fostered in Brandeis by American apostles of Theodore Herzl, the Austrian-born founder of modern Zionism, notably Jacob de Haas, Herzl's former secretary. Under his tutelage Brandeis absorbed books on the movement's history and aims as eagerly as his new Zionist friends could provide them. More than helping reach a goal for Jews, Brandeis saw in Zionism an opportunity to demonstrate the truth of one of the foundations of his political outlook: that ordinary men, bolstered by shared ideals, zeal, and courage, could establish a just commonwealth even against the greatest odds. Whatever benefits Zionism brought to Brandeis, he returned at least as much by his active involvement. Rising swiftly in the movement, he became chairman of its operating committee after 1914 when the world war forced the international Zionist organization to move its base to the United States. And his friendship with Woodrow Wilson, for whose 1912 presidential candidacy he had worked mightily, and whose New Freedom program he helped shape, enabled him to gain U.S. support for a Jewish homeland in Palestine.

In politics Brandeis considered himself an independent. Like most Jews of his station in life, he had started out as a Republican; but he had bolted to support the Democrat Grover Cleveland for president in 1884. He reverted to the Republicans to vote for Taft in 1908, a decision he soon regretted. In 1912 he turned to the Democrat Wilson, preferring his willingness to challenge the concentration of economic power to Theodore Roosevelt's more permissive approach. Although TR presented himself as an aggressive trustbuster, he preferred to sidestep the fundamental economic problems that confronted the country while focusing on his enduring need to prove himself. For the most part he avoided a direct challenge to the Republican hierarchy and the business community, and was anxious to avoid serious damage to the huge corporations that controlled his party and had funded his political career.

Brandeis's alliance with Wilson was a natural outgrowth of the Democrat's intellectual leadership of the progressive movement. More than that, the two men had certain common traits of character. As both realized when they first met in 1910, their gifts served to fill vital needs for each other. Wilson's personality was largely shaped by his Calvinist faith, which served as a counterpart to Brandeis's Puritanism. This stern doctrine endowed Wilson, like Brandeis, with a strong and unbending moral vision, which, combined with his belief in his own destiny and his devotion to morality, propelled him into the White House, making possible his greatest achievements. These were the same traits that would also underlay his rigid approach to peacemaking in 1918, contributing to the wrecking of his presidency and leaving his admirers and much of the citizenry disillusioned and embittered.

But these events were still sleeping somewhere in the future in 1912 when Wilson's alliance with Brandeis was formed. Once chosen the party's standard-bearer, Wilson realized that for all the sheen of his success as a reformer in New Jersey, he lacked the substantive knowledge on which to build a national platform. That was where Brandeis came in. The corporate attorney who was now heralded as the "people's lawyer" was attracted by Wilson's moralism and idealism, however hazily articulated. More than that, he realized that Wilson offered him an opportunity to wield the levers of power. Over the course of the summer and fall, in a series of memos and letters, Brandeis outlined to Wilson his strategy for curbing big business without enlarging government itself, by breaking up the large monopolies. As well as providing material for the nominee, Brandeis himself barnstormed the country on Wilson's behalf. After Wilson's victory, Brandeis played the freewheeling role of elder statesman and persuaded Wilson to adopt some of his pet ideas. They led to the creation of the Federal Reserve System and the Federal Trade Commission, along with passage of the Clayton Antitrust Act, all of which became ornaments of Wilson's presidency.

By now Brandeis had become the president's essential factotum. "I need Brandeis everywhere," Wilson told Rabbi Stephen Wise. "But I must have him somewhere." "Somewhere" would turn out to be the Supreme Court, but only after a bitter fight.

During the storm over his nomination, which broke immediately after it was announced, Brandeis publicly maintained silence. Privately he played a key role in his own defense. In a confidential memo to Wisconsin's Robert La Follette, one of the leaders of the Senate fight to confirm him, he noted that the stated objections of the opposition were that he lacked "a judicial temperament," had an "undesirable" reputation in the Boston bar, and was guilty of "unprofessional conduct." All of this was camouflage, Brandeis maintained, to disguise the real reasons: "He is considered a radical and is a Jew," Brandeis said, referring to himself in the third person. Indeed some Jews who opposed Brandeis's nomination did so because they feared it would exacerbate anti-Semitism. But Brandeis realized that his Jewishness would have been less of an issue if he had been a Jewish lawyer for Wall Street firms instead of a Jewish advocate who challenged the economic establishment at every turn.

Drawn to both sides of the fray were some of the luminaries of the legal, academic, and business worlds. Seven former presidents of the American Bar Association, including Elihu Root and William H. Taft, urged rejection. But nine of the eleven Harvard Law School professors backed his nomination, as did Harvard president emeritus Charles Eliot, a figure so revered that a leading Brandeis supporter said his endorsement could be bettered only by "a letter from God."

Following his confirmation by the Senate, Brandeis resigned his membership in a number of organizations, even the Massachusetts Bar Association. But he retained his position in the Zionist Organization of America because he thought he would be able to continue proselytizing for Zionism as well as advising Wilson on policy matters. When he supported Stephen Wise's newly formed American Jewish Congress in its battle with the American Jewish Committee, and attempted to enlist American Jews to help Jews in war-torn Europe, however, he drew criticism from the *New York Times*. The justice "should leave to others subjects of such controversial nature," the *Times* suggested. Within the week Brandeis relinquished his positions in the Zionist movement and in the American Jewish Congress, though he remained determined to help make their policies behind the scenes.

On a broader front, Brandeis now faced a huge problem. Even before he joined the Supreme Court he professed to be a judicial purist, and as a justice he seemed to revel in the Court's "splendid isolation" from the rest of the political universe. He made no public speeches, wrote no articles, and even declined to accept honorary degrees. Yet there was one major aspect of his life Brandeis could not and would not abandon—his political activism. In this case the solution to his dilemma was right at hand, in the person of his friend and associate Felix Frankfurter. Another brilliant product of Harvard Law, twenty-six years younger than Brandeis, Frankfurter would become his conduit to the political world beyond the strict confines of the judiciary. Frankfurter's professional life had already been greatly shaped by Brandeis. At a critical juncture in Frankfurter's career, Brandeis had arranged a teaching position for him at Harvard. This provided the financial security that allowed Frankfurter to pursue his own political and intellectual interests, which rivaled those of Brandeis himself in their variety and importance. Brandeis had also introduced Frankfurter to the Zionist cause and saw to it that he was installed in the upper echelons of the movement's leadership. Brandeis and Frankfurter had worked together for years because they shared common interests and beliefs, with Brandeis generally remaining in the background. They corresponded constantly. Brandeis, who liked to maintain a certain aloofness, began his letters to Frankfurter "Dear Felix," one of the few friends whose first name he regularly used. In one letter to Frankfurter, Brandeis described his view of his friend and accomplice as "half-brother, half son."

In a sense, Justice Brandeis's use of Frankfurter as a proxy for himself in the world of politics and government was simply an extension and expansion of their prior relationship in which the younger man had helped promote his mentor's ideas and purposes. Many members of the Harvard Law School community knew of the arrangement and did not seem to consider it unethical.* Others with less friendly inclinations toward the two men might have viewed the matter differently, but either they were unaware of the arrangement or did not consider it egregious.

Ever the practical man, Brandeis was quick to take account of the enlargement of Frankfurter's responsibilities. In November 1916, only a month after taking his seat on the Court, Brandeis sent Frankfurter a check for $250 to defray his expenses in carrying out Brandeis's political lobbying efforts. Brandeis made clear that more of the same would be forthcoming. Frankfurter, as Brandeis might have expected, returned the payment, saying he regarded its proffer as an honor. But Brandeis sent the money right back, along with a note that made clear what he

---

*More than sixty years after this arrangement began, in 1982, when the publication of Bruce Murphy's *The Brandeis/Frankfurter Connection* called attention to it, the *New York Times* reported these joint endeavors on its front page. In an editorial which noted that Brandeis had presented himself on the bench as an "awesome moralist and high priest of the separation of powers," the paper condemned both Brandeis's use of Frankfurter and the justice's involvement in politics as "wrong" and a violation of "ethical standards." In apparent mitigation the editorial acknowledged that "ethical standards have risen over the generations."

thought about Frankfurter's role. "In essence this is nothing different than your taking travel and incidental expenses from the Consumers League or the *New Republic*," he contended. "You are giving your very valuable time and that is quite enough. I ought to feel free to make suggestions to you, although they involved some incidental expense. And you should feel free to incur expense in the public interest." (Over the years Frankfurter would receive from Brandeis a total of $52,250, most of it paid directly into his bank account by Brandeis's financial secretary.) The key words here are "the public interest." With this phrase Brandeis justified—at least in his own mind and most probably in Frankfurter's—this departure from the ethics of the high Court he professed to revere. While this definition of "public interest" was convenient for Brandeis, it might have troubled those who were on the other side of the numerous controversies he sought to influence.

Whatever the ethical pros and cons of their arrangement, Brandeis certainly got his money's worth from his onetime protégé. He piled on the work: articles for the *Harvard Law Review* and the *New Republic*, items for the Zionist agenda, and a raft of domestic reforms included in a lengthy memo submitted to Frankfurter just as the Court was beginning its fall 1922 term, immodestly titled "What to Do About Capitalism." The suggestions ranged from expanding workers' compensation laws and banning injunctions against labor unions to encouraging consumer cooperatives and credit unions along with municipal ownership of utilities.

Once he took his seat on the Court, Brandeis made a point of not writing or talking directly to the president who had appointed him about matters of substance, though he did discuss policy issues with others in the Wilson administration. But Wilson got the counsel he wanted, even when he had to go to extraordinary lengths—as when he called on Brandeis in the justice's apartment to seek his advice on whom he should appoint to the new post of government chief of the railroads. Even when Frankfurter was at his beck and call, Brandeis continued to use his own network of contacts in the bureaucracy, which one biographer likened to "many invisible wires into many government bureaus."

Brandeis concentrated first on overhauling the jerry-built apparatus constructed to mobilize the U.S. economy for war. The justice's approach was serpentine if none too subtle. He had Frankfurter tell Colonel House, Wilson's top adviser, that if asked Brandeis would offer his view of the shortcomings of the War Department. The request was soon forthcoming, and so was Brandeis's advice, which essentially called for centralizing authority outside the department for such things as military production and labor relations. Brandeis avoided a direct role in the reorganized machinery, but he saw to it that his agent, Frankfurter, was in the thick of things as head of the newly created War Policy Board.

At least as important to Brandeis, and certainly closer to his heart, was the Zionist movement. There he continued to wield great influence despite his resignation from official positions. He continued to be listed as honorary president of the Zionist Organization of America, whose leaders made no important decision without consulting him. The Great War had created new problems for the dream of a Jewish homeland. Palestine itself was controlled by Turkey, an ally of Germany; Britain and France had secretly agreed to divide Palestine between them after the war ended. Seeking American help for his cause, the British Zionist leader Chaim Weizmann, the future first president of Israel, prevailed upon Brandeis to intervene. In May 1917, a month after the United States entered the war, Brandeis set aside his scruples and met with Wilson on the issue. The result was a statement from the president endorsing a Jewish homeland in Palestine under a British protectorate. Next day Brandeis met with British foreign secretary Arthur Balfour, lay-ing the groundwork for the Balfour Declaration which endorsed the concept of a Jewish homeland in the Holy Land. To carry this work forward, Brandeis went to Paris, site of the World War I peace conference, and then to Palestine. When he returned to Paris, he met again with Balfour, who as a result ordered the British regime in Palestine to change its pro-Arab stand. Brandeis then met in London with Wilson, whom he persuaded to ignore a recommendation by an international commission to restrict Jewish immigration to Palestine. In 1920, with the future of Balfour's promise once again shadowed by doubt, Brandeis wrote to Wilson pleading with him to intervene with French and British leaders. "Your word may be decisive," he declared.

In his disregard of fundamental protocols for judicial conduct during the battle for a Jewish homeland, Brandeis was impelled by one driving principle that he was fond of explaining to friends. "If you are 51 percent sure of the solution to a problem, it is far better to act than to leave the choice to others who are less sure of themselves." For Brandeis, a man singularly untrammeled by self-doubt, this axiom offered a green light into fields that knew no boundaries.

What did slow Brandeis down, or at least force him to alter his direct approach, was the change in administrations from Democratic to Republican, and from his friend and confidant Wilson to a series of Republican presidents who were relative strangers to him. Not that Brandeis halted his unrelenting efforts to promote his own ideas for government policy. But he was forced more and more to lean on Frankfurter to pave the way for what he was confident would be the Democratic party's ultimate return to power. In an era before the term "think tank" had been coined, Brandeis functioned as a one-man version of such an institution with Frankfurter as his emissary to influential senators in both parties. They had been his allies in the progressive movement, and he now sought to rally them behind a broad range of domestic programs.

With the election of FDR and the onset of the New Deal, Brandeis felt confident that his years wandering in the public-policy wilderness were at an end. Even before Roosevelt's election to the New York governorship in 1928, Brandeis alerted Frankfurter to his eagerness to connect with the man he believed would some day be the nation's president. For the next four years Brandeis was content to rely on Frankfurter to be his conduit to the governor's chambers in Albany.

Brandeis's patience was rewarded when, as Roosevelt's campaign for the presidency neared its victorious conclusion in 1932, FDR asked Frankfurter to arrange a meeting with Brandeis. After their first get-together, Brandeis told Frankfurter that Roosevelt seemed "well versed in most fundamental facts of the situation" and was "against the bankers." What was good for the new chief-to-be was just as valuable for his new lieutenants in waiting. During the tense weeks of the four-month interregnum before Roosevelt took office, key cabinet secretary designates sought out Brandeis's advice. Labor Secretary Frances Perkins consulted about a public works program and the staffing of her department. Interior Secretary Harold Ickes, who felt as if he had been "sitting at the feet of one of the fine old prophets"—an impression one can be sure Brandeis did nothing to undercut—agreed to appoint a Brandeis recommendation as his department's new counsel.

But Brandeis had bigger fish to fry. As Roosevelt's inauguration approached, Brandeis sent Frankfurter a broad blueprint for the New Deal based on all the ideas for reforming government and the economy that he had incubated for the past two decades. Among its four major thrusts were a public works program intended to create jobs for three million, a scheme for funding these projects, and proposals for overhauling the tax code and reforming investment and banking procedures.

Brandeis well knew that even the best-laid plans would come to naught without sufficient access to the president. For this

Brandeis could not count on Frankfurter alone. So he sought to develop other friendly sources, such as Raymond Moley, one of Roosevelt's "brain trusters," while circumventing other FDR confidants whom he believed less sympathetic to his ideas, such as Rex Tugwell. Indeed Tugwell viewed Brandeis as "a wolf in sheep's clothing," professing objectivity while promoting his own schemes for reform. Tugwell labeled Brandeis "an atomist," the foundation of whose philosophy was his faith in small social organizations in both business and government. He thus rejected the theories of Tugwell and other like-minded New Dealers who preferred federal government management and planning of the economy, as embodied in the original cornerstone of the New Deal, the National Recovery Administration.

But Brandeis pressed on. To strengthen his position he turned to Frankfurter—whom Tugwell referred to as "the first apostle"—to place other disciples in key federal posts. The most important of these were Tom Corcoran and Ben Cohen, two Harvard-trained lawyers who became, with Frankfurter's guidance and Brandeis's blessing, the two most important legislative architects of the New Deal. They gained influence with FDR not only because of their ingenuity and intensity but because their views were backed by Brandeis, then the most potent liberal on the Supreme Court.

Given Brandeis's involvement in the internal debate over how to combat the depression, it is not hard to understand why he did not welcome the chance to plunge into the new and unexpected crisis that developed abroad, in Hitler's Germany. Instead he chose for the most part to defer to Frankfurter, as he had done in response to the early protests against the Nazi boycott of Jewish businesses in April 1933.

The way Brandeis distanced himself from that fray was underlined on April 12, 1933. While Frankfurter was trying to talk Roosevelt into a concession on immigration for the sake of Germany's Jews, Justice Brandeis had what he described to

Frankfurter as "a very satisfactory" hour-long meeting with the president. They discussed a number of issues and events: the prospective appointment of Dean Acheson, former Brandeis law clerk, as undersecretary of the treasury; a scheme for a Post Office savings system, a pet Brandeis project intended "to free the Govt from the grip of the bankers"; and a recent visit from Myron Taylor, recently named as chief executive at U.S. Steel. This last gave Brandeis a chance "to put in a few words on Bigness and Overcapacity," two more of his favorite hobbyhorses. And in between all this there was time for FDR to "make an appreciative reference" about Brandeis's agent, Frankfurter, a comment that of course did not displease the justice.

As to the plight of Germany's Jews, Brandeis mentioned to Frankfurter that Roosevelt was to see Labor Secretary Perkins, "perhaps about your immigration proposal," a reference to a Frankfurter scheme for easing entrance requirements for refugees from Nazi persecution. Brandeis himself did not inquire about this matter. Indeed, he told Frankfurter, "there was no chance to talk to FDR about Jews," a remarkable comment given the lengthy session with the president at which the two appeared to have discussed everything short of "ships and shoes and sealing wax." Instead, the next day, in a brief note to Frankfurter, Brandeis proposed that Frankfurter suggest to the president that he "do something in re German Jews," though Brandeis did not explain what this should be.

Meanwhile the Jewish ordeal in Germany worsened. On April 12, the same day that Brandeis and Roosevelt had their White House meeting, the Germans announced that all Jews would be expelled from the civil service and all books by Jewish authors would be purged from libraries. The next day Roger Baldwin, head of the American Civil Liberties Union, called for the administration to ease immigration curbs against "political refugees," which was fast becoming the euphemism for European Jews. And on April 15 the *New York Times* reported that ten thousand Jews fleeing Nazi persecution had taken refuge in a number of European cities, mostly in Paris. The American Jewish Congress summoned a range of Jewish organizations to a conference intended to mount "vigorous resistance" to the Nazi actions.

Brandeis's only recorded response to these developments was in a note to Frankfurter on April 26, in which along with comments on half a dozen or so subjects he wrote: "I hope FDR will act soon. It is becoming a disgrace to us all that America does not act."

Yet for all his indignation, Brandeis still chose to position himself in a house by the side of the road. In an April 29 note to Frankfurter, he branded FDR's failure to ease immigration restrictions imposed by his predecessor, Herbert Hoover, a "disgrace to America and to F.D.'s Administration," though he said nothing to Roosevelt directly. In 1930, with the Great Depression in full swing, Hoover, without consulting Congress, had expanded the enforcement of an old provision buried in the immigration statutes. It barred visas to anyone "likely to become a public charge," in other words unable to support himself or herself because of mental or physical limitations. In a move that recalled the edict of New Amsterdam's Peter Stuyvesant three centuries earlier, Hoover broadened the interpretation of the "LPC" clause, as it came to be known, to apply to anyone unlikely to get a job under current economic conditions, thus turning it into a powerful weapon for denying visas to any potential immigrants, including Germany's Jews.

Brandeis said nothing to Roosevelt about his objections to Hoover's order. But he did note in his letter to Frankfurter that a former Austrian official, who had joined the Harvard faculty, had been "deeply moved, almost in tears about the German situation." He added, somewhat unfeelingly himself, "I guess the Jews of Germany had better make up their minds to move on, all of them. Of course, the nation is crazy now, but life there will never be safe, and it has been distinctly degrading to the present generation of Jews."

Whatever his musings about the fate of German Jewry, Brandeis could not escape the pressure on him, directly and through Frankfurter, to intervene with FDR, particularly from Stephen Wise, "If L.D.B. could talk for half an hour to FDR and Hull and bring the impact of that mighty conscience upon their souls, I really believe something could be done," Wise wrote to his friend Judge Julian Mack. With Brandeis as the point man, the effort could result in "not a battle won but half the war." Or so Wise seemed to think.

But Brandeis was not willing to risk his rapport with the president. The most he would allow was to arrange a meeting with Secretary of State Cordell Hull in May. Possessed neither of great imagination nor the gift of inspiring others, Hull nevertheless had during his years in Washington earned respect for his probity, his diligence, and perhaps most of all his durability. For these qualities, rather than his diplomatic skills or his comprehension of international affairs, FDR had selected Hull as his secretary of state. Tall, lean, white-haired, and intensely dignified, he seemed perfect for the part.

Hull's distinguished appearance belied a gritty interior and upbringing. He was first and foremost a survivor, the product of sturdy stock and a rigorous upbringing in the Cumberland foothills of Tennessee. His father had been shot and left for dead by a gang of Yankee guerrillas during the Civil War, but he recovered sufficiently to search out and locate his chief tormentor, whom he then summarily executed. For that deed no one ever raised a hand against him.

Born six years after the war ended, Cordell, one of five brothers, grew up wearing homespun. At fourteen he dazzled a countywide audience by arguing the case for George Washington in a debate over whether the first president or Christopher Columbus had contributed more to America's greatness. His delighted father thereupon dug into his savings to help his star debater go on with his education. The young man applied all his energies first to school, then to reading for the law, and finally to launching his political career with a position on the local Democratic county committee. Arriving in the U.S. House of Representatives, he soon gained fame for his dedication to the reduction of tariffs. More than any other factor, this issue drew Hull, freshly elevated to the Senate, to Roosevelt's presidential banner in 1931. Convinced that if Al Smith, Roosevelt's old ally and his chief rival for the nomination, had his way, the Democratic party would become a protectionist stronghold, Hull turned to Roosevelt whom he had first met during Roosevelt's Wilsonian years at the Navy Department.

In FDR's quest for the nomination, Louis Howe used Hull's Senate office as his Washington headquarters while Hull rallied support for the New Yorker throughout Dixie. After the election, when Roosevelt asked him to become his secretary of state, Hull claimed to be "thunderstruck." He had little experience in international affairs. This did not stop him from conditioning his acceptance upon having a major role in shaping foreign policy. Roosevelt did not skip a beat. "We shall each function in the manner you've stated," he blandly assured the old mountaineer. Hull, eager to believe what he was told, signed on.

The truth was very different. For the most part Roosevelt insisted on acting as his own secretary of state. The president, who considered Hull boring and indecisive, portioned out many of the remaining responsibilities to men with whom he was closer personally, notably Undersecretary Sumner Welles.

It would be some time before this reality became clear to Hull, but even then he was in no position to complain about being deceived. He himself had hardly been entirely above board with Roosevelt. A physical examination in the summer of 1932 had disclosed tubercular lesions in both of Hull's lungs. The White Plague, as it was then known, usually meant that patients would be shipped off to sanitariums, where most died within a few years. But Hull, with his eye on someday succeeding Roosevelt, kept the diagnosis a secret from the president and everyone else outside his immediate family. Nor was that the only part of Hull's personal life that he concealed. Hull's wife, Frances Witz, had attended an Episcopalian church while growing up in Staunton, Virginia, but her father was a Jewish immigrant from Austria. Fearful that having a half-Jewish wife, like tuberculosis, could ruin his chances for the presidency, Hull wrongly told *Who's Who* that his wife's original last name was not Witz but Whitney, which was in fact her married name from her first marriage. That deceit would not be discovered for several years, but meanwhile rumors about her lineage circulated. Anti-Semitic magazines published vicious articles that cited her ancestry as proof of a Jewish conspiracy to take over the government.

As he met with Hull, Brandeis knew nothing of the secretary's hidden life, though it probably would have made little difference. Brandeis often paid less attention to his audience than to what he thought needed to be said. And so he launched into what seems, by his account, to have been more of a sermon than a conversation. FDR should make the kind of statement that would have been made by Woodrow Wilson, whom Brandeis referred to as WW—this was the line Brandeis took with his guest, though it would have been hard for him to cite any such utterance by Wilson. For good measure the president should also relax strict immigration curbs to permit Hitler's victims to find sanctuary where the Statue of Liberty beckoned. To drive his point home, Brandeis told Hull that "he felt more ashamed of his country than pained by Jewish suffering," bemoaning the difference between current American attitudes and the nation's "nobler past."

There is no record of Hull's response to this visit. But Brandeis had been around Washington long enough to realize that if he wanted someone to pressure the president on this controversial issue, Hull was a most unlikely candidate. A man given to reading vast amounts of background material, and then rereading it, Hull was loath to make decisions. He was especially reluctant to decide anything that would involve him in controversy. This passive stance reflected his notable insecurity, feelings reinforced by Roosevelt's cavalier treatment of his role at State.

Five years after their 1933 meeting, in March 1938 following the *Anschluss*, Germany's takeover of Austria, Hull proposed an international committee to aid refugees from both countries, Brandeis wrote to Frankfurter, "Pity Hull was 5 years late in seeing the duty of America." His own lack of urgency he chose to overlook.

Years after the Hull-Brandeis conversation, Stephen Wise would also bemoan lost opportunity, though he placed the burden on Brandeis. "If only L.D.B. had taken hold in 1933 when some of us begged he should," he wrote Frankfurter. Referring to Brandeis as the "one and only," Wise allowed himself a dig at Frankfurter: "Were you not among those opposed to his doing so that time?" he asked pointedly, a reminder for which Frankfurter was not likely to thank him.

It is not clear whether Frankfurter or anyone else could have persuaded Brandeis to take a more active role. But his decision to remain on the sidelines did not keep him from carping about the roles others played. Thus in April 1933 he complained to Frankfurter that FDR had failed to deliver "much that seems to be essential" from the New Deal and had instead offered *kunstrucke*, or clever tricks, "of questionable value." He also grumbled that "the protests against Hitler had to rely upon Joe Robinson, Hatfield and Hamilton Fish." Senator Joseph Robinson of Arkansas, the Democratic Senate leader, had used the occasion of FDR's submitting the name of William Dodd, a prominent author and scholar, as ambassador to the Third Reich to denounce the German persecution of Jews, a policy he called "sickening and terrifying." "Such cruel policies," he warned, "will bring their own penalties." Despite Brandeis's belittling reaction, Robinson's comments, because of his leadership role, his Southern roots, and his conservative leanings, seemed a significant development.

Adding impact, Robinson's criticism was echoed by other senators from both sides of the aisle, including Henry Hatfield of West Virginia, a state that like Robinson's Arkansas had no significant Jewish population. As for Hamilton Fish, a Republican congressman from Roosevelt's very own neck of the woods in Dutchess County, New York, who would later become a bitter foe of the New Deal on foreign policy, he had the month before introduced a concurrent resolution calling upon the president to make "friendly representation" to the German government to respect the civic, economic, and political rights of Germany's Jewish citizens.

It must have puzzled Wise to learn that while he pleaded with Brandeis to seek an audience with FDR in November 1933, Brandeis somewhat offhandedly turned down an invitation from the president for the justice and his wife, Alice, to lunch with the president and the first lady. "I supposed he was wiping off his slate in preparation for his leaving for Warm Springs," Brandeis wrote to Frankfurter. "It seemed wise to express our regrets," he said without explaining, except to add: "There would have been no fair chance to talk policies with F.D."

Over these years of uncharacteristic passivity, Brandeis offered no clearer explanation for his reticence. Certainly his role on the Court did not seem to provide much of an excuse, given his unrelenting efforts to press his policy ideas first on Woodrow Wilson and then on FDR. And these were issues, such as the shape of the New Deal, that were far more likely to come before his fellow justices than any effort to succor the Jewish targets of Nazi persecution. Rather, Brandeis seemed to be rendered inactive by his own anxieties about the Jewish role in American society. These misgivings reflected his own experience of being shunned by Boston's upper strata and nearly denied appointment to the Supreme Court, and they persisted despite his own achievements and ultimate widespread acceptance. Brandeis was not reluctant to advocate a wide range of social and economic reforms, however controversial, since they were intended to benefit society generally. But to argue for a cause that specifically benefited Jews, at the expense, some would argue, of other Americans, was a higher-risk proposition. It might place American Jewry, and Brandeis's own exalted status, in jeopardy.

Zionism was a different matter. Brandeis was at pains to equate Zionism with Americanism. "Let no American imagine," he said, "that Zionism is inconsistent with patriotism." In his advocacy of a Jewish homeland in Palestine he had to argue with the British and with the Arabs but not against the interests of other Americans.

While Brandeis agonized from a distance over the unfolding tragedy in Germany, he had no problem challenging the president on other matters from his position on the Supreme Court, which during Roosevelt's first term emerged as the principal nemesis of the New Deal. While Brandeis was seen as a liberal bulwark on the conservative-dominated Court, his resentment of the centralization of government power, encouraged by the New Deal, drove him to the ranks of the enemy. On "Black Monday" in 1935 Brandeis joined with the conservative majority in overturning the National Recovery Administration, whose regulatory codes and Blue Eagle logo represented the salient initiative in FDR's efforts to overhaul the economy. The agency affronted Brandeis's deep suspicions of expanded federal power. The Court's decision was a particular blow to organized labor, whose cause Brandeis had long espoused. To union leaders, the NRA, for all its high-handedness, represented the first action by the federal government to protect the right of workers to organize. Many were particularly outraged at Justice Brandeis's vote with the majority. Sidney Hillman, then a leader of the needle trades unions in New York, recalling Brandeis's long battles on behalf of social reform, complained that "having closed the sweatshops, he now clears the way for their reopening."

Roosevelt himself was stunned by the decision and uncomprehending of the depth and breadth of opposition on the bench. When his aides brought him word of the ruling, he asked, "Well, what about Old Isaiah?"—the honorific that New Dealers affectionately accorded to Justice Brandeis, long the patron prophet of liberal reform. If the president had better understood Old Isaiah's judicial philosophy, he would not have needed to ask the question. No sooner had the decision been read from the bench than Brandeis spelled out its meaning in blunt terms to New Deal lawyer Tom Corcoran. Brandeis had known him since Corcoran clerked at the Court for Justice Holmes. Summoning him to the justices' robing room, Brandeis told Corcoran: "This is the end of this business of centralization, and I want you to go back and tell the president that we're not going to let this government centralize everything. It's come to an end."

Brandeis's scolding only added to Roosevelt's dismay. The broad thrust of the ruling was such that FDR and his close aides felt, as one of them, Jerome Frank, put it, "that it was going to be impossible for him to carry out his program." Two years later the NRA decision and similar judicial debacles led FDR to launch his ill-fated plan to "reform" the Court by packing it with justices more to his liking. Given advance warning by Corcoran, Brandeis told his young friend plainly that he was dead set against the plan and warned that the president was making a serious mistake. More than that, working behind the scenes he engineered the release of a letter from Chief Justice Hughes forcefully disputing FDR's claim that the Court was overworked (the rationale for the president's proposal), which many viewed as the decisive blow in killing the idea.

It was a year later, in October 1938, more than five years after FDR and Hitler came to power, that Brandeis made his first call on FDR on behalf of the Jews. But in keeping with his conduct, Brandeis's purpose was not to aid the persecuted Jews of Europe but rather to bolster hopes for a Jewish homeland in Palestine. He was prompted by the recommendation of a British commission that Palestine be divided into separate Jewish and Arab states. Zionists opposed the idea, and the British themselves ultimately found it infeasible, though years later a similar approach made possible the state of Israel. Fearful that this proposal might lead Britain to reduce the number of Jews it allowed into Palestine, Brandeis sought to convince FDR that Palestine could accommodate a great many Jews. "FD went very far in our talk in his appreciation of the significance of Palestine—the idea of keeping it whole and making it Jewish," Brandeis wrote Frankfurter. "Possible refuges for Jews elsewhere he spoke of as 'satellite,' and there was no specific talk of them." In the event, Roosevelt did nothing to persuade the British to change their policy.

The following month came *Kristallnacht*, the Nazi pogrom that recalled the horrors perpetrated by the tsars. Roosevelt condemned the violence but refused even to consider asking Congress to ease immigration restrictions, though he did agree to a six-month extension of visitors' visas that had been granted to twelve thousand German-Jewish refugees.

So far as Brandeis was concerned, that was sufficient. Told that Rabbi Wise was considering pressing the president to amplify his objection to *Kristallnacht*, he wired Wise: "Think Skipper should not be called upon to make suggested protest he expressed himself fully."

It was difficult to find any among FDR's friends and allies who were willing to criticize him on these grounds. Roosevelt's interior secretary, Harold Ickes, a vigorous foe of the Nazi regime, made a point during a visit with Brandeis of blaming the lack of protest of Nazi persecution not on Roosevelt or the

United States but on "the cowardice on the part of the rich Jews of America." As Ickes later told his diary: "I said that I would like to get two to three hundred of them together in a room and tell them that they couldn't hope to save their money by meekly accepting whatever humiliations others chose to impose on them."

Brandeis, according to Ickes, "agreed completely." As Ickes recounted the justice's views in his diary, "He said there was a certain type of rich Jew who was a coward. According to him these are German Jews and he spoke of them with the same contempt that I feel for them."

One has to wonder what Brandeis was thinking of. Perhaps he was trying to humor Ickes, a man as willful and dogmatic as Brandeis himself. But on their face his comments about the cowardice of American Jews carried more than a whiff of hypocrisy, coming from a man who had chosen the public stance of bystander. By the time Ickes' diary was published in 1953, "Old Isaiah" had died twelve years earlier. Well before his passing at age eighty-five, the leadership of the President's Jews had fallen to the hands of exactly the man Brandeis would have chosen for the task, his protégé Felix Frankfurter.

IV

THE SOUL OF
DISCRETION

On the face of things, American Jewish leaders outside government had as much reason to look to Felix Frankfurter to persuade FDR to help targets of Nazi persecution as to Justice Brandeis. While Frankfurter did not match Brandeis's renown in the pantheon of Jewish political leaders, he was closer to the president than his mentor. Moreover he was free of the shackles of judicial robes, which to some minds restricted Brandeis's freedom of action, even if the justice himself did not seem to take this inhibition seriously. And Frankfurter's closeness to Brandeis created the potential for two profoundly gifted comrades working hand in hand for the Jewish cause.

This design, however, was flawed by one troublesome reality. Frankfurter, as ultimately became clear, was just as reluctant as Brandeis to jeopardize his own relationship with the president by assuming an active role in a difficult controversy. And so the Brandeis-Frankfurter connection, instead of providing a mechanism for Jews to pressure or cajole the president they so much admired into helping their German brethren, became a sophisticated apparatus for fending off such efforts. Faced with pleas to seek the president's aid, Brandeis would explain that he had relayed these requests to his and Roosevelt's friend, Frankfurter. And Frankfurter would dutifully pursue these matters, but often with someone else instead of Roosevelt and almost invariably with a restraint that was hard to distinguish from simple reticence.

In a letter to a friend in April 1933, Rabbi Wise speculated about Frankfurter's inaction. "I think he feels a certain disinclination to step out into the open at this time," Wise wrote. "Perhaps his very great influence with the Administration ought to be reserved. He knows best."

He conveyed that same understanding in a letter to Frankfurter himself. "It seems to me you have been most effective in the discreet exertion of the weight of our government on behalf of elementary decencies," he wrote Frankfurter. "More power to you." That was just the sort of attitude that Frankfurter appreciated.

And so Frankfurter, who early in life had earned a reputation as a liberal firebrand, now made discretion his watchword, as far as the fate of Jewish refugees was concerned. As long as Rabbi Wise and other Jewish leaders respected his discretion, the convoluted role Frankfurter had created for himself would be much easier to fill. In any event, it should have been relatively familiar for him. It was shaped by a combination of deep-rooted insecurity and consuming ambition, and in one way or another, and in various venues, he had been playing it most of his life.

Operating in an era before the term became part of the idiom, Felix Frankfurter had nevertheless become the first great headhunter in American politics. As a result of this proclivity and his closeness to FDR, one high-ranking early New Dealer, General Hugh Johnson, pronounced Frankfurter "the most influential single individual in the United States." He did not offer the judgment as a compliment. Frankfurter, Johnson contended, had "insinuated" his "boys" into "obscure but key positions in every vital department" of the New Deal. In his instinct for spotting talented young lawyers and helping them rise, Frankfurter was following in the path blazed by his patron and friend Louis Brandeis, who had promoted Frankfurter's own career. Not that Frankfurter necessarily needed Brandeis's help to get ahead, as his early years demonstrated.

Born in Vienna in 1882, Frankfurter grew up in a family that had achieved a measure of prominence within the isolated community of Austrian Jews. His father, Leopold, descended from a long line of rabbis stretched out for centuries, and an uncle was head librarian of the University of Vienna. Leopold Frankfurter had himself studied for the rabbinate but in a step characteristic of his irresolute personality had abandoned this venture when it did not bring early success. He immigrated to America in 1893. Next year his wife, Emma, and their six children, including twelve-year-old Felix, steerage passengers all, joined him in New York.

Felix spoke no English, but according to family lore he learned the language in six weeks. Leopold Frankfurter sold linens and did well enough so that after a few years he was able to move his brood from Manhattan's lower East Side to a middle-class neighborhood farther uptown. The elder Frankfurter was an outgoing, gregarious man, something of a romantic dreamer but not very ambitious, thus limiting his family's economic horizons and his influence on his son.

Felix's future was shaped more by his mother, a hard-driving and serious woman. "Hold yourself dear," she told her children: set worthy goals and take pride in your Jewish heritage. In the face of meager finances she prodded her children to make the most of what they had—native intelligence and a stable and supportive home background. Even in a family whose members applied themselves to reading and education, young Felix stood out for his bookishness. He spent hours at the nearby Cooper

Union library, reading newspapers from around the country and developing an interest in politics and current affairs.

Looking back, unburdened by excessive modesty, he considered himself a child prodigy, likening his precocious absorption with world events to the childhood achievements of Mozart and John Stuart Mill. However valid these comparisons, Frankfurter did make the most of New York City's public education system and his omnivorous reading. He swept through the demanding curriculum of City College of New York at the age of nineteen, finishing third in his class. At CCNY he won particular acclaim for his debating skill. Indeed the college debating society, which had restricted its annual tournament to seniors, changed its rules during Frankfurter's junior year to permit him to compete.

An important aspect of Frankfurter's developing personality was his stature, or rather lack of it; he stood less than five feet five inches tall. His command of expression—he was not only thoughtful but quick-witted—and his intellect helped the young man win attention in a world dominated by taller men.

As he made his way through school, Frankfurter discarded his links to the Jewish religion that, like Brandeis's, had been tenuous at best. Despite his family's background in the Old World, religion had not played a large role in Frankfurter's early life. Later, without denying his ethnicity as a Jew, he described himself as an agnostic. His main concern now was not with religion but with finding a way to enter his chosen profession, the practice of law, a natural choice for a bright young man with a gift for public speaking and a scholarly bent.

After graduating from college in 1902 he spent a year clerking in the city's Tenement Housing Commission at $1,200 per year to earn tuition money, and in 1903 he entered Harvard Law. At Harvard the study of law and the experience of life at the university became for Frankfurter a sort of substitute for religion. "I reveled in the place," he later recalled. "I ate up not only the law but attended lectures, went to concerts, went to the library, read, roamed all around and just satisfied a gluttonous appetite" for intellectual and cultural life.

Frankfurter was attracted not only to this feast for the mind and the soul but to the freedom Harvard offered to outgrow the restrictions of his immigrant origins. "What mattered was excellence in your profession, to which your father or your face was equally irrelevant. And so rich man, poor man were just irrelevant titles to the equation of human relations. The thing that mattered was what you did professionally."

In this meritocracy the short young man, less than a decade removed from his steerage passage to the New World, flourished. He compiled a brilliant academic record, which won him election to the *Law Review* and entrees to distinguished Harvard faculty and alumni, among them Oliver Wendell Holmes, recently appointed to the U.S. Supreme Court. His contacts and reputation at Harvard also gained him a job at a white-shoe Wall Street law firm that had never before hired a Jew. Even so, one of the senior partners advised Frankfurter that to assure acceptance in the real world of law practice, as distinguished from academe, he should change his name. Frankfurter had little incentive to take such a step, though, since he did not find lawyering in the WASP world nearly as congenial as Harvard. The private practice of law, he liked to say, involved mainly "getting money for people who already had plenty of it."

Frankfurter soon left his Wall Street firm to take a job in the U.S. Attorney's office in New York, then headed by Henry L. Stimson, to whom he had been recommended by faculty at Harvard Law. This would be a watershed in his life. By 1906, when Stimson took on the twenty-four-year-old Frankfurter, he was already on his way to becoming a legendary figure in his country's governing establishment. Like Frankfurter, Stimson had been raised in New York City but under circumstances that could hardly have been more different from the young man whose life he was to help shape. He was born in 1867 to a family of substantial means. After graduating from Yale, and then Harvard Law in 1891, his breeding and academic background commended him to Elihu Root, Theodore Roosevelt's secretary of state and most trusted adviser. Root brought Stimson into his New York law firm where he thrived and prospered. Meanwhile Stimson caught the eye of President Roosevelt, who persuaded him—at financial sacrifice—to accept appointment as U.S. Attorney for the Southern District of New York, in the heart of the financial beast that trustbuster TR wished to tame.

Stimson brought Frankfurter with him and made him his right-hand man, involving him in a series of mostly successful prosecutions for railroad rebating, winning convictions and big fines against such prominent targets as the New York Central and American Sugar Refining. Frankfurter's contributions to this effort so impressed Stimson that he took him to the White House to meet TR, an experience that enhanced Frankfurter's already flattering view of the Rough Rider president as one of the heroes of American history.

Stimson and Frankfurter left government when William Howard Taft succeeded to the presidency in 1909. But the next year Stimson allowed Roosevelt to persuade him to run for governor of New York, once again with Frankfurter by his side. It was a role for which he was ill-suited. Neither Yale nor Harvard nor his tony Manhattan upbringing had prepared Stimson for the hustle and clamor of a political campaign or for the delivery of a stump speech. As disastrous as the campaign turned out to be for Stimson, Frankfurter found the hustings a stimulating place, particularly when Roosevelt joined the fray on the candidate's behalf.

The impact of Stimson's influence on Frankfurter went beyond the excitement of rubbing shoulders with a president. Stimson was a compelling figure—intelligent, cultured, and an avatar of traditional values. As Herbert Hoover's secretary of state in 1929, with the Japanese already on the march in Asia,

Stimson, true to his Presbyterian upbringing, shut down the State Department's code-breaking division, explaining curtly, "Gentlemen do not read each other's mail." With his old-school commitments and allegiances, Stimson embodied just the sort of establishmentarian background that Frankfurter sought as a link to bolster his own emerging new identity. When Taft named Stimson as his secretary of war, Frankfurter signed up for his first stint in Washington. Stimson made him his all-round aide, dealing chiefly with the overseas possessions of the growing American empire.

On the side, the ever-aspiring Frankfurter developed relationships with two men who would play crucial parts in his professional and intellectual development, Louis Brandeis and Oliver Wendell Holmes. Both served Frankfurter as role models, in addition to Stimson, on his own road to the top of his profession. One of the ways in which Frankfurter sought to strengthen his relationship with such great men was by expressing his admiration of them in effusive terms. He "was an artist in adulation and sometimes, forgetting the artistry, he laid on flattery with a trowel," observed Max Freedman, Frankfurter's sympathetic biographer.

"Men no differently from women have to be told with great frequency that you love them," was the way Frankfurter rationalized his idolatry. Practicing what he preached, he wrote to Stimson after a notable courtroom victory as U.S. Attorney: "No one can testify so appropriately as I to your disinterestedness and tender fairness, but above all your thoughtfulness, generosity and loyalty toward your subordinates." After Taft's defeat in the 1912 presidential campaign and Wilson's ascension to the presidency, Frankfurter accepted an offer from the new secretary of war to stay on in his post at the War Department.

His enjoyment of the capital's social milieu helped him get through this transitional period. He joined a number of other young bachelors, among them Walter Lippmann, then a junior government official, in renting a ramshackle old house on Washington's Nineteenth Street, which Justice Holmes, among the many distinguished guests, wryly dubbed the "House of Truth." This abode became the center, as one resident described it, of "endless talk and an even more endless flow of casual guests." They included, besides one sitting justice, Holmes, the nation's outstanding private attorney, Louis Brandeis. Another guest, less prominent but who nevertheless attracted more of Frankfurter's attention, was a bright, irreverent, and beautiful young newspaper reporter named Marion Denman.

Frankfurter's courtship of Denman was no easy challenge. Their backgrounds could not have been more different. She was the daughter of a Congregational minister whose family had been in the country since pre-Revolutionary times. What they did have in common did not make their romance smoother. Like Frankfurter, the object of his affections was tense, high-strung, and driven by ambition. The six-year courtship resulting in marriage reflected and intensified Frankfurter's struggle to establish his identity apart from his family and his cultural background.

Meanwhile a new horizon and a new life opened for Frankfurter at Harvard. Aided by a good word from Brandeis and his own scintillating reputation as a former student and as a skilled young assistant to Stimson, Frankfurter was offered a teaching position at his alma mater. From the beginning he vowed that teaching would not cut him off from the struggle in the outside world over politics and ideas. He would use Harvard to strengthen his hand in the fray. "I am not a cloistered scholar," he wrote to Holmes, "and not even Cambridge, I think, can spoil my zest of life." He was true to his resolve. As a legal mainstay for the newly formed National Consumers League and similar public-spirited groups, he commuted to New York and Washington two or three times a week while churning out articles for magazines, notably the newly created *New Republic*.

America's entry into World War I brought Frankfurter back to Washington once again in the War Department as a jack of all trades. His first major assignment had its bizarre aspects—to accompany Henry Morgenthau, Sr., father of FDR's future treasury secretary, on a secret mission to Turkey to attempt to persuade the Ottoman Empire to break with the Central Powers.

How this was to be accomplished was never clear. Morgenthau, who had been Wilson's ambassador to Turkey but had resigned in despair over the Turkish slaughter of the Armenians, clearly had his differences with the Turkish government. Frankfurter was pressured into taking the assignment because, or so he later concluded, it was hoped he could keep Morgenthau's imperious temperament under control. Nothing came of the mission, which was fortunate for the Zionist movement in which Frankfurter was becoming increasingly involved as a result of his friendship with Brandeis. Given that Palestine was then part of the Ottoman Empire, if Turkey had joined the Western Powers as an ally instead of remaining an enemy, the chance of Palestine becoming a homeland for the Jews would have become even more problematic.

After the war Frankfurter made another trip abroad, this one more directly involved with Zionism. In 1919 as a private citizen he accompanied Brandeis to the Paris Peace Conference, participating in negotiations that improved the prospects for a Jewish homeland in Palestine. The experience added to Frankfurter's growing sense of his own importance. This self-regard was reflected in a letter to Wilson, then also at the peace conference, in which he pleaded for the president's support of the Balfour Declaration. Wilson ultimately agreed. "Circumstances have made me the trustee of a situation that affects the hopes and the very life of a whole people," Frankfurter wrote to Wilson, though he was only a very junior player in a drama with a full cast of senior statesmen. "Therefore I cannot forebear to say that not a little of the peace of the world depends upon the disposal, before your return to America, of the destiny of Palestine."

Between these two foreign trips, Frankfurter had plenty to do in the United States. His most controversial undertaking was an investigation of the trial of Tom Mooney at President Wilson's behest. A militant West Coast labor leader, Mooney had been convicted in the bombing of a 1916 Preparedness Day parade in San Francisco. Frankfurter concluded that Mooney's trial was a miscarriage of justice. This and similar activities by Frankfurter on behalf of left-wing causes triggered the outrage of Frankfurter's onetime hero Theodore Roosevelt, who likened Frankfurter to "Trotsky and the other Bolsheviki" for "excusing men who are murderers and encouragers of murder." But TR's disapproval in no way dampened Frankfurter's zeal for jousting against the forces of the legal establishment, which continued after he returned to his teaching post at Harvard in 1919.

The controversy that most engaged him was the battle to prove the innocence of Sacco and Vanzetti, the two Boston anarchists who were charged with a payroll robbery and murder, and sentenced to death. The case became one of the great causes celebres of the 1920s, with Frankfurter in the van of those forces fighting to reverse the verdict. After years of struggle, the tragic pair was executed in 1927. Frankfurter rarely spoke of the case afterward, but when he did he would say flatly that the two anarchists were murdered.

Throughout the 1920s, a decade distinguished for its complacency, wherever progressive forces were pitted against the status quo, Frankfurter could often be found on the left side of the barricades. On his own or in collaboration with Brandeis, and often with the latter's financial backing, Frankfurter carried on the struggle pioneered by Brandeis for minimum wage and hour laws and other labor and social welfare reforms.

Widely criticized for his espousal of what many at Harvard and elsewhere deemed radical causes, Frankfurter remained firm in his beliefs, even when he was challenged by TR and Henry Stimson. Responding to a note from Stimson who accused him of jeopardizing the reputation of Harvard Law School by his activities, Frankfurter responded: "If a professor at the Harvard Law School should refuse to associate himself with causes that seek the vindication of the law, simply because for the moment such vindication runs counter to popular opinion, how much respect would you have for the character of such a teacher?"

Although he brushed off such establishment criticism, Frankfurter was concerned about attacks that might stem from his identity, as he himself phrased it, as "a Jew of alien origin." And he was sensitive to the sometimes precarious position of Jews in the legal world. To a friend in a law firm that had hired a number of his referrals but had turned down a particularly bright prospect, he wrote: "I assume that you have all the Jews that the traffic can bear." His defensiveness was illustrated by a letter to Stimson in which he wrote: "I am deeply interested in Zionism which I suppose I am entitled to be interested in, and to give as much time to it as though I were a prominent Mason, or an important lay member of a church."

His sensitivity about his Jewishness was no doubt heightened by his struggles to defend his academic career against Harvard's president A. Lawrence Lowell, whose anti-Semitism was evidenced by his effort to impose a quota on Jewish students admitted to Harvard. When Frankfurter sought appointment to the committee on admissions, to oppose Lowell's move, Lowell rejected him, claiming that he lacked the "solid judgment" required for such a position. Although Lowell failed to establish a formal quota, he achieved much the same result by changing Harvard's admissions policy to lower the standards for applicants outside the North and East where most Jewish applicants lived.

As he pursued his advocacy of insurgent legal causes, Frankfurter's political loyalties also moved leftward. He had supported

Wilson in 1916 and the Cox-Roosevelt ticket in 1920, but the nomination of Wall Street lawyer John Davis by the strife-torn 1924 Democratic convention was too much, or rather too little, for him to accept. Instead he backed the Progressive party candidacy of Bob La Follette, whose defeat left Frankfurter adrift in the political seas. He would ultimately chart a course that would alter the shape of his life, guided by the rise of a bright Democratic star in the East, Franklin D. Roosevelt.

Frankfurter and Roosevelt had been casual acquaintances since the world war, when FDR had sought Frankfurter's advice on labor problems in the Navy Department. In 1924 Frankfurter, like many others in the world of politics, was impressed by Roosevelt's "Happy Warrior" speech nominating Smith. And when Roosevelt made his return to political life emphatic by capturing the governorship of New York in 1928, Frankfurter was glad to provide him with advice on a variety of matters.

But Frankfurter drew the line at anything more permanent, turning down the chairmanship of a judicial commission. He made clear that he preferred to serve as an ad hoc adviser rather than accept the responsibilities and burdens that came with a more formal commitment. Apart from his characteristic reluctance to be pinned down, Frankfurter had his doubts about FDR's credentials for the White House. He had supported Al Smith, not Roosevelt, in the contest for the Democratic presidential nomination, and his misgivings about Roosevelt persisted even after FDR had won that fight.

"I know his limitations," he wrote Walter Lippmann, who had famously made public his own skepticism about Roosevelt. "Most of them derive, I believe, from lack of incisive intellect and the kind of optimism that sometimes makes him timid, as well as ambition that leads to compromise. If he is elected, I think he will often do the right things, as it were, on inadequate and not wholly sturdy grounds. I don't expect heroic action from him."

Frankfurter's detachment from FDR may well have reflected the injury to his ego at not having been asked to join the coterie of Roosevelt campaign advisers dubbed the brain trust. Whatever his doubts, they did not deter him from dispensing the adulation he offered to other distinguished leaders he claimed as friends. "No predecessor of yours, not even TR, brought to the presidency so extensive and intimate a knowledge of his countrymen as you have," Frankfurter wrote in congratulating FDR on his 1932 election to the presidency. Once Roosevelt took office, he asked Frankfurter to become solicitor general, the government's chief advocate before the Supreme Court. But Frankfurter turned him down, maintaining that he would be more useful—and, he might have added, more influential—as an adviser without portfolio. "Frankfurter is a stubborn pig," the peeved Roosevelt complained.

Frankfurter was not so much stubborn as canny. Although he may have been miffed at not being recruited for the brain trust, he was shrewd enough to realize that given his own temperament and ego he was probably better off as a lone-wolf counselor. He knew that the effort to influence Roosevelt, one way or another, often turned into an ideological tug-of-war among his brain trusters and appointees. Donald Richberg, the labor lawyer who crafted the ill-fated National Industrial Recovery Act, which established the NRA, so despised by Brandeis, recalled how a dozen or so bright and ambitious men would stand around FDR's desk, "shooting ideas into him" in rapid fire, while Roosevelt, puffing on his long cigarette holder, would turn his head from one side to another to skim the cream of the crop.

This was just the sort of free-for-all Frankfurter preferred to avoid. Not that he made himself scarce during those yeasty early days of the New Deal. In the celebrated First One Hundred Days, and in the ensuing months, he commuted to the capital from Cambridge almost every weekend. But by holding himself apart from the formal structures in which most other advisers were embedded, he often managed to win special attention and influence for his views. And there was no doubt about which way Frankfurter sought to use his influence: sided with Mr. Justice Brandeis in his unrelenting crusade for smallness and decentralization. He opposed the thrust toward big government and a planned economy favored by other key New Dealers such as Raymond Moley and Rex Tugwell, two early members of the brain trust.

Most of Frankfurter's effectiveness in this struggle came from his unofficial role as recruiter-in-chief for the New Deal in its opening years, drawing on the pool of talent generated by Harvard Law School. Among the more prominent Frankfurter protégés who helped carry the load for the New Deal in its open years were Tom Corcoran and Ben Cohen, FDR's two leading legislative draftsmen; Dean Acheson in the Treasury Department; James M. Landis at the Securities and Exchange Commission; and Jerome N. Frank, law officer for the Agricultural Adjustment Agency. By and large Frankfurter's referrals won the favor of other New Dealers. At dinner with some of her cabinet colleagues who were complaining about the inefficiency at one branch of the Labor Department, Frances Perkins said bluntly, "We mean to put in one of Frankfurter's men pretty soon and get things straightened out in that division."

Not surprisingly, Frankfurter ascribed the influx of talent to lofty motives, mainly the desire for public service among talented young professionals, fostered by the depression. "More and more, the ablest of them—in striking contrast to what was true thirty years ago—are eager for service in government," he wrote in *Fortune*. "They find satisfaction in work which aims at the public good and which presents problems that challenge the best ability and courage of man."

But Frankfurter's achievements in running a sort of New Deal employment agency irritated some officials, who pointed out that the professor's recruits were impelled not only by altruism but also by ambition, which sometimes conflicted with the goals of their bosses. Notable among the critics was James Farley, Roosevelt's postmaster general, the office traditionally regarded as the dispenser of patronage. "I don't see why I am here as Postmaster General," grumbled Farley, who had been FDR's campaign manager, "since Frankfurter seems to hand out all the patronage."

The resentment of other New Deal officials at times seemed aimed not only at Frankfurter but at his coreligionists who made up a good part of the influx. "A plague of lawyers settled on Washington," complained George Peek, a crusty farm specialist who had been given charge of the Agriculture Adjustment Agency, a major player in FDR's efforts to deal with the farm crisis. "They claimed to be friends of somebody or other, mostly of Felix Frankfurter and Jerome Frank," Peek observed. Frank, the AAA's general counsel who was also Jewish, himself viewed the relatively large number of Jews among his staff attorneys as a problem. He once scolded an aide who brought him a list of Jewish lawyers as potential appointees: "Goddam it, you've got too many Jews here now. The people will begin to say that I am just selecting Jews."

Frankfurter's consciousness of the deep strains of anti-Semitism in American society inevitably colored his attitudes as Nazi persecution of Germany's Jews heightened, and contributed to his reticence to respond. When he did act it was often for defensive reasons. Thus in early April 1933, when he received word that Stephen Wise's American Jewish Congress was actively planning to organize public protests against Nazi persecution, Frankfurter sent word to the rabbi that he had arranged a meeting with FDR on the issue. Next day he hastened to phone Wise. "I have seen General Headquarters [another of the sobriquets used for FDR] and I feel sure he is watching the thing with understanding and sympathy," he reported. "Action followed very speedily upon our talk."

It seems clear that the real purpose of Frankfurter's meeting with FDR was to forestall further protests, particularly a visit to Washington by Wise. Frankfurter acted in part to protect Roosevelt from being hectored. But he was also protecting Roosevelt's confidence in him as an influence with the Jewish community, a rapport that would be threatened if the Jews were to get out of hand. The "action" that Frankfurter promised came on the day of his meeting with FDR on April 11, when Roosevelt instructed Labor Secretary Perkins and Secretary of State Hull to arrange a "moral gesture" of admitting a small number of prominent victims of Nazism.

Hull appears to have shrugged off the assignment, but Perkins characteristically threw herself into the affair. She did this even though she herself was on politically shaky ground. Her appointment had stirred disappointment among FDR's union supporters who challenged her credentials; they wanted one of their own in the job, and certainly not a woman. And she had no particular connection with Jewish issues or organizations. But in thirty years of public service, Madam Perkins, as she was called, had never turned her back on a humanitarian cause.

Born in Boston in 1882 to a prosperous upper-middle-class family, she graduated from Mount Holyoke College and adopted the activism in social causes characteristic of a number of privileged educated women during the era. A few years after college she began working closely with Jane Addams at Chicago's Hull House, where she observed firsthand the poverty and social isolation confronting the immigrants who flowed into America at the turn of the century. Moving to New York to earn a master's degree in social economics from Columbia University, she then became a reform leader seeking legislation to protect children and improve unsafe working conditions—which was how she first met State Senator Franklin Roosevelt. Galvanized by the Triangle Shirtwaist fire in 1911, over the next two decades she committed herself to reforming the horrendous conditions under which the working poor of New York labored.

Perkins married Paul Wilson, a New York City official, but defied the conventions of the day by continuing to use her maiden name professionally. In 1916 she gave birth to a daughter and thought her career was over. But two years later Al Smith, whom she had known from her lobbying days, won the New York governorship and made her chairman of the state's Industrial Commission. Franklin Roosevelt, when he succeeded Smith, chose her to head the state's Labor Department. Determined to be taken seriously, Perkins dressed modestly, habitually wearing a simple black dress with a white bow and a small tricorn hat that became her trademark. Despite her demure manner she was not easily browbeaten, and her dry sense of humor helped ward off gender bias. When a reporter asked if being a woman was a handicap, she answered coolly, "Only when climbing trees."

Taking on this new challenge of arranging to admit selected victims of Nazi persecution, she turned for help to Frankfurter, whom she had come to know when both had worked with the National Consumers League. The problem Frankfurter faced, created by President Hoover's broadening of the "likely public charge" provision in the immigration law, challenged even his formidable legal and political skills. As possible solutions Frankfurter drafted for Perkins two alternate executive orders, either of which would have circumvented the "LPC" barrier for visa applicants who were seeking to avoid racial or religious persecution. But instead of arguing his case with Roosevelt, Frankfurter chose an indirect approach. He sent the proposals to Raymond Moley, who had been made an assistant secretary at the State Department. His suggestions, Frankfurter argued to

Moley, were nothing more or less than "an enunciation of the traditional domestic policy of the United States. And it would be tragic beyond words if narrow, moralistic views, based on vague timidities, would deflect and defeat the high and wise purposes of the president."

If Moley supported Frankfurter's arguments, he lacked the clout to gain approval from the rigid bureaucracy that controlled immigration policy at State and reflexively resisted any attempt at liberalization. Undersecretary William Phillips, an old friend of FDR's, passed the word to the president that his department viewed any such change with disfavor.

Perkins fought back in conversations with the president. She took courage when at one point Roosevelt remarked, "You know, population never made a country unprosperous," adding that "some day" immigration policy might have to be redrawn in more generous terms. But "some day" never arrived for FDR. Whatever sympathy he may have had for the beleaguered Jews of Germany was overshadowed by strong resistance in Congress and among the public to the relaxation of immigration barriers. Attempting to challenge or defuse this political opposition involved expending political capital that FDR did not wish to invest on this issue. And neither of his two leading Jewish advisers, Brandeis and Frankfurter, directly urged him to take the plunge. Thus the intransigent State Department carried the day.

Conceding defeat, for the moment anyway, Perkins wrote to Frankfurter that the administration refused to issue a public statement or an executive order about refugees. Indeed the president did not even mention the word "refugee" in any of his public statements then or later in his presidency, except for a brief reference to Americans made homeless by the flooding of the Mississippi River. Only in 1938, in the wake of the *Anschluss*, did FDR refer to European refugees. The most Perkins could gain in the way of a concession was a promise that the State

Department would confidentially instruct its overseas consuls to interpret the "likely public charge" provision liberally.

Frankfurter was indignant. "It is rather heart-breaking that the President's desire and what I understood was a cabinet decision should be postponed by considerations of prudence which at the time occurred neither to the President nor the cabinet," he wrote Perkins. Attached to the letter was a news clipping quoting Nazi propaganda minister Joseph Goebbels as warning the Jews that they faced even more stringent measures from the Nazi regime. "It isn't any good to have confidential relaxation of visual rules," Frankfurter argued. "To do the right thing in the dark is the wrong way to do it." In a personal context, Frankfurter called the decision particularly painful to him "as one who is more attached to Franklin Roosevelt's Administration than he has been attached to any other. It grieves me beyond words," he added, "that the human and wise forthrightness of Franklin Roosevelt should be impeded—I refuse to believe it will be permanently frustrated—by the formal timidities of the Bill Phillipses." But the "forthrightness" of FDR seems to have been more apparent to Frankfurter than to Moley, Perkins, or anyone else, since the expression of these sentiments had been limited to a few elliptical words about a "moral gesture" cloaked in the confidentiality of a conversation with cabinet members.

In any event, Frankfurter's outburst to Perkins begged a question. Given the strength of his feelings and his arguments, his closeness to the president, and his faith in Roosevelt's wisdom and forthrightness, why did he not make his case directly to the Skipper instead of to Secretary Perkins? Frankfurter appears to have provided part of the answer in another paragraph of his letter to her. "For once in my life I wish that for a brief period I were not a Jew," he wrote with characteristic self-absorption. "Then I would not have the appearance of being sectarian in writing you as I have written."

Jewish leaders were not satisfied with FDR's sub-rosa gesture. "It will not be long" before American Jews would "insist something more meaningful come from the Administration," Rabbi Wise wrote to his confidant Julian Mack. In a letter to Frankfurter, Wise noted the sentiment among Jews for a full-scale boycott of German goods and said he would have a hard time opposing the idea without a word from FDR to bolster his case. He pointed out that he had sought to discourage protest resolutions in Congress to avoid embarrassment to the president, but "I cannot feel that I have the right to stand out any longer against the possibility of the American people making their voice heard in the halls of Congress."

That got Frankfurter's attention. Once again, as with the threat of a Jewish boycott earlier in the month, he was eager to shield FDR and preserve his own relationship with the president. He phoned Wise immediately, and soon a telegram came from Wise, evidently suggested by Frankfurter, repeating the same arguments Wise had made in his earlier letter. But it closed with this powerful plea: "Time is of the essence prayerfully hope for *some word* by the President in *whatever* form he may choose to express his own deep feeling and that this word will be spoken at once" (emphasis in the original). Frankfurter immediately forwarded the telegram to FDR. But the only response came from Secretary Hull, thanking him for his "courtesy" in bringing Wise's message to the administration's attention. Frankfurter allowed none of this to shake his loyalty to Roosevelt or threaten his own position in the inner circle.

When Jewish leaders asked him to help arrange a meeting with FDR to discuss easing visa restrictions for European Jews, Frankfurter demurred. He would be unwilling to act as "a conduit," he explained, because it would create "wholly unwarranted implications" about his relationship with the president. His counterproposal was delicately nuanced. He would not join such a delegation, Frankfurter said, though he would be willing to accompany it. But he added a condition. "My presence should be the result of an expression of desire on the part of the President," he wrote Joseph Proskauer of the American Jewish Committee; he would attend only "if it be agreeable to the president to have me present at the interview."

For the administration's inaction, Frankfurter, probably at this point FDR's most influential adviser, took no responsibility. Instead he blamed others. One target was the State Department. "It really is disheartening that the human and courageous determination of the President should have failed of execution somewhere along the route," he wrote to Raymond Moley, echoing the refrain of his earlier letter to Perkins. "Can't you have the wise and brave determination of the president vindicated promptly?"

Jewish leadership also came in for censure, particularly the American Jewish Committee. It had been relatively sedentary in the controversy, in contrast to the activism of the American Jewish Congress, which Wise had helped create. In his letter to Proskauer, Frankfurter blamed "the internal rows" among New York Jewry for undercutting efforts to persuade the administration to protest the persecution of Germany's Jews.

Frankfurter of course knew better than to believe this. Rather, the administration's policy reflected its own priorities in domestic and foreign policy in the light of public anxiety over a new wave of immigration. But his note to Proskauer does demonstrate Frankfurter's internal conflicts at the time. Whatever the divisions among Jewish organizations, they were no greater than Frankfurter's struggles within himself. "For once in my life I wish that for a brief period I were not a Jew," he wrote to Cordell Hull in May 1933, repeating his plaint to Perkins the month before. "Then I would not have even the appearance of being sectarian."

Amid his blame-placing and internal agonizing, except on rare occasions Frankfurter avoided using his best asset in the fight to aid Germany's Jews, his closeness to FDR. He abstained from appealing directly to the president even when importuned by Brandeis. Instead he wrote to Perkins and Moley urging the easing of immigration restrictions. But his letters implicitly acknowledged the futility of this exercise.

Responding to a State Department memorandum on the immigration controversy sent to him by Perkins, which referred to refugees seeking to flee "political" discrimination, he wrote that it had "no application to the present Germany situation." "I am sure that the president and you are aware that the line that is now being drawn in Germany is not a political line," Frankfurter wrote. "Implacable and systematic extermination of people of Jewish faith and race is the avowed objective of the present German government. I shall continue to refuse to believe that alone of all Western governments this Administration will remain without public actions or utterance in the face of such an assault on the decencies of civilization."

But for all its lofty indignation, Frankfurter's letter ignored the basic reality, which he surely must have recognized. For the U.S. government to respond to the "assault on civilization," Frankfurter's friend Franklin D. Roosevelt would have to lead the way. And Roosevelt, mindful of the political calculus fostered by the depression, did little to alter the State Department's resistance to substantial change.

No figure was more influential in shaping the department's position than Assistant Secretary of State Wilbur Carr, a longtime acquaintance of the president who supervised the foreign service, including the U.S. consuls stationed abroad. Called by one critic the "epitome of the bureaucrat," Carr's rise was quite different from that of most in the U.S. diplomatic service, men who came from backgrounds of wealth and privilege. Carr was a poor Ohio farm boy who learned bookkeeping at a commercial college and worked his way up through the ranks to the directorship of the Consular Service in 1909. He established and maintained control of the service through tight discipline implemented by periodic inspections which rated officers for such qualities "as honesty, morality and loyalty" as well as the number of visas granted. In addition, Carr's command of minutiae made him invaluable to his superiors on fiscal and budgetary matters. By the time FDR took office, many regarded Carr as the grand old man of State.

Carr's diary reveals a visceral anti-Semitism. Traveling to Detroit he complained that the city was filled with "dust, smoke, dirt, Jews." After a boat trip to Albany he grumbled that most of the passengers were Jews "of one kind or another" and found it "appalling to observe the lack of appreciation of the privilege they are having." Naturally he was eager to enforce Hoover's new tightening of the immigration rules, and he advised colleagues to ignore the protests of American ethnic organizations.

Carr and Roosevelt had known each other since World War I days when they had offices in the same corridor of the old building that then housed the War and Navy departments along with State. FDR had been impressed with Carr's command of detail, so much so that on his first day in office in 1933 he asked Carr's advice on whether his directive closing the banks should be issued as an executive order or a proclamation. A proclamation, Carr concluded, for this unprecedented move. FDR took his advice. Roosevelt, relentless philatelist that he was, also enjoyed Carr's promise to get him stamps from related official documents for his personal collection. With this chummy rapport with the president, Carr had no hesitation in maintaining the barriers to immigration despite FDR's "moral gestures." He would continue to do so until he left his post in 1937 to become ambassador to Czechoslovakia.

In this attitude he was strongly supported by his nominal superior, Undersecretary William Phillips, who disliked Jews at least as vehemently as Carr. In his diary Phillips complained that his favorite resort, Atlantic City, was "infested with Jews," and he wrote disparagingly of Jewish business associates. But Phillips's relationship to FDR went back even farther than Carr's to their days at Harvard, and he did not leave his post until 1936 when Roosevelt made him ambassador to Mussolini's Italy.

For Jews and their supporters to challenge the State Department's attitude was made more difficult by the seeming intensification of anti-Semitism in the United States, partly because of the depression, partly in response to the rise of Nazism, and partly because of the New Deal's accessibility to Jews. At first Jews took pride and encouragement from the prominence of Jewish appointees in the government and the influence they appeared to wield. But those feelings were soon undercut by anxiety.

The *American Hebrew*, which had been worried about Jewish bloc voting in the 1928 New York governor's race, took pains in the second year of the New Deal to debunk "the myth of a 'Jewish Hierarchy.'" Washington correspondent Arthur T. Weil set out to refute the proposition advanced by Nazis and other anti-Semites that "under the Roosevelt New Deal a disproportionate number of Jews are holding pivotal positions in Washington, dangling the major strings that make the rest of the nation hop skip and jump." Weil pointed out that only one Jew, Henry Morgenthau, held a cabinet position, and that no Jews were in the "little cabinet" made up of a score or so assistants and undersecretaries. No Jew, wrote Weil, held a prominent position in any of the independent agencies. The article briefly passed over the role of unofficial adviser Felix Frankfurter and a number of officials, such as Ben Cohen and Jerome Frank, whose influence outweighed their relatively modest position in the organizational charts. Weil concluded: "With 4,000,000 Jews in the United States there could hardly be fewer appointees; certainly this is anything but over-representation."

Despite this defensive calculus, it was not difficult to see how anti-Semites could make a case that Jews wielded significant influence in the Roosevelt administration. Whatever the exact number of Jews in the upper echelons of the government, no one could deny there were more of them there now than in the past. "Unlike previous administrations where the Protestant ethic both reigned and ruled," one sympathetic analyst wrote, "Roosevelt sought young, ambitious and idealistic people to lay the groundwork for a more socially just society."

That was one way to look at it. But many in the corporate world and in the middle class viewed the supplanting of the "Protestant ethic" with grave misgivings. These skeptics found it easy to equate the construction of a "socially just society" with socialism or some more radical form of left-wing ideology with which they tended to link young Jewish idealists. As a result, regardless of the mathematics involved, the allegedly excessive influence of Jews in the New Deal was an argument that served as a double-edged sword: it could be used against Jews *and* against Roosevelt, who had himself become the most controversial figure on the American scene. "Most presidents," *Fortune* observed as the 1936 election approached, "even in a period of potential anti-Semitism like the present, would be allowed to enjoy the friendship of intelligent and honorable Jews exactly as they would be permitted to enjoy the friendship of any man of mind and honor."

Not so with FDR. His ties to Frankfurter, Morgenthau, and other prominent Jews "are held against him in many quarters." The magazine cited former NRA chieftain Hugh Johnson's description of Frankfurter as "the most influential single individual in the United States" in a tone that suggested "what he means is the most dangerous." But *Fortune*, echoing the refrain of the *American Hebrew*, contended that Jews were not really much of a factor in the New Deal. Conceding that Frankfurter was arguably Roosevelt's most influential adviser, the magazine contended that with the exception of Morgenthau and Ben Cohen, "no other Roosevelt Jew disposes of anything which could remotely be called power." Still, *Fortune* went on to acknowledge a fundamental truth about the complaints of excessive Jewish influence: "The point is not that the accusation of pro-Semitism is true or untrue. The point is that it is made."

Because of his own relationship to Roosevelt, Frankfurter was in a rare position to provide a counterweight to the State Department, where Carr and Phillips held sway on immigration policy. But he avoided any such intervention that might affect his own rapport with the president. To the contrary, in 1938 after the *Anschluss,* when at FDR's urging an international conference was called to consider the refugee problem, Frankfurter wrote to congratulate his friend. This despite Roosevelt's announcement that none of the nations attending would be expected to change their immigration laws to allow entry by refugees from Hitler. In apparent acknowledgment, Frankfurter conceded in his letter that most of the Nazi victims "won't find a haven of refuge here or elsewhere." Lest Roosevelt take offense at this implicit criticism of his initiative, Frankfurter added, "But what you have done will help sustain their souls in the material enslavement."

There was a time in his life when Frankfurter would have poured his energies, his eloquence, and his legal skills into challenging the immigration quotas that denied escape to the victims of Nazism. But the zeal that fired the young man to battle for the rights of Tom Mooney, Sacco and Vanzetti, and the like had been sapped by myriad anxieties about himself and his status as a Jew, along with his hopes for professional advancement. In addition to preserving his relationship with FDR, there was the possibility of an appointment to the Supreme Court to consider. Although Frankfurter had avoided directly promoting himself for the post, he could not have been unaware of the opportunity, particularly since Roosevelt had twice mentioned that he intended to select him when the time was ripe. But he had to worry that he could jeopardize his chances, either by creating friction with the president directly or by taking public positions that would make it hard for FDR to appoint him.

The sensitivity of Frankfurter's situation became clear after the death of Justice Benjamin Cardozo, a Jew, in 1938 created a vacancy on the Court. Frankfurter's contributions as a policy adviser had won him many friends in high places, including Ickes, FDR confidant Harry Hopkins, and Robert Jackson, then U.S. solicitor general and a future justice himself. All lobbied hard for Frankfurter's nomination to the Court after Cardozo's death. And all realized that Roosevelt was reluctant to nominate Frankfurter in part because of his liberalism and also because of his religion. Cardozo's death left one Jewish justice still on the Court in Brandeis, which some thought was already one Jew too many. A group of prominent Jews, among them Arthur Hays Sulzberger, publisher of the *New York Times*, called on Roosevelt to urge him not to nominate Frankfurter because, they maintained, it would foster anti-Semitism.

This infuriated Frankfurter, but he was saved from the anxiety of his coreligionists by the endorsement of Senator George Norris of Nebraska, with whom he had worked on labor legislation and who had the advantage in this situation of being both a Protestant and a Republican. Norris wrote a long letter to the president urging Frankfurter's selection, and just as important issued a public statement. Frankfurter would later refer to his being chosen by Roosevelt as "a bombshell," which led Ben Cohen to observe: "I don't know why Felix was so surprised." Cohen pointed out that Frankfurter protégé Tom Corcoran had lobbied vigorously for Frankfurter's selection "and would call him every night to report what had been done."

Frankfurter's indignation when he himself came close to being victimized by anti-Semitism, albeit fostered by other Jews, in no way altered his temporizing when confronted with the consequences of Nazi persecution. He maintained his stance even when the long arm of the Gestapo reached into his own family. In 1938, following the *Anschluss*, Frankfurter's uncle, Dr. Solomon Frankfurter, a renowned Austrian scholar, was arrested and sent to a concentration camp by the country's new Nazi rulers after he protested a Nazi clampdown on scholarship. Rather than seeking the help of his own government, Frankfurter appealed to Britain's Lady Astor. She was a leading member of her country's notorious "Cliveden Set," named for Astor's spacious estate sited above the Thames, where she and her upper-class, right-wing cohorts planned efforts to placate Hitler. Thus she was on good terms with the Nazi regime. Sure enough, a good word from her ladyship effected the old man's release. Three years later, when Solomon Frankfurter died, news accounts incorrectly attributed his release from the concentration camp to the U.S. State Department.

Frankfurter, by now a justice on the Supreme Court, was greatly upset and immediately wrote FDR to set the record straight. He had not asked the State Department for help, Frankfurter emphasized, "precisely because I wanted to avoid the criticism even of the evil minded and hardhearted against any charge of favoritism by your administration." Roosevelt wrote back to remonstrate: "I think that even a Justice of the Supreme Court is entitled to ask his own government to help out persecuted people, even though they be his own relatives, in any part of the world."

But this was a proposition Frankfurter was reluctant to test, as he had demonstrated on numerous occasions. The vacuum he left created an opportunity for another of the President's Jews to wield influence, in a way that further frustrated the attempts of American Jewry to help their beleaguered brethren in Europe.

V

THE TROUBLESHOOTER

As IF Rabbi Stephen Wise did not have his hands full enough
trying to help the persecuted Jews of Germany in 1937, a new
threat to Jews loomed in, of all places, Brazil. Since Hitler's rise
to power, Brazil had been a haven for Jewish refugees from
Europe. But in November 1937 its president, Getúlio Vargas,
staged a coup and assumed dictatorial powers. In an attempt to
foster stronger economic ties with Nazi Germany, as a market
for Brazilian exports, he ordered the deportation of hundreds of
Jewish refugees. "We have had a terrible cry of alarm from the
Jews in Brazil," Wise wrote to Felix Frankfurter. Wise claimed
that he was concerned not just about the fate of Brazil's Jews but
more broadly about what Vargas's new revolutionary regime,
which bore all the hallmarks of incipient fascism, portended
for the Western Hemisphere. Who could get the president to
address this issue?

Wise said his own views "would not avail," presumably
because he lacked the necessary influence with FDR. But once
more he was willing to let Frankfurter off the hook when it came
to pressuring the president directly. "I feel that you may not be
ready to take it up with him," he wrote. That left another of

the President's Jews, Sam Rosenman, who since the 1936 election had been playing a much more prominent role in the inner workings of the New Deal. Wise quickly rejected that possibility too. "Rosenman isn't a serious enough person to be able to handle this problem," he wrote, about as damning a judgment as the rabbi could make of a potential ally and prominent Jewish political figure. Rather than trust Rosenman, he would consider appealing to Idaho senator William Borah, a Gentile and a Republican.

As it happened, Vargas was more pragmatic than power mad. He shifted with the economic winds away from anti-Semitism and toward greater friendship with the United States, and would eventually join the Allies in declaring war on Hitler.

But while the situation of the Jews in Brazil improved, Wise's opinion of Sam Rosenman did not. In January 1938, in another letter to Frankfurter, he found reason to take an even dimmer view of the man who, except for Louis Howe and Morgenthau, had been closer to Franklin Roosevelt than any other during his tenure as New York governor. During a recent visit to Washington, Wise reported to Frankfurter, his friend David Niles, a Jewish progressive from Boston and an aide to Harry Hopkins, had mentioned attending a White House tea at which Rosenman was also present. "I have a hunch that he is there too much and that his influence is not good," Wise wrote. "I suppose he is some kind of liberal, had to be in order to be near F.D.R. But I am sure that Jewishly his influence is all to the bad."

In his judgment of Rosenman, Wise had more than a "hunch" to rely on. In the spring of 1933, three months into Roosevelt's presidency, when many American Jews were pleading with their government to protest Hitler's anti-Semitic binge, Rosenman, a member of the American Jewish Committee's executive committee, called upon his fellow members to remain silent. "On the basis of direct information," Rosenman assured his auditors, FDR was "concerned over the German situation"—whatever that meant.

On the same day, June 5, 1933, Republican Representative James M. Beck of Philadelphia, a former U.S. solicitor general, called upon the nations of the world to protect Germany's Jews "by the mighty forces of world opinion. The Jewish race in Germany has made great and noble contributions to civilization which will be gratefully remembered when the name of Hitler will be, even in Germany, a shameful memory," Beck added.

The next week Herbert Lehman, FDR's successor as governor of New York, launched a campaign to raise $1 million for the relief of German Jews victimized by the Nazis. "Hundreds of thousands of men and women in all walks of life have been ruthlessly and without pity deprived of their means of livelihood and of the primary rights of citizenship," Lehman declared. "We cannot permit our co-religionists to suffer needlessly and endlessly when we have the means, at least in some slight degree, to mitigate their distress."

But growing tragedy abroad was not enough to impel President Roosevelt to speak out, a circumstance that Rosenman sought to explain to American Jewish Committee leaders. Roosevelt was keeping silent to avoid ruffling the waters before the forthcoming international conferences on disarmament and economic policy that year, Rosenman explained. Should those conferences fail, he warned, "the result for the world at large and the Jews in particular would be extremely unfavorable." Assistant Secretary of State Raymond Moley, who was not Jewish, saw things differently. He told one Jewish leader that neither conference posed "an insuperable obstacle in the way of a direct statement from the White House" on the Jewish persecution in Germany.

But Rosenman did not consult Moley. Instead he echoed his comments to the American Jewish Committee meeting in messages to Wise, who had been thinking of organizing a delegation to visit the president. "You should not ask the President to make any declaration or public act," Rosenman wrote. And furthermore, "receiving a delegation or deputation" by the president "is out now."

As events developed, both conferences turned into debacles, as might well have been foreseen given the attitudes of FDR in one case and Chancellor Hitler in the other. The economic conference failed in large part because Roosevelt refused to make any agreement with other nations that might limit his freedom of action at home. And Hitler, bent on rebuilding Germany's military power to equal that of Britain and France, torpedoed the disarmament conference. These outcomes could hardly have been affected by any criticism from FDR of the Nazi spree of anti-Semitism, though such a statement might have given Hitler pause and certainly would have offered hope to the Jews.

Well before Rosenman's attempt to muzzle anti-Nazi protest, he had crossed swords with Wise when Roosevelt was still governor of New York. Just as he prepared to launch his drive for the Democratic presidential nomination, FDR found himself forced to contend with the ugly controversy over alleged political corruption at Tammany Hall. Fanning the flames of public indignation against Tammany was a new adversary, Stephen Wise, head of a citizens committee pushing for civic reform. With his political future in jeopardy, in part because of Wise, Roosevelt had placed his fate in the hands of the same aide who had helped bail him out a number of times during his service as governor. This was Samuel I. Rosenman, a thirty-four-year-old troubleshooter seasoned on the battlefronts of both law and politics. On that occasion he had once more rescued Roosevelt and in the process frustrated Wise.

Rosenman was the son of Ukrainian Jews who had immigrated first to San Antonio, where the paterfamilias, Sol Rosenman, tried his hand as a peddler. When that did not work, Sol moved his wife and five children to New York City's lower Harlem, then a heavily Jewish neighborhood. While the elder Rosenman earned a living as a storekeeper, his youngest son, Sam, made a fine record for himself at Townsend Harris, New York's elite high school, its City College, and then Columbia University.

Although Sam Rosenman resented the social discrimination against Jews that he found at Columbia, it did not dissuade him from going on to Columbia Law School. After taking two years off for stateside duty as a U.S. Army first lieutenant during World War I, Rosenman earned his law degree in 1919. He soon met and ultimately married Dorothy Reuben, with whom he had two sons. But this was only after their courtship had been prolonged by the misgivings of the bride's father about the ability of his prospective son-in-law to support his daughter appropriately. Father Reuben need not have worried; Rosenman had ambition to spare and energy to match. No sooner had he passed the bar than he obtained a job clerking for a prosperous Manhattan lawyer. But he had his eyes on bigger things, in particular a slot on the bench, where long-term tenure offered relative shelter from the shifting tides of the legal profession, and he concluded that politics was his best route.

While practicing law he threw his energies into precinct organizing for Tammany Hall in his local assembly district. Its leader was a third-generation machine politician named James J. Hines, a prototypical Tammany operative who would later come to a bad end. Originally a blacksmith, Hines took pride in his physical strength and did not hesitate to deploy it to advance Tammany's interests in the rough-and-tumble of New York city government. Hines and Rosenman worked closely for a number of years, even living in the same apartment house, while Rosenman learned the ropes of big-city politics. Hines had "great energy," Rosenman said of him years later. "I was a great admirer of his personality and really his ability to understand things for which he wasn't trained." Rosenman thought so much of Hines that in 1929 he arranged a meeting with Governor Roosevelt, "who was quite taken" with the ward boss. "I'm sure that if Hines had stayed straight he would have been a very powerful political figure in the Roosevelt Administration," Rosenman said. Indeed, until the forces of law and order caught up with him in 1938, Hines functioned as the man to see about Roosevelt's preferences in the labyrinth of New York politics.

Hines "fell into bad company" and learned from racketeers how to make "soft money," was how Rosenman explained his former patron's ultimate downfall. Hines did have at least one sterling quality, from Rosenman's point of view: he was "very particular not to involve innocent people around him," Rosenman noted gratefully. So on election day, when Hines's minions were dispatched to stuff ballot boxes, bully their opponents, and otherwise rig the voting results, Hines would never allow Rosenman in the clubhouse. "I would only hear about it later from others," Rosenman said. Of course, after hearing about these activities for several elections, Rosenman did not ask himself how "innocent" he was entitled to feel. In any event, when Hines was convicted of racketeering by prosecutor Thomas E. Dewey in a trial that dominated New York tabloids and sent the accused to Sing Sing prison, Rosenman's name never came up in the proceedings.

Before his fall, Hines picked Rosenman to run for the state assembly. Rosenman's largely middle-class home district in Manhattan had always been represented by a Republican. But Hines shrewdly concluded that Rosenman's Ivy League background gave him a chance to break the GOP stranglehold. Aided by a small group of friends who called themselves the "Flying Squadron of Debutantes," Rosenman shocked the Republicans by winning the election.

He served five years until he saw a better opportunity as a result of the resignation of the Democratic member of the legislature's bill-drafting commission, whose job was to provide technical expertise on lawmaking. With the help of his allies at Tammany, Rosenman arranged to have himself appointed to fill the vacancy. As he put it, he was getting "a little tired" of the assembly, and opportunities for advancement seemed nil. His new job gave him a chance to work with and do favors for the state's most influential politicians. And he could earn more money by supplementing his salary with freelance legal and political work when the legislature was out of session.

Rosenman's legal acumen and political savvy on the bill-drafting commission caught the eye of the redoubtable Belle Moskowitz, chief adviser to governor Al Smith. In 1928, when Smith was busy running for president, Moskowitz dispatched Rosenman to help newly nominated Democratic gubernatorial candidate Franklin Roosevelt by providing background on state issues. Initially Rosenman, who had been hoping to work on Smith's presidential campaign, was crestfallen. But his disappointment soon faded as Roosevelt found good use for his skills. And Rosenman realized that his rapport with the candidate offered him his best chance yet to get the judgeship he still yearned for. As FDR stumped the state with Rosenman at his side, he tutored his new aide on speechwriting as he preferred it to be done. "Knock out a draft of what you think I ought to say, and we'll go over it in the morning," was the offhand way Roosevelt typically handled the matter. Rosenman readily adapted to this nonchalant approach and soon took over the main burden of writing FDR's speeches.

The two men got on so well that after Roosevelt narrowly won election he kept Rosenman on in the elevated position of counsel to the governor. But first he had to talk Rosenman into accepting. Rosenman was reluctant to give up his post on the bill-drafting commission with the ample opportunities it offered for financial reward. In addition, he knew that under Smith, most of the governor's significant legal work was done by unofficial advisers. "It really was a sinecure," he told

Roosevelt, adding, "I was too young to be immersed in that kind of post." But Roosevelt promised Rosenman that he would abolish the "kitchen cabinet" Smith had relied on and turn over all their work to the counsel.

Rosenman took the job, and FDR lived up to his word. "There was practically nothing that the governor was doing officially that escaped my attention," he recalled. "There were no secrets, either with respect to state affairs or the public maneuvering for the presidency."

The two spent a great deal of time together. During Roosevelt's final two years as governor, Rosenman lived at the executive mansion in Albany while his growing family stayed in New York. "I had a room at the mansion and lived there with him, used to go to work with him, and come back have breakfast with him and have dinner with him and spent a great many evenings with him," Rosenman recalled. "It's a hard job being governor, and being governor's counsel is also a full-time job, and I think we understood each other very well."

The governor's house guest earned his keep, handling a range of administrative chores, advising on policy issues, and writing speeches. But his most crucial role involved the deepening legal problems of Tammany Hall, which soon became Governor Roosevelt's political problems. The legal and political fracas that involved both FDR and his trusted aide, Rosenman, had a long-term significance that reached beyond the New York political-arena of the time. The two-year imbroglio proved to be a crucible that tested and ultimately strengthened Roosevelt's bond with his counsel and contributed importantly to the influence Rosenman would wield during FDR's White House tenure.

There was much irony in this situation for both men. In his political career before going to work for Roosevelt, Rosenman had always had Tammany backing, starting with Jimmy Hines. Although FDR had feuded with the leadership of the New York County Democratic Party, as Tammany Hall was officially known, he too had benefited from the machine's support, particularly in his campaign for governor.

Tammany's iron-fisted control of patronage, and its free-and-easy attitude toward graft, had always provided ready political ammunition to the GOP and provoked demands for investigation. Matters seemed to boil over after the 1930 elections for state and local office, with the fires of indignation stoked by two civic-minded and outspoken clergymen, Rabbi Wise and his close colleague, Reverend John Haynes Holmes, a crusading Unitarian minister. The two presented FDR with a long list of charges against New York's Tammany-backed playboy mayor, James J. Walker, and demanded his resignation. After six weeks, in a statement drafted by Rosenman, the governor bluntly rejected the charges, an action which many of his own supporters would come to consider a blunder since it made him seem insensitive to the excesses of Tammany.

Moreover FDR's action did not end the furor. A new investigation commissioned by the state legislature led to further charges against Tammany. Again Roosevelt turned to Rosenman while staying in the background. As Rosenman well understood, FDR was in a pickle. "Remember, starting in 1930 he was a candidate for the presidency," Rosenman told an interviewer years later. "He knew that he was walking a very tight rope in New York." He had to choose between incurring Tammany's wrath or being stigmatized as a creature of the machine. No wonder Roosevelt decided that the better part of valor was to let his faithful aide take the spotlight and the heat. Rosenman's inquiry into the charges against New York County sheriff Thomas Farley, a pillar of Tammany corruption, led to Roosevelt ordering Farley's ouster from office, which earned the organization's resentment of both Rosenman and his boss. Rosenman's handling of the matter, as Ray Moley pointed out, was "a tribute to his devotion to Roosevelt." It was also a reflection of his keen sense of opportunity and his willingness to take a short-term setback in exchange for the prospect of a long-range advantage, in this case FDR's gratitude.

Roosevelt rewarded his counsel in March 1932 by nominating him for a vacant seat on the New York Supreme Court, thus fulfilling Rosenman's longtime ambition. FDR described the appointment as one of the most unselfish acts of his life, "because I am cutting off my right arm." Confirmed by the legislature, Rosenman was nevertheless rejected by Tammany a few months later when the Hall nominated someone else as its candidate to serve the full judicial term he had filled on an interim basis. On this occasion Roosevelt used his arm in another striking metaphor. Wiring his disappointment to Rosenman, he added, "I have a long memory and a long arm for friends"—which is what Rosenman was counting on. Rosenman was not absent from the bench for long. In 1933, a year after Tammany's failure to support him forced Rosenman off the bench, New York's new governor, Herbert Lehman, renominated him to the court. This time Tammany went along, and Rosenman won election to a full fourteen-year term.

In the interim, though Rosenman had officially left Roosevelt's service in April 1932, FDR found plenty of chores for him. One with considerable importance for the launching of Roosevelt's candidacy for the presidency was the organization of the so-called brain trust, whose members, most recruited from academe, constituted FDR's chief guides to policy during the tumultuous early days of the New Deal.

Perhaps even more far-reaching in its own way was Rosenman's contribution to Roosevelt's address accepting his party's presidential nomination. Moley, functioning in his role as senior member of the brain trust, had given the governor a draft of the speech, but as was his custom he had not bothered to provide a peroration. Rosenman was asked to write a suitable conclusion. He did so early in the morning while the convention was still deadlocked and FDR's nomination was by no means a certainty.

A prodigious eater, Rosenman fortified himself for the task with several home-cooked hot dogs and a pot of coffee and scribbled out two paragraphs containing a phrase that would come to embody Roosevelt's presidency. "I pledge you," Rosenman wrote, "I pledge myself to a *New Deal* for the American people." It was a phrase that had a special resonance for FDR: for those Americans with strong memories it recalled the "Square Deal" propounded by the first Roosevelt in the White House.

The impact of this new cognomen, which would become one of the most enduring political trademarks in the nation's history, was greatly enhanced with the appearance the next day of a drawing by the widely syndicated liberal cartoonist Rollin Kirby. With artful strokes, Kirby depicted a figure resembling Edwin Markham's "Man with the Hoe," as captured in Millet's famous painting, gazing hopefully at an airplane above with the words "New Deal" emblazoned on its wings.

The airplane had special meaning because of Roosevelt's unprecedented decision to fly to the convention to accept his nomination, a gesture intended to demonstrate his disdain for stodgy tradition. Even before the cartoon appeared, Roosevelt had rewarded Rosenman for his efforts by inviting him to join him at the convention in Chicago. Given the shaky status of air travel at the time, the flight was considered a daring move and caused particular uneasiness for Rosenman's wife, Dorothy. When she asked Roosevelt at an informal press conference whether her husband would go to Chicago, FDR wisecracked that Sam Rosenman would indeed go to the convention but would skip the plane trip and travel by tricycle.

Once the convention ended, Rosenman was conspicuous by his absence from the Roosevelt entourage. His New York judicial duties continued through the year. Beyond that, the competition for Roosevelt's attention and favor among the growing legion of brain trusters and other advisers led Rosenman to remain in the background for the time being. A particular barrier was the scarcely concealed hostility of Raymond Moley, whom Rosenman himself had brought into Roosevelt's inner circle. After six months in power, Rosenman complained to Henry Morgenthau that Moley, a man "who used to hang outside my office with the hope that I would pass on some of his papers to Governor Roosevelt, had turned into someone who acted as if he was running the government." Whatever the reasons, as Rosenman later acknowledged, his visits to Washington during the momentous days of FDR's first term were "almost exclusively social"—occasional formal dinners, weekend and holiday visits, and trips along the Potomac on the presidential yacht.

One exception to this pattern was his talk to the American Jewish Committee's leaders in June 1933, urging them to avoid pressing FDR to protest the Nazi persecution of the Jews. While Rosenman did not officially represent the president it was clear that he was looking out for Roosevelt's interest. He took pains to give the impression that he was fully informed about FDR's attitude.

What he told the Jewish leaders also reflected his own beliefs. Unlike most members of his generation of Jews who entered politics and public affairs, and unlike most Jews of Eastern European origin, Rosenman chose to identify himself not with the activism of Stephen Wise's American Jewish Congress but rather with the cautious approach of the older American Jewish Committee. Rosenman had not gotten where he was in life by accident. From the start, as a servant of Tammany, he had made no move without calculating the risks and rewards for his career.

Now, with Roosevelt in the White House, he reckoned that continuing to argue the Committee's view as opposed to the more aggressive stance of the American Jewish Congress was his best course. Like many of his American Jewish Committee colleagues, Rosenman saw the answer to the problems of American Jews through long-term educational efforts to improve public attitudes. It was tantamount to the Booker T. Washington approach to combating racial bigotry. Thus Rosenman arranged for the endowment of a special professorship in human relations at Newark University to monitor anti-immigration statements in textbooks.

And he came to head an organization called the Jewish Education Committee, backed by a $1 million endowment, whose objective, as Rosenman described it, was "to show the Jew the right way to prepare himself for a self-respecting life in a Christian community. The way is to know himself, his background, his race's contribution to civilization. These things we do through Jewish religious education." Those who saw the problems of Germany's Jews as requiring more urgent and aggressive responses faced Rosenman's determined opposition.

As Roosevelt resisted immigration change and active protest against Nazi persecution, and Rosenman kept busy with his judicial chores, the Nazis expanded and intensified their torment of the Jews. The idea of the "final solution" remained buried in the recesses of Hitler's mind. But the enactment of the Nuremberg Laws in September 1935 foreshadowed the apocalypse. These decrees codified the racial policies that Hitler had envisioned in *Mein Kampf*. Under the Reich Citizenship Law, the status of German citizenship was conveyed only to those belonging to "a national of German or related blood." The Law for the Protection of German Blood and Honor forbade marriage and sexual contact between Jews and Aryans. Jews were forbidden to fly the German flag. And Jews were stripped of all basic civil rights, classifying them as state subjects rather than as citizens. They were defined as a separate race. The Nazis had laid a foundation for a chain of measures, one leading to another, escalating in severity and leading ultimately to the physical destruction of European Jewry.

By the time the Nuremberg Laws had been promulgated, more than 75,000 German Jews had fled the country. Fewer than

10,000 managed to get into the United States while thousands of others found a haven in Canada and South Africa. Meanwhile Jewish concern about anti-Semitism in the United States mounted, as *Fortune* noted in a lengthy article. "The apprehensiveness of American Jews has become one of the important influences in the social life of our time," the magazine reported early in 1936, only a few months after its discussion of Jewish influence on FDR as a 1936 campaign issue. But *Fortune* claimed there was "no reason for anxiety so far as concerns the record to date of the organized forces of anti-Semitism." Indeed, the magazine concluded that "American organized anti-Semitism is a poor thing indeed." And for evidence it cited a recent survey by the National Conference of Christians and Jews in which those questioned overwhelmingly believed there was less anti-Semitism in their communities now than before the onset of the depression.

Such reassurances, however, did not stop Jews from worrying, among them Rosenman. And in his response to the possibility of his own personal exposure to anti-Semitism, Rosenman was as self-effacing as his colleague and coreligionist Frankfurter would be two years later when he refused to ask his own government to intervene on behalf of his imprisoned uncle.

Although he had been called back into FDR's service as the principal speechwriter for the 1936 campaign, Rosenman suggested that he and his wife be left behind when the president toured the Midwest Bible Belt. "That's no way to handle anti-Semitism; the way to handle it is to meet it head-on," Roosevelt said. Or so Rosenman remembered, though Roosevelt's record as president was filled with abundant evidence of his determination to avoid meeting "head-on" issues of any kind, particularly anti-Semitism. Despite polls indicating disturbing evidence of anti-Semitism at home, not to mention the horrors perpetrated by Hitler abroad, there is no public record of Roosevelt addressing the issue during the long course of his presidency.

In any event, Rosenman stayed with the campaign. And in the second term that followed Roosevelt's overwhelming victory, in which he captured all forty-eight states except Maine and Vermont, Rosenman's role and influence in the White House grew. In part this was due to attrition among other early advisers, some of whom had fallen out of favor with the president or were victims of the constant internecine warfare that consumed the ranks of White House aides. Raymond Moley was not around for the second term after quarreling with FDR over the means and ends of the New Deal. Neither was Rex Tugwell, who had provided much of the ideological context for the early reforms. Even such shining lights as Tom Corcoran and Ben Cohen seemed to have lost their early luster as a result of internal feuding and FDR's shifting tactics.

Rosenman, though, persevered. He even acquired a status symbol of sorts, a presidential nickname bestowed by FDR. Thus "Sammy the Rose" took its place alongside "Tommy the Cork" for Tom Corcoran, "Harry the Hop" for Harry Hopkins, and "Henry the Morg" for the treasury secretary, sobriquets that reflected the heavy-handed jocularity that typified FDR's sense of humor.

Rosenman held a relatively secure position in the New Deal firmament in part because he was a commuting adviser. As a sitting New York state judge, he kept his out-of-town base and stayed out of sight much of the time and thus out of the line of fire. Rosenman also made it plain to FDR and anyone else who paid attention that his role was to advance by serving the president, a point he had already established by helping Governor Roosevelt wiggle out of his difficulties with Tammany Hall. With the exception of his views on Jewish refugees, he kept his opinions on political issues to himself, meanwhile striving to conform to FDR's whims and caprices, even on small matters.

For example, Rosenman was a formidable trencherman. By the time he reached his forties, during Roosevelt's second term, he had accumulated more than two hundred pounds on his five-foot-seven-inch frame, and his stockiness verged on corpulence. He came by this weight honestly, as White House staffers realized. During government conferences he refreshed himself from an endless stream of sandwich trays and malted milks. Even after polishing off a full-course dinner he would often send out for sandwiches to stanch a new hunger attack. A friend once observed that if Rosenman's intake of alcoholic beverages approached his consumption of food, he would have wrecked his career and his liver at an early age.

But Rosenman rarely drank anything stronger than a beer or sherry. And his disinterest in hard liquor created something of an etiquette problem for him when dining with Governor Roosevelt, who liked to ply his guests with cocktails before dinner, invariably more than one. Rather than seeming ungracious by refusing the drink, Rosenman took to emptying his glass into one of the flowerpots in the governor's study. Someone evidently reported this to Roosevelt, and on the next such occasion he archly informed Rosenman that his plants had become discolored, leading to the discovery of an abnormal percentage of alcohol in the soil. After joining in the general laughter, Rosenman retorted: "Well, governor, if you don't want to lose all your plants, you'd better pass me up on seconds." Roosevelt, who himself rarely took more than two drinks on such occasions, agreed to do so.

Such badinage did not deter Roosevelt from relying more and more heavily on Rosenman in a variety of situations. Thus Rosenman's first important assignment of FDR's second term had to do with the president's proposal to overhaul the Supreme Court to make it more to his ideological liking. Roosevelt had been understandably frustrated by a series of decisions by the Court's "Nine Old Men," which threatened to wreck the New Deal. Instead of presenting his plan to add new justices to the Court as a way to freshen the outlook of the tribunal, as Rosenman suggested, Roosevelt insisted on justifying his idea as a way to help overworked justices. For all his seeming confidence, though, the president was apparently troubled by misgivings. On the night before he was to make his plan public, as Rosenman was preparing to return home to New York, FDR's secretary Marguerite LeHand called him aside and told him: "The president is terribly nervous about this message. I think it would be helpful and comforting to him if you stayed over until the thing is finally completed and put to bed."

The president's lawyer was fast becoming his security blanket. In the days that followed it became clear that Roosevelt would have been better off listening to the advice offered by Rosenman and others and taken a direct approach to his problems with the Court. His Court-packing plan turned into a political disaster that reversed the fortunes of the New Deal. The combination of this debacle and a severe economic relapse plunged Roosevelt into deep difficulty midway through the second term that had begun so triumphantly.

Late in 1938 the respected liberal journalist and historian Walter Millis delivered a somber verdict on the New Deal. It had been, he wrote, "reduced to a movement with no program, with no effective political organization, with no vast popular party strength behind it, and with no candidate." As for Roosevelt himself, he seemed nothing more than a lame duck politician who had lost his grip, facing the dead end of his career. In the spring of 1939 a *Fortune* magazine survey showed that little more than one-third of the electorate would support Roosevelt if he ran again. Ultimately it was the burgeoning crisis abroad, stemming from the aggressive acts of Hitler's Third Reich, that would save FDR's political bacon and make possible a third term.

Not that Roosevelt planned it that way. Instead, as the European crisis heightened he clung to the isolationist tendencies he had brought with him to the White House. Rooted deep in the country's history, American isolationism, buttressed by the Monroe Doctrine, drew support from groups with sometimes sharply contradictory beliefs. Among them were the populist farmers of the South and West, resentful of British financial interests which they viewed as allied with reviled Eastern bankers. More benign but no less impassioned were the pacifists and social reformers who saw international involvement as leading to war. Not only did they regard war as an evil in itself, they also denounced it as a corrupting influence on society and a diversion from efforts to deal with social and economic problems at home.

From these two groups in both parties Roosevelt found his first-term isolationist allies. Their votes helped transform New Deal plans into law to benefit farmers, small businessmen, and debtors, and restrain the excesses of big business and finance through regulations and taxes. They freely lent their support on domestic issues in large part because they knew they could count on having Roosevelt as a silent, though sometimes reluctant, partner on foreign policy.

Typifying the often coy collaboration between FDR and the isolationists was the passage of the Johnson Act in 1934. It prohibited Americans from making loans to nations that had defaulted on war debts, and thus limited aid to Britain and France if they faced future aggression. While debate on the measure swirled around Capitol Hill, the president kept his silence. Although backers avoided saying they had the president's support, they believed, as the bill's sponsor, Republican Senator Hiram Johnson of California, put it privately, that Roosevelt "really favored the bill" to use "as a weapon in dealing with these European welshers." Any doubts about the president's real sentiments vanished when, shortly after signing the bill in April 1934, he invited Johnson and his wife to the White House for dinner and later favored Mrs. Johnson with an autographed picture of himself.

Gradually FDR moved toward recognition of the threat Hitler posed not just to the nation's old World War I allies, Britain and France, but to the United States itself. But as to the shift, "I don't think it was Roosevelt who did it," Rosenman said later. "It was Hitler, Mussolini and the Japanese war lords, and the front page of the newspaper."

The threat to world peace and to the welfare of European Jewry was greatly magnified in March 1938 with the *Anschluss*. Immediately the 250,000 Jews of Austria became targets for the same brutal persecution inflicted upon 500,000 German Jews. Fearing political pressure, and unwilling to expend the political capital it would take to fight for the liberalization of immigration laws, FDR organized an international conference on the refugee problem. At the French resort town of Evian, the conference turned into a well-publicized exercise in futility. The meeting of more than thirty nations was doomed from the start when the State Department made clear that no country attending, including the United States, would be expected to change its laws to allow an increase in immigration.

By the time of the conference, more than 250,000 Jews had fled Germany and Austria; but more than 300,000 were still seeking shelter from oppression, driven by desperation but with little hope to sustain them. As the Zionist leader Chaim Weizmann remarked, "The world seemed to be divided into two parts, those places where the Jews could not live and those where they could not enter."

Untroubled by the international community and its empty expressions of concern for the plight of the Jews, Hitler's crusade reached new levels of brutality. In October 1938, just days after the Munich agreement sealed the doom of Czechoslovakia, more than twelve thousand Polish-born Jews were expelled from Germany on Hitler's orders. They were driven from their homes in a single night and allowed one suitcase per person for their belongings. Eventually four thousand were permitted to enter Poland; the rest were forced to remain at the border under conditions so harsh that some actually tried to escape back into Germany and were shot.

The seventeen-year-old son of one deported family, Herschel Grynszpan, was living in Paris when his sister Berta sent him a postcard pleading for help. Having none to offer, the young man bought a revolver and bullets, and on November 8, 1938, went to the German embassy in Paris and shot the third secretary, Ernst von Rath. In Grynszpan's pocket police found a postcard addressed to his parents with the message "May God forgive me. I must protest so that the whole world hears my protest, and that I will do."

Grynszpan was held by the French police out of German reach. But the Reich had its own paths to revenge. On the same date von Rath was shot, the German government halted publication of Jewish newspapers and magazines and banned Jewish children from attending German state elementary schools. On November 9, von Rath died of his wounds. That night, under orders from Hitler delivered by Goebbels, the violence began. "The Führer has decided that demonstrations should not be prepared or organized by the party," Goebbels declared. But he added that "insofar as they erupt spontaneously, they are not to be hampered." Within the next few days storm troopers shattered the storefronts of some 7,500 Jewish stores and businesses, giving the pogrom its lasting name as *Kristallnacht*, the Night of Shattered Glass. Throughout Germany, Jewish homes were ransacked. As the London *Daily Telegraph* correspondent Hugh Carleton Greene reported: "Racial hatred and hysteria seemed to have taken complete hold of otherwise decent people. I saw fashionably dressed women clapping their hands and screaming with glee, while respectable middle-class mothers held up their babies to see the 'fun.'"

At least ninety Jews were killed in the streets; hundreds more committed suicide. An estimated two thousand were murdered in concentration camps. The persecution and economic loss did not stop with the pogrom. Even as their businesses were ransacked, Jews were also forced to pay *Judenverm gensabgabe,* a collective fine of 1 billion marks (equal to roughly $5.5 billion in today's currency) for the murder of von Rath. This penalty was levied by the state's compulsory acquisition of 20 percent of all Jewish property. Six million deutschmarks of insurance payments for property damage due the Jewish community were to be paid to the government instead as "damages to the German Nation."

The number of emigrating Jews now surged as those who were able left the country—a desirable outcome for the Nazi party. In the ten months following *Kristallnacht,* more than 115,000 Jews emigrated from the Reich. Most went to other European countries, the United States, and Palestine, and at least 14,000 made it to Shanghai. As part of government policy, the Nazis seized houses, shops, and other property the emigrés left behind.

Roosevelt's response was to pronounce himself "deeply shocked," adding, "I could scarcely believe that such things could occur in a 20th century civilization." That was by far the strongest statement FDR had yet made about the Nazi persecution of the Jews. He also recalled for consultation the U.S. ambassador to Berlin, Hugh Wilson, who had replaced William Dodd earlier in the year. But when he was asked whether he could think of any place in the world that would accept a mass emigration of Jews, the president responded, "No, the time is not ripe for that."

Would he recommend relaxing U.S. immigration restrictions to admit Jewish refugees?

"That is not in contemplation," Roosevelt said. "We have the quota system," he added, as if that were a blueprint ordained by God and carved in concrete.

Later Rosenman discussed his own reaction to the tragic events in Germany. "I think every Jew felt it more deeply than the Christian did," he said. As for the president, Roosevelt seemed struck by what Rosenman described "as the Jewish willingness to take this sort of thing lying down in Germany. It struck FDR as a particularly undesirable attitude. One of the things he couldn't understand was why didn't some Jew assassinate Hitler, even realizing that it would mean his own death." Roosevelt did not seem to grasp the improbability of any Jew with a deadly weapon getting close enough to Hitler to do him harm. Or, given the horrors of *Kristallnacht*, what disaster the Jews of Germany would suffer if any such attempt were made. And Rosenman apparently made no attempt to explain this to him.

Instead, without being asked, in the wake of *Kristallnacht* Roosevelt's longtime adviser sent the president a memo supporting his continued refusal to relax immigration restrictions. "I do not believe it is either desirable or practicable to recommend any change in the quota provision of our immigration law," he wrote Roosevelt. Expanded immigration, Rosenman suggested, would worsen unemployment and produce a "Jewish problem" in the countries that increased their quotas. FDR's own political instincts had already inclined him against relaxing immigration restrictions. Polling data that Roosevelt followed closely certainly seemed to argue against such a move. In March 1938, at the time of the *Anschluss,* a majority of Americans told pollsters that the persecution of German Jews was either wholly or partly their own fault. In light of such indicators, would different advice from Rosenman, in whom he reposed so much trust, have given Roosevelt pause to reconsider? The world will never know.

Nor will we ever know what would have happened if Roosevelt had sought to make the changes in immigration that Rosenman opposed. Certainly conventional wisdom held that an increase in immigration would swell unemployment, thus creating the "Jewish problem" that Rosenman worried about. But plenty of evidence exists to counter the assertion that the admission of foreigners would have increased the ranks of jobless Americans. Often overlooked in the phobia about immigration and unemployment was the fact that most immigrants belonged to family units that included more consumers than breadwinners. The increase in aggregate demand created by immigrants, it could plausibly be argued, would likely generate more jobs than they filled.

The polling data that influenced judgments by politicians, presumably including FDR, was not necessarily definitive or reflective of deeply held feelings. Polling analysis that probed deeper than the surface head counts revealed a high degree of volatility and suggestibility. For example, when one survey asked which groups or organizations had "too much to say about running this country than they should," only 4 percent of those interviewed mentioned Jews. But when asked directly whether Jews had "too much power and influence," 67 percent agreed. The contrast indicates how easily resentment against a particular group can manifest itself when attention is focused on that group. But it also implies that if a positive case were made for a group, it might have an ameliorative impact on attitudes toward that group, particularly if the case were made by the President of the United States.

More broadly, what Kenneth S. Davis argued in his magisterial biography of FDR was the potential for "bold, frank leadership" by the president. He might not only have responded to the understandable economic concerns of Americans but also mobilized the humanitarian instincts of his fellow citizens, instincts which were much in evidence in the shocked reaction to *Kristallnacht*. For a chief executive who had famously declared in his first campaign for the White House that the presidency was "preeminently a place of moral leadership," this would have seemed a reasonable course. But he chose not to try it, nor is there any evidence that Rosenman suggested he do so.

Instead of immigration, Rosenman saw colonization as the answer for the Jews, provided a large enough expanse of land could be obtained. He suggested as a possibility a "new and undeveloped land in Africa and South America." FDR had also expressed some vague interest in colonization, if only because it offered a possible alternative to easing immigration barriers. But neither Roosevelt nor Rosenman showed much interest in pursuing the idea toward a concrete plan. For example, Treasury Secretary Morgenthau, another of the President's Jews, brought Roosevelt a proposal that the United States acquire British and French Guiana in return for canceling the World War I debts of their colonial landlords. But FDR rejected the idea out of hand. "It's no good," he said. "It would take the Jews five to fifty years to overcome the fever."

As a substitute for the Guianas, Roosevelt suggested that refuge for the Jews be found in the Cameroons, then a British West African territory. Morgenthau immediately commissioned a feasibility study, but his experts concluded that the cost of such a project would be excessive and the potential for economic development slim. Both ideas were soon buried, with no evidence of any interest by Rosenman.

Then another cabinet member, Interior Secretary Ickes, came forward with an idea that on its face seemed more promising. This was the resettlement of Jewish refugees in what was then the territory of Alaska. The Interior Department would seem far removed from the issue of Europe's desperate Jews. But Harold Ickes was no respecter of bureaucratic boundaries or other conventions. A longtime Republican, he had deserted the GOP in 1912 to campaign for the first President Roosevelt on the Bull Moose ticket. He had switched sides again in 1932 to join Franklin Roosevelt's campaign and then his cabinet. There he fiercely advocated conservation and resolutely opposed the forces of privilege, in the process often trying the patience of the president. Roosevelt, though, valued his interior secretary's integrity and dedication enough to humor him during his intermittent sulks and outbursts and to shrug off his ominous grumbling.

Ickes was a man of many passions, petty and grand. A self-described curmudgeon, his irascibility was rivaled by his imagination, his ambition to expand Interior's domain, and—of particular significance at this moment in history—his intense distrust of Adolf Hitler. In 1937, after the hydrogen-fueled German dirigible *Hindenburg* exploded in midair while landing in New Jersey, Congress acted to permit the secretary of interior to sell helium to foreign countries to use in airships instead of hydrogen, provided they were not used for military purposes. But when Germany subsequently contracted for the purchase of a huge amount of helium, Ickes, defying the president who approved of the deal, refused to go along. He insisted that given the helium, the Germans would certainly find a way to make military use of it. "Who would take Hitler's word?" he asked Roosevelt. The deal died.

Now Ickes saw the crisis facing Germany's Jews as offering him a double opportunity—to enlarge the scope of his department and at the same time disrupt the Führer's agenda for persecuting the Jews. His notion of making Alaska a haven for Jews stemmed in part from a tour of the vast territory that Ickes had conducted in the summer of 1938, looking for ideas from local officials to attract settlers to develop the region.

But it wasn't only Alaska's economic development that offered Ickes a rationale for the proposal. Japan's aggression against China and the likelihood of war in Europe intensified American concerns about Alaska's strategic importance and, with its tiny population, its vulnerability. Washington had been trying to lure settlers to "Seward's Folly" ever since 1867 when Andrew Johnson's secretary of state had made himself a target for ridicule by negotiating the purchase of the territory from

Russia. But every effort had failed. *Kristallnacht* suggested to Ickes and other political leaders, including Democratic Senator William King of Utah, that the Jews might be more willing than most people to brave the desolate north country.

Refugees from Hitler, when confronted with the hardships of frontier life, King reasoned, "would not be thinking of the comforts of life in the States that they had sacrificed, but in terms of the savagery and hopelessness of the conditions abroad from which they had been rescued." At a press conference on Thanksgiving eve, 1938, two weeks after *Kristallnacht*, Secretary Ickes proposed Alaska as "a haven for Jewish refugees from Germany and other areas in Europe where the Jews are subjected to oppressive restrictions." Alaska was "the one possession of the United States that is not fully developed," Ickes pointed out. He noted that impoverished families had recently relocated from the dust bowls of the American West to the three-thousand-mile Matanuska Valley in south central Alaska, and predicted their pioneering efforts would "open up opportunities in the industrial and professional fields now closed to the Jews in Germany." It all seemed like an extension of American tradition, proponents argued. Like the *Mayflower* Pilgrims who landed at Plymouth Rock, the Jews would flee intolerance in Europe and carve out a new life for themselves in the New World.

Determined to promote the idea to the limit, Ickes arranged for the Interior Department to issue an extensive report that pointed to two advantages for the United States. In addition to the opportunity to develop the territory's vast economic potential, immigrants would reduce the military risk of leaving the area dangerously underpopulated. "Hundreds of thousands of pioneers" from other countries would come, the report predicted. And, best of all, regular immigration quotas would not apply since Alaska was only a territory, not part of the United States proper.

Senator King and California Democratic representative Frank Havenner introduced legislation in both houses of congress to transform this blueprint into reality. Meanwhile supporters created a National Committee for Alaskan Development, which forged an ecumenical coalition of national leaders and groups to back the legislation. Backers included the Academy Award–winning Hollywood actors Luise Rainer and Paul Muni, the theologian Paul Tillich, the Quakers, and the Federal Council of Churches.

Yet some Jews held back out of their persistent fear of being seen as too self-interested. Rabbi Wise worried that the Alaska plan "makes a wrong and hurtful impression, that Jews are taking over some part of the country for settlement. Just because small numbers of Jews might settle there," he argued, "was not sufficient reason to support it." The Labor Zionists of America became the only Jewish organization publicly to endorse the King-Havenner Bill.

But there was plenty of opposition from nativists and super-patriots who charged that the legislation would open the door to Trojan horses, such as Jews who believed in "the Marxian philosophy." The most important opposition came from the State Department, which regarded the bill as an attempt to sneak aliens into the United States through the back door. Ickes realized that only the president himself could help overcome the opposition. But when he sought FDR's help, nearly a year after he first broached the idea, Ickes discovered that the president would support allowing only ten thousand new settlers per year for five years, and of that number "not more than 10 percent would be Jews." That minuscule figure, Ickes explained, "would avoid criticism that we would be subjected to if there were an undue proportion of Jews." Of course it would do little to help the masses of European Jews threatened by Hitler.

In the end, Roosevelt was not willing to call for even those few immigrants; he refrained from saying anything publicly about the Alaska issue. Without the backing of the White House, the Alaska plan died. As for Rosenman, the self-professed advocate of colonization, there is no record of his uttering so much as a word to FDR in support of the plan.

By the time Roosevelt put an end to Ickes' Alaska project in November 1939, Europe was already at war. After a few months of "phony war" or *Sitkzkreig*, Hitler's panzers smashed through France, Belgium, and Holland, as they had Poland earlier, and brought Britain to the brink of defeat. Americans feared they might be next. With these series of disasters dominating the horizon, concern over European Jewry faded, and so did prospects for their escape. Against this background Rosenman, busy with his growing speechwriting responsibilities at the White House, had little further to do with the crisis of Jews abroad. But another of the President's Jews decided that for him, at least, it was time for a shift in strategy. Instead of concentrating on trying to save the Jews from persecution, a cause that given the president's attitude seemed all but hopeless, Ben Cohen decided to promote a controversial scheme to counter the military might of their persecutors.

VI

BUNDLES FOR BRITAIN

HAVING BEEN MENTORED by Felix Frankfurter and inspired by
Justice Brandeis, Benjamin Cohen shared many of their convictions as well as their Harvard background. But for all his
achievements in the early years of the New Deal, Cohen did not
match the public stature of these two giants. In the end, though,
what he achieved in the struggle against Nazism far overshadowed anything these two more prominent figures accomplished
or even attempted.

One advantage of his relative lack of celebrity was that Cohen
was not besieged, as Frankfurter and Brandeis were, by American Jews seeking FDR's help for the Jewish targets of Hitler's
hatred. Not that he could escape entirely from such pleas. In
the wake of *Kristallnacht*, as Sam Rosenman was advising FDR
not to ease quota restrictions for European Jews, Stephen Wise,
the most prominent Jewish American, asked Cohen's advice on
how to get Roosevelt more directly engaged in the battle for the
victims of persecution.

Cohen had small comfort to offer. The Jews "cannot again
rush to Washington to ask the Bishop of Washington who is a
great friend to go to the Skipper," he wrote Wise, an apparent

reference to the Right Reverend James E. Freeman, the Episcopal bishop of Washington, who had conducted a national prayer service at Roosevelt's first inaugural. Now, Cohen believed, that gambit had been overused.

Similarly in June 1940 when Wise asked Cohen to set up a meeting between the president and officials of the World Jewish Congress, created by Rabbi Wise to aid Jewish refugees, Cohen declined. "I don't feel I should push myself into Jewish matters when the skipper does not ask my advice," he explained. "Why don't you speak to LDB [Brandeis] & FF [Frankfurter] about it? They are high moguls and I am only a nobody."

But this response to Wise camouflaged the intensity of Cohen's true feelings about the plight of the Jews. They had been revealed earlier, in the tragic year of 1938, when, following the *Anschluss*, FDR set in motion at Evian the international conference on the refugee crisis. Although Cohen was not a member of the U.S. delegation, he nevertheless went to the conference as a private citizen to observe the proceedings. Cohen was no naif. As a disciple of Brandeis and Frankfurter, a veteran of the Paris Peace Conference of 1919, a Wall Street operator who had made a fortune in the market and escaped before the crash, and a designer of the New Deal's most important reforms, it did not take him long to see that the much ballyhooed meeting would produce nothing of consequence. But he stayed in Evian and relayed information about the proceedings to his friends among the leaders of the American Jewish community. While in Europe, Cohen also met with David Ben-Gurion, the future first prime minister of the state of Israel, who was then chairman of the Jewish Agency for Palestine, which sought to promote development in the incipient Jewish homeland. Fearing correctly that the British would restrict Jewish immigration to its mandate in order to avoid conflict with the Arabs, Ben-Gurion sounded out Cohen on American reaction if the Jews turned to armed resistance to get their way on Palestine. Cohen told him that neither American Jews nor the U.S. government would back such a strategy.

Ben-Gurion then pleaded with Cohen to persuade Brandeis to take up the Jewish cause with Roosevelt. But Cohen would make no such commitment. He was willing only to arrange for FDR to invite Justice Brandeis to the White House in 1938 for a discussion of British policy on Palestine. The meeting encouraged Brandeis at the time, though it led to no specific results.

Cohen was not well suited by personality or background for the more overt role in supporting the refugee cause that some Jewish leaders wanted him to fill. If Rosenman, whose specialty was speechwriting, was Roosevelt's rhetorician-in-chief, Ben Cohen, whose expertise was legislation, was the president's chief technician. Often he teamed with Tom Corcoran in assembling the major legislation of the New Deal.

Born in 1894 and raised by comfortably middle-class Jewish immigrants in Muncie, Indiana, Cohen was bright enough to gain admission to the University of Chicago at sixteen. At Chicago's law school his grades were the highest ever recorded, an achievement that made graduate work at Harvard all but inevitable. In Cambridge, Cohen studied under Felix Frankfurter, who remained a longtime influence. After World War I it was Frankfurter who exposed Cohen to Zionism, just as Brandeis had done for him. Frankfurter helped arrange Cohen's appointment as counsel to the American Zionist Organization just after the Armistice. This drew the young man into participation in the postwar peace negotiations over attempts to establish a Jewish homeland in Palestine. Cohen's upbringing in Muncie had left him with only a casual knowledge of Jewish holidays and customs, and like many other assimilated Jews of that time he saw himself more as an American than a Jew. His work for Zionism did not intensify his religious ties to Judaism, even though it did bolster his concern for the welfare of the Jewish people, particularly abroad where they were most threatened, as well as his interest in international affairs.

Settling in New York after the peace conference, Cohen entered private practice and made himself an expert in corporate reorganization. In addition to the fat fees he collected from Wall Street clients, he played the stock market freely, as did many others in the booming twenties. Indeed at one point Chrysler stock made him so wealthy that he pointed with satisfaction every time one of the company's cars rolled by on the street. But then the Chrysler bubble collapsed, and Cohen had to scramble for legal odd jobs to remain solvent. Still, he found time to help Frankfurter draft model legislation establishing minimum wages for women, which was adopted by several states.

When Frankfurter brought him to Washington in 1933, the introverted Cohen, then thirty-nine years old, found the perfect complement in Corcoran, another Frankfurter protégé. The two men worked well in harness. The glib, convivial, accordion-playing Corcoran's greatest strength was as a lobbyist on Capitol Hill, where he could make the most of his Irish charm. The brooding, introspective Cohen did his convincing on paper, interpreting the law to give the advantage to whatever client or cause he represented. His shyness kept him out of the limelight, which at any rate would have made him miserable. It is a measure of Cohen's solemnity that even the ebullient Roosevelt did not attempt to coin a nickname for him as he did for several of his colleagues.

Corcoran and Cone worked together so closely that their names were often pronounced together as if they made up one word—"corcorandcone." Their first joint accomplishment was the Truth in Securities Act, centerpiece of the New Deal's reforms of the financial industry. That set the pattern. Dubbed the "Gold Dust Twins" after an advertising slogan for a popular brand of powdered soap, they cleaned up the Augean stables of capitalism with landmark legislation regulating stock trading, public utilities manipulation, and wages and hours. Much of their work, in curbing the excesses of the Wall Street power brokers, seemed to epitomize the doctrines of their intellectual godfather, Justice Brandeis.

Officially Cohen was associate counsel to the Public Works Administration and later general counsel to the National Power Policy Committee in Harold Ickes' Interior Department. But in reality he served as legal adviser to an array of New Deal lawyers and officials who formed the habit of "talking it over with Ben." Both he and Corcoran worked grinding schedules that left them little time for anything else, even sleep. To relax, Cohen went to the movies but almost invariably dozed off in his seat. His frantic agenda and his shyness discouraged friendships with women from ripening into romance. "The only way you are ever going to sleep with Ben," the young New Deal lawyer Joe Rauh told one frustrated young woman, "is to go to the movies with him."

In a government brimming over with ambition, Cohen and Corcoran naturally inspired jealousy. Henry Morgenthau complained to Eleanor Roosevelt that the two men "were wielding the greatest influence" on the president, which he feared would somehow lead to his being forced out of government. The passage of time eased Morgenthau's anxieties. When Roosevelt's activist agenda was exhausted during FDR's second term, the team broke up and Corcoran and Cohen lost their major roles in the New Deal drama. Corcoran tried to drum up enthusiasm for a third term for Roosevelt, but his aggressiveness boomeranged, leaving lasting resentments among conservatives and turning him into a political liability.

Cohen, while maintaining the respect of insiders, faded into the background with little in the way of recognition or reward. His friends had put his name forward for promotion to more prestigious positions than his relatively obscure job at Interior. But Roosevelt passed over him for a position on the Securities and Exchange Commission and as assistant secretary at Treasury, where he would have worked under another Jew, Morgenthau—it was suspected by some New Deal insiders, for fear of an anti-Semitic backlash.

With the administration's ideas for domestic reform stalemated, Cohen's attention turned abroad, to the peril of the Jews and the threat of war, both of which were steadily growing.

In January 1938 Herman Göring, who had been placed in charge of the "Jewish question," ordered SS leader Reinhard Heydrich to speed up the expulsion of Jews from Germany. A week later in a Reichstag speech the Führer issued a stark warning to the Jews of Europe: "If the international Jewish financiers in and outside Europe should succeed in plunging the nations once more into a world war, then the result will not be the Bolshevizing of the earth and thus the victory of Jewry, but the annihilation of the Jewish race in Europe."

In March Hitler, who had seized the Sudetenland from Czechoslovakia six months earlier as a result of the Munich agreement, gobbled up the rest of Czechoslovakia, which soon enacted its own version of the Nuremberg Laws. In May the *St. Louis*, a ship crowded with more than nine hundred Jewish refugees from Austria and Germany, was turned away by Cuba, just as the first Jewish immigrants had been rebuffed three hundred years before. But unlike their seventeenth-century brethren who were permitted to land in New Amsterdam, the *St. Louis* passengers were rebuffed by the United States and a number of other countries before returning to Europe where most ultimately met their deaths.

Meanwhile Roosevelt was struggling to find a way for the United States to cope with the growing crisis in Europe that would not damage him politically by provoking isolationist protests. In June 1936 the platform adopted by the Democratic convention that renominated FDR for a second term, dictated by the president himself, might have been written by any of the country's numerous isolationist leaders. It pledged "to work for peace, to take the profits out of war, to guard against being drawn, by political commitments, international banking, or private trading, into any war that may develop anywhere." This was the foreign policy route Roosevelt had followed since his speech at the opening of the 1932 campaign repudiating the League of Nations.

But soon after his second term began, events at home and abroad forced him to veer off course into uncharted seas. On the domestic front his misguided effort to recast the Supreme Court undermined his alliance with progressive isolationists who had backed his domestic reforms but viewed his move against the Court as overreaching. But the greatest pressure on Roosevelt came from the growing threat of aggression overseas. In response he followed no consistent set of beliefs or values. Instead he steered an erratic course that left the country confused and divided by the ominous march of events abroad.

In October 1937, groping for a more effective answer to Japan's invasion of China and to the escalating threat from Hitler, Roosevelt delivered the first major foreign policy address of his presidency. He accused a few unnamed countries of "threatening a breakdown of all international law and order." Likening this to "an epidemic of physical disease," he seemed to call for "a quarantine" of aggressor nations. The speech stirred controversy, drawing both strong support and opposition. But when pressed to elaborate, the president decided to drop the subject, leaving the isolationists to dominate the debate. When the Munich crisis of 1938 seemed to bring the world to the brink of war, the president assured Hitler that the United States had "no political involvements in Europe" and "would assume no obligations for the conduct of the present negotiations."

This made clear to Hitler that he had nothing to fear from the nation that had fought World War I to keep the world safe for democracy. The next day, responding to word that Neville

Chamberlain had accepted Hitler's invitation to meet with him at Munich, Roosevelt sent the British prime minister a two-word cable of congratulations: "Good man." And he hailed the temporary peace of Munich negotiated with Hitler by Chamberlain at the sacrifice of Czechoslovakia. "I fully share your hope and belief that there exists today the greatest opportunity in years for the establishment of a new order based on peace and law," he cabled Chamberlain.

The optimistic glow generated by Munich soon faded, however. Within a month of the signing of the agreement, Roosevelt asked a visiting British politician to assure the prime minister that he could count on having "the industrial resources of the American nation behind him in the event of war with the dictatorships." But that would depend, of course, on the president's ability to manage such a commitment. He wanted Chamberlain "to know that privately," the president said, but he "couldn't say it publicly." Chamberlain, taking the assurance for what it was worth, did not put great stock in it.

When war did break out in September 1939, the president told Americans: "This nation must remain a neutral nation." But in pointed contrast with the previous Democratic president, Woodrow Wilson, who in an oft quoted phrase called on Americans to be "neutral in thought as well as deed," Roosevelt said: "I cannot ask that every American remain neutral in thought as well. Even a neutral cannot be asked to close his mind and conscience." Nevertheless the president added reassuringly: "I hope the United States will keep out of this war. I believe that it will. And I give you assurance and reassurance that every effort of your government will be directed toward that end."

This hazy doctrine sufficed during the early "phony war" stage that followed the swift collapse of Poland in the fall of 1939. But in May 1940, when Hitler's armored legions crushed France and the Low Countries, U.S. confidence that the broad Atlantic would save it from involvement in the European war collapsed. Hitler's massive offensive commanded the nation's attention. In New York City an extra platoon of police directed Times Square traffic jammed by the great crowd that assembled to read the news bulletins flashing across the top of the *New York Times* annex. Headlines blared the news of German advances. From correspondents stationed in the warring capital cities, radios carried static-ridden accounts of the fighting into the nation's living rooms.

At the New York World's Fair in Flushing Meadows, the fog of war shrouded the bright hopes nurtured when the fair had opened in the ill-fated year of 1939 with the slogan "World of Tomorrow." The chief Belgian representative at the fair said his government would maintain its exhibit regardless of the war's outcome. On May 14, the day his country's capital surrendered, Reink Bekkering, manager of the Dutch exposition, vowed that "Holland will never cease to exist."

A similar note was sounded that same night by Lord Lothian, Great Britain's ambassador to the United States, in an address to the English-Speaking Union. "Despite all the murk and gloom of the time, I am not afraid," Lothian told an audience of fifteen hundred, which included among other notables J. P. Morgan. As he did in every speech he gave, Lothian emphasized the U.S. stake in the struggle abroad. A Hitler victory, he claimed, would "leave America isolated and alone to champion a free way of life."

Secretary of State Hull warned in a speech to the American Society of International Law that the world was threatened by "an orgy of destruction" and called for "a wholly united opinion" to support the government's response. But unity was hard to achieve. Most Americans wanted Britain to survive, but few were willing to go to war to prevent England from joining Hitler's growing list of conquered lands. British sympathizers in the United States preferred to offer their support through organizations like Bundles for Britain, which sent medical

supplies, clothing, and other nonmilitary supplies to the beleaguered island. But Britain's doughty new prime minister, Winston Churchill, was not satisfied with bandages and blankets.
He wanted the tools of war. In a blunt cable to FDR he warned
the president that his country was in grave peril, adding, "The
voice and force of the United States may count for nothing if
withheld too long." Churchill needed help of all sorts, but most
urgently he wanted the "loan" of fifty World War I vintage
U.S. destroyers to help stave off an anticipated cross-channel
invasion. Roosevelt, facing strong isolationist sentiment in the
country and now determined to seek an unprecedented third
term, dragged his feet before responding.

Meanwhile Churchill's destroyer request became the
focal point of a great national debate over the American role
in Britain's lonely struggle against Hitler. Those who believed
the United States could not afford the risk of helping the British contended against those who said the nation could still less
take the risk of allowing Britain to perish. While this argument
raged in public, Roosevelt searched for a resolution behind
the scenes.

As it turned out, FDR's quest for a solution to this international dilemma was greatly expedited by the skill of his
erstwhile master of domestic reform, Ben Cohen, who threw
himself full tilt into the battle to aid the British. Throughout
all his pleadings for a destroyer deal, Cohen never—so far as
is known—linked the issue to the plight of Europe's Jews, a
connection that he certainly knew would have damaged if not
doomed his cause.

To be sure, one did not have to be Jewish to want to help
Britain against the Third Reich. Much of the impetus for a
destroyer deal came from the Century Group, an informal
aggregation of Eastern lawyers, journalists, and businessmen,
most of them of Anglo-Saxon origin, who were more concerned
with saving Great Britain than rescuing Jews. To one of their

members, the journalist Joseph Alsop, the Centurions represented what he liked to call the "WASP ascendancy," made up of privileged individuals whose connections with the elite of government and business gave them "substantially more leverage than other Americans." Alsop's own most impressive connection was his blood tie to the president's family: his mother was a first cousin and close friend of First Lady Eleanor Roosevelt.

Cohen was no WASP, though like many Americans he might have had other reasons for opposing Nazi Germany than the plight of the European Jews. But it was clear from his involvement in Zionism and his visit to the Evian conference that he was intensely concerned with the threat to European Jewry. Their predicament, more than anything else, seems to have shifted the attention of this self-described "nobody" from domestic affairs, on which he had focused most of his life, into the international arena.

Initially it was Century Group member Alsop, who often acted as the British embassy's unofficial liaison with the Roosevelt administration, who drew Cohen into the destroyer controversy. In this case Alsop realized that because of his post at the Interior Department, Cohen would have ready access to Secretary Ickes, who was known to favor helping the beleaguered British. Sure enough, Ickes relayed Alsop's arguments backing a destroyer deal to FDR, who rejected his suggestion because of anticipated congressional opposition. FDR cited a recent provision adopted by the Senate that banned the release of the destroyers or other military equipment to the British unless it could be shown that the proposed gifts were not needed for the defense of the United States itself. This was clearly a tough standard to meet while the U.S. Navy was desperately trying to build its own peacetime fleet into what was bravely called "a two-ocean navy."

But Cohen refused to give up. He decided to approach the president on his own and spent the next few days polishing a legal memorandum which he titled "Sending Effective Material Aid to Great Britain with Particular References to the Sending of Destroyers." In it he analyzed the destroyer issue much as he had examined New Deal legislation he had drafted and sustained in the courts. He drew on his political insight and a knack for circumventing seemingly overwhelming legal obstacles. Early in the New Deal, for example, in successfully defending the Holding Companies Act that had cracked down on the financial empires of electric power companies, Cohen decided not to ask the Supreme Court to overturn adverse decisions on the law from two lower courts. Instead, realizing the conservative justices would overturn the law itself, he asked the Court to withhold its decision pending further appeal. Two years later, after Roosevelt's appointments had moved the Court to the left, Cohen filed his appeal and won a decision reversing the lower courts and upholding the constitutionality of the act.

Similarly, in trying to justify the transfer of destroyers to Britain, which everyone believed was prohibited by law, Cohen relied on his political instincts more than constitutional principles. Employing hairsplitting technicalities and unprovable assertions about national defense, his memorandum stretched the law, creating a loophole wide enough for the fifty warships to steam through on their way to join the Royal Navy.

In his covering letter to the president, Cohen drove to the heart of his case. The legal barriers to the destroyer transfer would disappear, Cohen maintained, if the transaction "would, as at least some naval authorities believe, strengthen rather than weaken the defense position of the United States." Elaborating, Cohen first pointed out "that in the present state of the world the maintenance of British sea power is of inestimable advantage to us, in terms of our own national defense." He acknowledged that the Senate had recently ruled out releasing destroyers unless the chief of naval operations first certified that the ships were "not essential to the defense of the United States."

He contended, though, that "it would seem the most specious sort of legal argument" to insist that these old ships were essential to the national defense if in fact "the present requirements of national defense would be best served by their release." Of course this assertion, while it sounded impressive, was impossible to prove. Nevertheless Cohen insisted that a view contrary to his, while technically appearing to be in compliance with the law, would actually undermine its fundamental purpose, and he cited three Supreme Court decisions to back up his claim.

Cohen then turned to another apparent bar to the deal—a 1794 statute that prohibited "the arming of any vessel with intent that such vessel shall be employed in the service of any foreign prince or state." This restriction, Cohen pointed out, was initially designed to prevent the United States from equipping French privateers in American harbors with vessels they could use to raid British shipping; it "was in no way aimed at the *sale* of ships to belligerents."

With similar logic Cohen disposed of a more recent statute, the Espionage Law of 1917, which declared it a crime "to send out of the jurisdiction of the United States any vessel built, armed or equipped as a vessel of war . . . with any intent or under any agreement or contract . . . that such vessel shall be delivered to a belligerent nation." On its face this language would seem to most laypersons to be an airtight prohibition against a destroyer deal. Not so, Cohen argued, pointing to the phrase "with any intent or under any agreement or contract." Those words, Cohen insisted, restricted the ban to vessels that had initially been built or equipped for delivery to a belligerent nation, in this case the British. The destroyers, on the other hand, were not covered by the ban because they had been built to fly the Stars and Stripes, not the Union Jack.

Relying on such split hairs, Cohen argued that the proposed destroyer deal accorded so well with statutory law and legal precedent that it did not require congressional approval. Still,

Cohen noted, "even if Congressional approval is not required, Congressional opinion would have to be taken into account." But approval from Capitol Hill could be counted on, he claimed, because the maintenance of British sea power was obviously essential to U.S. national defense.

On July 19, 1940, while Cohen's boss Ickes was in Chicago for the Democratic convention and while Roosevelt himself was polishing his acceptance speech, Cohen sent his handiwork to the Oval Office. "Dear Missy," he wrote in a brief covering note to Roosevelt's secretary Marguerite LeHand, "Could I trouble you to give the President the enclosed letter with attached?" At first his imaginative contrivance fell on deaf ears. Cohen's old collaborator, Tom Corcoran, told him he was off base. So did his boss, Ickes. And the president himself was no more enthusiastic, at least at first. He passed the memo on to Navy Secretary Frank Knox with a note that described it as "worth reading," but he added that despite Cohen's arguments to the contrary, "I fear Congress is in no mood at the present time to allow any form of sale."

Secretary of State Hull took his customary stolid stance and shied away from Cohen's argument. The mere act of sending legislation to approve a destroyer deal would, as Hull put it to Roosevelt, "stir up considerable isolationist antagonism." Then too, the legislation would face "many weeks of discussion before it could be enacted."

While the president deliberated, Britain's plight worsened. On August 4, the same day he talked with Roosevelt, Hull learned from Lord Lothian that the British had lost five more destroyers the previous week, further sapping their ability to stand off the German invasion flotilla whose arrival in the English channel was expected momentarily. On July 21, 1940, Hitler had issued a new directive that all invasion plans be completed by September 15 in time for landings to take place the following week. In Africa, heightening the pressure against the

Franklin D. Roosevelt
(AP/Wide World Photos)

Louis D. Brandeis
(Library of Congress)

Felix Frankfurter
(Library of Congress)

Samuel I. Rosenman
(Library of Congress)

Benjamin V. Cohen
(Library of Congress)

Rabbi Stephen S. Wise
(Library of Congress)

Henry Morgenthau, Jr.
(Library of Congress)

David Niles
(Harry S. Truman Library)

British, the Italians invaded British Somaliland with an army seven times larger than the defending force of 25,000.

In Washington, Roosevelt continued to tread a narrow line. At his August 2 press conference he had favored enactment of the first peacetime draft in the nation's history, calling it "essential to national defense." The president allowed reporters to quote only one sentence from his remarks, however, as he tried to distance himself from the emotional battle over the issue raging on Capitol Hill.

The president had other worries. Although he had won his party's nomination for a third term, his presidential candidacy was off to a slow start. A new Gallup poll showed the Republican standard-bearer, the charismatic Wendell Willkie, leading in twenty-four states with a majority of electoral votes. As for a destroyer deal, despite all the earnest consideration it had received, at the moment it seemed as dead in the water as if struck by a U-boat torpedo.

It might have sunk without a trace except for Cohen's determination and the restless mind of another of the President's Jews, Cohen's longtime friend and adviser, Felix Frankfurter, to whom he now turned for help. One of the fundamental principles of the American system of government holds that members of the nation's highest Court should stand apart from politics, out of respect for the Constitution's insistence on separation of powers and the Supreme Court's special need to maintain its independence and the confidence of the public.

Cohen of course knew that. But he also knew that, since Frankfurter's appointment to the Court the year before, the justice had behaved as if he considered himself an exception to the rule, among other things advising FDR on the appointment of his old friend Henry Stimson as secretary of war. This was much the same attitude taken by his revered mentor Brandeis, who had been eager to advise both the president who appointed him, Woodrow Wilson, and also to influence Franklin Roosevelt, whose aims in office seemed to offer potential for the fruition of many of Brandeis's strongest beliefs. Once on the Court, having begun advising the Roosevelt presidency as a Brandeis collaborator, Frankfurter saw no reason to abandon that role when it came to the destroyer deal.

Frankfurter was a willing collaborator for good reason. In addition to his distress over Hitler's persecution of the Jews, his heart belonged to Great Britain. An academic year at Oxford had given him many British friends. Prominent British scholars such as Harold Laski and John Maynard Keynes called on him during their visits to the United States. And he had opened his home to three children of a British lawyer and former student, refugees from the Luftwaffe's assaults.

Frankfurter realized that the key to convincing Roosevelt to accept Cohen's argument would have less to do with the law and a literal reading of the statutory code than with politics and public opinion. In legal terms, Frankfurter could easily see that some court of law would judge Cohen's artful argument to be as flimsy as the paper on which it was typed. What counted, though, was whether Cohen's rationale would win backing in the political arena. Cohen himself could not advocate his cause because of his post in the Roosevelt administration, not to mention his background as a liberal reformer and a Jew. With a provocative case—as Frankfurter recalled from his own Senate confirmation, which had received a crucial boost from George Norris of Nebraska—the proper sponsor was crucial. Norris's Midwestern Americanism could scarcely be questioned. Frankfurter needed a Norris counterpart, someone who could lend Cohen's argument added credibility and command public attention.

He found the right man in Dean Acheson, the epitome of the Protestant establishment. Tall, elegant, and self-assured, the forty-seven-year-old Acheson looked the part that Frankfurter wanted him to play. His prestige was such that he had been retained to represent the New York Stock Exchange in

1938 during federal hearings stemming from the disclosure of monumental embezzlements by the exchange's former president, stockbroker Richard Whitney. After laboring each day at the hearings in New York City, Acheson unwound on the train back to Washington while sipping a drink in the club car and writing limericks lampooning the proceedings.

Along with Acheson's demonstrated political and legal sagacity, his previous relationship with FDR made him particularly well qualified for the role Frankfurter and Cohen wanted him to play. Chosen by Roosevelt to be his undersecretary of the treasury, Acheson became acting secretary but then quit after a bitter dispute over monetary policy that brought the president's wrath down on his head. True to his gentleman's code, Acheson wrote a gracious letter of resignation and even showed up at Treasury for the swearing-in of Henry Morgenthau to the job he would have had if not for his quarrel with the president.

When that ceremony ended, Roosevelt motioned Acheson to his desk. "I have been awfully angry with you," he said in a stage whisper. "But you are a real sportsman." Several months later, when another Treasury official quit in anger, publicly denouncing Roosevelt's fiscal policies, the president suggested that the malcontent "read Dean Acheson's letter of resignation and learn how a gentleman resigns." Just as Acheson's background was tailored to the role of Cohen's collaborator, his beliefs were equally well suited as evidenced by his active role in the pro–destroyer deal Century Group.

Once Acheson signed on as Cohen's partner, the two men, the self-assured Episcopal bishop's son and the shy Jew from Muncie, closeted themselves in Cohen's New York apartment to draft a public letter that would build support for their objective. They produced a hodgepodge of lawyerly precedents and military theories which closely tracked Cohen's prior thesis that the president had the authority in his own right to sell the destroyers without congressional approval. Hoping to shield

FDR against criticism that he was disregarding Congress, Acheson and Cohen declared that they would not advocate action without congressional approval if they thought a majority in Congress was opposed to such a transaction. "But believing as we do, that the preponderant opinion both in and out of Congress favors such action," their letter said, "we are loath to see time lost to secure authority which already exists when time may be vital to the preservation of our own liberties."

Acheson and Cohen would have been hard-pressed, if asked, to support their claim of congressional and popular approval. According to one informal survey of the Senate in early August, to which Cohen was privy, twenty-three senators, twelve of them members of the president's own party, opposed the sale of destroyers to Britain; only seven were "probably" in favor, with the remaining sixty-six undecided. While overall public sentiment favored aid to Britain, no one yet had any basis for measuring attitudes toward a destroyer sale.

Untroubled by such fine points, Acheson now set out to recruit three additional signatories for the letter with prestige comparable to his own: Charles Burlingham, a patriarchal figure in the New York Bar; Thomas D. Thatcher, a former U.S. District Court judge and a good enough Republican to have been Herbert Hoover's solicitor general and Acheson's own law partner; and George Rublee, a progressive Republican who had served in the Wilson administration. These prestigious co-signers made it relatively easy for Acheson to persuade the *New York Times* to publish the letter. So did his longtime friendship with Charles Merz, editor of the *Times*, whom he had known since they were undergraduate classmates at Yale.

The letter ran on Sunday, August 11, 1940, under a three-column headline that would have given the casual reader the impression that the Cohen-Acheson brief had the *Times*'s own endorsement: "No Legal Bar Seen to Transfer of Destroyers. Ample Authority for Sale of Over-Age Naval Vessels to Great

Britain Exists in Present Laws, According to Opinion by Legal Experts." Given its prominent display, occupying nearly half a page in the Sunday *Times*, the letter predictably attracted widespread public attention. "But that was not the purpose of the exercise," as Acheson said later. He and Cohen had aimed their missive mainly at two men, and they did not wish to depend on either of them reading it in the newspaper.

The first target was Attorney General Robert Jackson, who at the moment was camping out in the Pocono Mountains of Pennsylvania with his daughter. Since the campsite had no phones, a messenger was dispatched to ask Jackson to call Acheson on a matter of urgency. Within a few hours the attorney general was on the line. "To say that he was in a happy state of mind would not be truthful," Acheson acknowledged later, "but friendship helped him control annoyance and listen." Acheson pleaded "the dreadful urgency of the President's knowing that he had the power, and with it the responsibility to act," and outlining his legal argument for a destroyer deal. Jackson said he would take it under consideration. Ultimately the attorney general would produce an advisory opinion for the president that accepted Cohen's arguments and endorsed the transaction.

The other target for the letter was of course the president. Ben Cohen took on that assignment. On August 12, the day after the letter ran in the *Times* and little more than three weeks after his initial memorandum, Cohen sent a copy of the letter to Marguerite LeHand with a one-sentence covering note suggesting that the president "might be interested to glance" at the letter he was enclosing.

The next day FDR summoned Secretary of War Stimson, Treasury Secretary Morgenthau, and other cabinet members to the White House. Now, though the president made no direct reference to the letter in the *Times*, its influence on his thinking could be readily inferred from the way he framed the all-important question of how to deal with Congress: Should he make the deal with Churchill first and then tell Congress, or vice versa? This was a dramatic turnabout. For three months, in every discussion of the destroyer issue, Roosevelt had invariably referred to the difficulty of getting congressional approval before he could act. Now for the first time he had indicated, as Cohen and Acheson had contended, that this was a problem he might not need to solve. Act first and tell Congress later was the burden of the counsel he got. And this was exactly what he wanted to hear.

Meanwhile, to placate isolationists worried about U.S. defenses, the president concluded weeks of haggling with the British by accepting an offer for long-term leases on naval bases along a string of British possessions from Newfoundland to the West Indies. Instead of just a loan of destroyers to the British, the deal now could be cast as a trade of aging destroyers for strategic bases that would bolster U.S. defenses in its home waters.

Even so, Secretary of War Stimson continued to have misgivings about the legal rationale, as set forth in the Cohen-Acheson letter. Who better to turn to for guidance than his friend for more than thirty years, his former special assistant and protégé, Mr. Justice Frankfurter? Frankfurter was glad to help. Remarkably though, in discussing the merits of the Cohen rationale, the justice did not find it relevant to mention his own active role in the legal controversy over the destroyers. After all, Frankfurter had encouraged and helped arrange for publication of the document that had become the principal vehicle for the argument to allow the transaction to proceed. Instead Frankfurter simply said that after "thinking it over hard for two or three days," he had concluded that the issue over the destroyers really turned on the question of national defense. From that point of view, as a result of Britain's offer of bases as a quid pro quo for the destroyers, the United States would be "tremendously strengthened" by the transaction. Anyway, he told Stimson, this situation was entirely different from the cases that the statutes under discussion were intended to cover.

Stimson, himself a pillar of legal rectitude, was of course assuming that his old friend was dealing with him in good faith, and he was grateful for the advice. "It was very good of him to have taken all this trouble to help me out in this way," he wrote in his diary. When he called the president to share his good feelings, Roosevelt was "greatly pleased" and Stimson judged was "about ready to push it ahead."

So it was that three weeks after publication of the Cohen-Acheson letter, on September 3, 1940, Roosevelt announced the destroyer-for-bases trade proclaiming the transaction as "probably the most important thing that has come for American defense since the Louisiana Purchase." When reporters pressed him for details, he brushed their questions aside, suggesting the deal involved "all kinds of things that nobody here would understand, so I won't mention them." The only thing to bear in mind, he insisted, was that "It is a fait accompli; it is done this way."

Cohen's ingenuity at getting around the law conceivably could have been deployed to circumvent the immigration restrictions that kept European Jewry on the other side of the Atlantic. But for all his own commitment, Cohen sensed that the political will for such a maneuver was lacking in the White House.

In political terms the destroyer deal was a triumph for the president. It established him as a commander-in-chief, not just a candidate for reelection. Even the *Chicago Tribune* and other isolationist publications, agog over the prospect of acquiring the bases from the much resented British Empire, hailed the bargain.

Overseas the British were jubilant, and not just because of the addition to their depleted fleet. More important, they recognized that the agreement represented what Churchill privately called a "long step" by the United States toward entering the war on the British side.

The point was not lost on the Third Reich, as made clear by Hitler's top naval commander, Grossadmiral Erich Raeder. He underlined this view in a meeting with the Führer and with General Alfred Jodl, chief of staff of the Armed Forces High Command on September 6. The transaction, he said, "represents an openly hostile act against Germany" and the prelude to "the closest cooperation between Britain and the U.S.A." The situation required "an examination of the possibilities for active participation in the war on the part of the U.S.A." and of the German response to that event.

The next month Hitler, together with Mussolini, reached a pact with the United States' natural enemy in the Pacific, Imperial Japan. The three powers pledged to come to one another's aid if any of them were attacked "by a power at present not involved in the European War or the Sino-Japanese Conflict." Since the agreement specifically stated that the pact did not affect relations with the Soviet Union, that left only one country to which this ominous provision could be relevant. The treaty was a dagger aimed at the United States. Fifteen months after the agreement was signed, Hitler's new ally drove the blade home at Pearl Harbor.

Overlooked by most in the hoopla over the transaction with the British were fundamental questions of legality and the democratic process. Asked for an advisory opinion, Attorney General Jackson, in the helpful tradition of attorneys general advising presidents, gave Roosevelt the green light for doing what he wanted to do. Jackson's case rested on the president's role as commander-in-chief, about which the Constitution is notably vague, and on the president's even more elliptically defined powers in foreign relations.

Not everyone was persuaded. In a lengthy letter to the *New York Times*, a leading political scientist, Edward S. Corwin, pointed out that Jackson's opinion overrode the power specifically delegated to Congress over government property—in this case the fifty destroyers—with the hazy authority claimed for the president. To take that argument to its logical conclusion, Corwin asked, "Why may not any and all of Congress's specifically delegated powers be set aside by the President's 'executive power' and the country be put on a totalitarian basis without further ado?" That question would become more acute in decades to come when, as Cohen's biographer, Clemson University historian William Lasser, pointed out, Roosevelt's "fait accompli," would serve later chief executives "with a blueprint for ignoring Congress, manipulating public opinion and bending domestic law to the exigencies of foreign policy," thus helping lay the foundation for the imperial presidency.

These were future events that a president facing an exploding global conflict might not wish to spend time pondering. But Roosevelt's handling of the destroyer deal also sheds light on his response to other contemporary problems he already faced, including the danger to European Jewry. The United States could not deal effectively with that problem in isolation; it would have to be part of an overall approach to foreign policy, sufficiently coherent to rest on the support of an informed public. Yet Roosevelt's foreign policy in his first two terms was marked by temporizing and dissembling, as illustrated by the destroyer-for-bases trade. In implementing the deal FDR followed a pattern of manipulation and concealment. His bargaining with the British—who at times feared they were getting the short end of the deal—to arrange for the lease of naval bases, as well as negotiations with GOP standard-bearer Wendell Willkie to persuade him to refrain from denouncing the deal, were shrouded in secrecy. And this was capped by his presentation of the transaction as "a far-reaching act of preparation for continental defense." By emphasizing the U.S. acquisition of the bases while scarcely mentioning the grant of the destroyers to the British, the president camouflaged the extent to which the deal set the United States on the road to war. According to State Department adviser Breckinridge Long's contemporary account, the president saw greater danger from the transaction than he let on to the public. "Germany may take violent exception to it and declare war on us," Long wrote in his diary on August 31, three days before the deal was announced, after talking with Secretary of State Hull. "Cordell realizes that—specifically said he did, and says the President does, too."

In this and other instances Roosevelt feared being more candid with the public about the likelihood of war because of the supposedly irresistible strength of isolationist sentiment. Thus in his struggles to secure revision of the Neutrality Act and repeal of the arms embargo in the fall of 1939, because they restricted aid to Britain and France, Roosevelt decided to rest his case on the dubious claim that his proposals would keep the nation out of war. If instead he had chosen to make the argument that repealing the embargo would help Britain and France and thus strengthen American security, he would have been more honest and would have helped pave the way for future assistance to the allies. Afterward Cordell Hull argued that even though he and Roosevelt realized that a German victory over Britain and France would leave the United States in "utmost danger," they also believed that "with isolationism still powerful and militant in the U.S. it would have been the peak of folly to make aid to the democracies an issue in connection with neutrality legislation." As the journalist Herbert Agar, a Roosevelt admirer and sometime confidant, observed, "It seems a pity to say that the peak of folly would have been to tell the truth." Roosevelt assumed, Agar noted, that "an uproar would have been the price of truth telling. Such an assumption raises questions about the durability of democracy."

Called into question in this case is not the quality of democracy but the quality of Roosevelt's leadership, which much of the time made the avoidance of "an uproar" its supreme objective. FDR's zeal to suppress disagreement often led him to conceal disturbing realities. Despite the air of self-assurance he generated, he seemed to lack the necessary confidence in his own skills to lead the public in the proper direction. This same caution doomed hopes that he would deal effectively with the Jewish refugee crisis.

The recognition of this tragic reality impelled Ben Cohen's involvement in the destroyer controversy. The successful outcome of that transaction allowed him to feel that at least he was doing what could be done to hamstring the Nazi military machine. In a way, Cohen was in a desperate race, trying to stop the Nazis before they finished off the Jews. But time was running out. An unimaginable horror was beginning to unfold in Hitler's Europe. And when word slowly filtered back to the United States, this appalling knowledge would make even more torturous the quandary facing American Jews.

VII

THE PRESIDENT'S RABBI

IN THE SPRING of 1940, Reichsführer Heinrich Himmler ordered the building of a concentration camp near the Polish city of Oswiecim to hold Polish prisoners and provide slave labor for new German-run factories to be built nearby. It was called Auschwitz, and soon it would have an even more terrible mission. Later that year, as Franklin Roosevelt announced the destroyer trade with the British, Hitler, having conquered most of Western Europe, began systematizing his response to the *Judenfrage*, or Jewish question. With Teutonic efficiency the Nazis tightened controls over all the Jews under their thumb, requiring them to register their assets.

In June 1941, in a life-or-death gamble for the Third Reich, Hitler invaded the Soviet Union, telling his generals beforehand that the battle to come would be a "war of annihilation." Communists and Jews would be targeted for death; normal rules of military conflict would be junked. Hitler's new enemy contained an estimated three million Jews, many living in rural *shtetls*. As Hitler's armies swept through Russia, special units of the Nazi SS elite guard, known as *Einsatzgruppen*, systematically rounded up and shot the inhabitants of the *shtetls*, aided in their grisly rounds by German police units and local ethnic Germans.

The next year, 1942, saw the beginning of unprecedented mass murder. In January at the Wannsee Conference in Berlin, the Nazis coordinated plans for the Final Solution: all Jews would be deported to occupied Poland where new extermination centers were awaiting them at Belzec, Sobibor, Treblinka, and Auschwitz-Birkenau.

The extent of this awful enterprise made it inevitable that even under the rigid silence imposed by Himmler, news would get out. The systematic extermination of the Jews of Europe had been under way for several months when word reached a Breslau industrialist named Edward Schulte. Although himself a closeted anti-Nazi, Schulte nevertheless had cultivated excellent contacts within the party hierarchy. On a visit to Zurich in July 1942, Schulte passed on what he knew to another businessman, Isidor Koppelmann, a Swiss national and a Jew.

The information that Schulte relayed was not entirely accurate. As Schulte told the story, the plan for total mass murder was still under consideration, when in fact the first Nazi extermination squads had already been unleashed. But Schulte's account was close enough to the truth to stand the test of history. While pledging Koppelmann to keep his identity secret, Schulte urged him to get the information to the Allied governments. Through an intermediary, Koppelmann contacted a man well suited to the task. He was Gerhart Riegner, the Swiss representative of the World Jewish Congress, formed by Stephen Wise in 1936 to exert pressure across international boundaries on behalf of Jewish refugees.

A young German Jew who had left his homeland soon after Hitler took power, Riegner's credentials included a degree in international law at the Graduate Institute of International Studies in Geneva. He soon demonstrated that he was up to his mission. As eager as he was to get Schulte's tragic news out,

Riegner was determined first to make certain he was not setting off a false alarm. Quietly he looked into the background of the initial informant, Schulte. He learned that Schulte had twice before provided the Allies with important leads that turned out to be accurate—advance word on the Nazi invasion of the Soviet Union and on shifts in the German High Command. Moreover, as far-fetched as Schulte's information might seem, it fit with what Riegner had heard from other sources about the Nazi campaign against Jews deported from their native lands.

For Riegner, the choice of who to inform was obvious. It was Rabbi Wise, who now chaired the executive committee of Riegner's employer, the World Jewish Congress. A harder problem was how to get a message to Wise. On August 7, armed with a letter of introduction from a former professor, Riegner went to the U.S. consulate in Geneva to ask their help. But his proposed communication met with great skepticism from the assistant consul, Howard Elting. This reaction foreshadowed the attitude of the State Department at every level for months to come, which would greatly impede efforts to sound the alarm about the mass killings. For several days consulate officials pondered what to do with Riegner's message. Finally, on August 11, sufficiently impressed with Riegner's diligence and sincerity, Elting agreed to cable Riegner's dramatic news to Rabbi Wise in New York by the only means possible, via the State Department in Washington.

In a covering message, however, Elting's boss, the U.S. minister in Geneva, Leland Harrison, strongly questioned the accuracy of Riegner's warning. In Washington, where the State Department was already predisposed to discount such reports of mass murder, Harrison's message amounted to a red flag. Consequently the department did not transmit the message to Wise. Instead it sent a summary to the Office of Strategic Services, forerunner of the Central Intelligence Agency, describing it as a "wild rumor inspired by Jewish fears." In a message to his colleagues that encapsuled the State Department's thinking, Elbridge Durbrow of the European Division asserted: "It does not appear advisable in view of the Legation's comments, the fantastic nature of the allegation and the impossibility of our being of any assistance if such action were taken, to transmit the information to Dr. Stephen Wise as suggested."

Uncomfortable about cutting off the rabbi's mail, officials in Washington drafted a message to Minister Harrison in Geneva admonishing him in effect not to accept any more such "fantastic" reports without a firmer foundation. Cooler heads prevailed, and the warning to Harrison was toned down simply to explain that the department had not passed on Riegner's message to Wise. Howard Elting, Riegner's initial contact in the Geneva legation, suggested to him that the department might reconsider if he could provide substantiating information.

At about the same time these exchanges between the State Department and its Geneva consul were taking place, on August 21, 1942, President Roosevelt told reporters that he had received reports of Nazi policies from several governments-in-exile of Nazi-occupied countries. According to these accounts, Roosevelt told a press conference, the Nazi measures "may even lead to the extermination of certain populations." Roosevelt wanted it known that any such "barbaric crimes" would be avenged and added that the U.S. government welcomed information "from any source that is reliable of the continuation of atrocities." What the president apparently did not know was that such information was already in Washington, under lock and key at the State Department.

Meanwhile Gerhart Riegner was not idle. In response to the prompting from Elting he gathered more information about mass arrests and deportations of Jews in France and what had once been Czechoslovakia. State Department officials in Switzerland nonetheless continued to discount the reports. Some thought the Jews were exploiting mere rumors in order to provoke a response from the United States and Britain. Meanwhile the days dragged on, with Wise still in the dark about Riegner's message.

But Riegner had not been not naive enough to rely on the good offices of the State Department alone. Figuring that his cable to Wise might be sidetracked, he had sent the same message to the rabbi via Sidney Silverman, a Labor MP and the British representative of the World Jewish Congress. He reasoned that while the British Foreign Office might wish to hold up Riegner's warning, as the State Department had done, the Foreign Office would not dare suppress a message from a member of Parliament. Sure enough, on August 28, nearly three weeks after Riegner had first gone to the consulate in Geneva, Wise finally received a copy of his message, relayed by Silverman.

Now the rabbi had to decide what to do with it. Stephen Wise was then sixty-eight years old. For nearly half a century he had played a leading role in every controversy of importance touching on American Jewry, many with the potential for grave consequences. Now, though, the receipt of Riegner's delayed cable confronted him with a challenge far more portentous than anything he had experienced. How he dealt with it would reflect the triumphs and trials of a full lifetime.

For all his public career Stephen Wise had been known not just for his intellect, which helped make him a national figure, but for his relentless combativeness, which also elevated his public profile. He used to boast that his grandfather, one of seven rabbis among his forebears, fought with his congregation in Hungary for forty years. His point was that his own battles were part of a family tradition, presumably helping legitimize them. But in the past decade, with European Jews facing the greatest crisis in their history and several million American Jews looking to him for leadership, he had restrained his natural instinct toward conflict. Instead he seemed to have concluded that the best course for American Jews and for himself was to rely on the goodwill of Franklin Roosevelt.

More and more, Wise now filled a role not dissimilar to that played by Brandeis, Frankfurter, and Rosenman, that of enabler. By not arguing with the president publicly or privately, they allowed FDR to look the other way when the danger facing the Jews was brought to his attention. Strictly speaking, Wise could not be counted as one of the President's Jews because his roots were in the Jewish community while theirs were in government. But Wise was important to FDR. Because of his role as the nation's preeminent Jewish leader, he served in effect as the president's rabbi, continually validating FDR's bona fides with the Jewish community, whether Roosevelt responded to their concerns or not.

Born in 1874 in Budapest, Wise had been brought to the United States from Hungary when he was seventeen years old, traveling in steerage like his latter-day friend Felix Frankfurter. His father assumed the pulpit of a Manhattan congregation, and the family prospered, moving from their first home, a lower East Side tenement, to more comfortable quarters uptown. Given his heritage, his pursuit of a rabbinical career was all but inevitable, and he was helped along by his family's connections in Europe and the United States and by his father's tutoring.

After graduating from Columbia University and concluding his rabbinical studies under no less a personage than Adolf Jellinek, the chief rabbi of Vienna, Wise returned to New York City and an appointment as an assistant rabbi at a Manhattan synagogue. Within a few months the death of the chief rabbi led Wise to assume the full responsibilities of rabbi when he was not yet twenty years old, meanwhile earning a doctorate at Columbia.

Not satisfied with intellectual accomplishments alone, Wise soon plunged into a variety of political and social causes early in his career. He saw them as a way of linking his faith in Judaism with the principles of his adopted country. After he moved to Portland, Oregon, in 1899 to become rabbi of Temple Beth El, his concern with social causes became a dominant motif in his ministry, and his involvement in local politics helped bring about a reform candidate's election as mayor of Portland.

Wise's achievements in Portland soon brought him an invitation from New York's prestigious Temple Emanu-El to give "test sermons," in effect auditioning as a replacement for the synagogue's venerated but aging rabbi. It took only one sermon from Wise to convince the Emanu-El trustees that they had found their man. Tall, broad-shouldered, and handsome with craggy features, Wise's deep, sonorous voice and flair for language captivated audiences of Jews and Gentiles alike. But when he was offered the job, Wise shocked the trustees by turning it down because they would not meet his demand for a "free synagogue." He wanted total authority to decide on the subject and content of his sermons, including political issues. What's more, he composed an open letter to the trustees giving his reasons for turning down their pulpit, then published it as a pamphlet. All this infuriated the trustees, including their most prominent member, Louis Marshall, who had helped found Emanu-El and who had earned his own battle stripes fighting on behalf of the American Jewish community. But as Wise surely reckoned, the publicity attendant to the episode generated attention and support that helped him carry out his next move, to found the "free synagogue" he wanted in New York.

The differences between Wise and Marshall were broader than the dispute over the offer of the pulpit at Emanu-El. They stemmed mainly from the conflict between German Jews, like Marshall, many of whom now lived in fashionable uptown Manhattan, and East European Jews who dwelled in Manhattan's distinctly unfashionable lower East Side, for whom Wise sought to speak. Wise knew that only time could reconcile these differences. Meanwhile he sought to draw the two groups together in a common cause, the growth of the Free Synagogue. Uptown he met privately with wealthy Jews to seek funding and goodwill. He got plenty of both, including substantial donations from leaders of Temple Emanu-El where his trial sermons had ended in acrimony. The uptown Jews were impressed by the intellectual strength of the sermons he offered in the Free Synagogue's first home, a Universalist Church on the upper West Side. But Wise also opened a branch of the Free Synagogue in an auditorium on the lower East Side, where he held forth on Friday and Sunday evenings.

Two years after the Free Synagogue opened its doors, Wise had attracted sufficient attention in New York and elsewhere to rate a feature story with photos, spread out over seven full pages of *Harper's Weekly*. The magazine's description of this clerical celebrity made him seem like a matinee idol: "Imagine a tall, spare, active, swarthy athlete of early middle age, his frame well covered with muscle. The whole surmounted by a massive head, framed in a leonine mass of wavy, blue-black hair. The ring of his clear baritone sounds like the booming of a deep-toned bell." This panegyric conceded that the icon had faults too, but managed to make his chief shortcoming sound like a virtue. This was his "readiness to fight to the last ditch rather than surrender one jot or tittle of what he regards as right." But, the author contended, Wise's belligerence was overshadowed by his "ever present wish to be of real and lasting benefit to all mankind."

The success of the Free Synagogue allowed Wise to move his temple to a more prestigious address, Carnegie Hall, which could seat three thousand. More important, his pulpit served as a springboard for Wise to promote other causes. One was the American Jewish Congress, which he organized in 1916 over the opposition of Marshall and other American Jewish Committee leaders. Another was the crusade for a homeland for world Jewry, through Zionism. Finally there was his pursuit of a lifelong interest in politics. Although he had been at least a nominal Republican until well into his thirties, Wise had been one of a number of progressives attracted to the promise of reform as set forth by Democrat Woodrow Wilson. Deserting the GOP in 1912 to support Wilson for the presidency, he was in frequent touch with the new chief executive once he reached the White House.

In local politics Wise had a harder time maintaining good relations with the Democrats because of his antipathy toward Tammany Hall. As a child he had seen the influence of Tammany at work in the streets of New York; as an adult he discovered that the machine had not changed its heavy-handed ways. The rabbi organized a citizens group and over the next decade crusaded in a series of municipal elections, winning notoriety and influence. He formed a lasting alliance with one Democratic politician, Al Smith, who despite his Tammany connections Wise considered a reformer at heart. Disappointed by Smith's crushing defeat nationally in 1928, Wise took hope from Franklin Roosevelt's victory in the state, and at first he and the new governor got along famously.

After Wise had testified before the legislature in favor of an FDR proposal for aid to the aged, the governor thanked him for "a splendid piece of work," adding, "I wish you could come up here once a week regularly to give me courage and enthusiasm." But Wise's honeymoon with Roosevelt did not long survive the 1928 election, mainly because of New York City's Democratic mayor Walker, whom many voters viewed as an engaging rogue and whom Wise considered a contemptuous scoundrel.

This led to Wise's leadership of a an anti-Walker reform group and his 1930 clash with Rosenman and FDR. Even before Roosevelt rejected Wise's demand for Walker's ouster, he gave Wise a piece of his mind in a face-to-face encounter, a tongue-lashing that both men long remembered.

In two years Walker was forced to exit the political scene, to Roosevelt's relief. But Wise was not willing to call it quits on their feud. In 1932, as Roosevelt campaigned for the Democratic presidential nomination, the rabbi rejected suggestions from political associates that he back the governor for the presidency. FDR was "a pseudo liberal who has not given an iota of support and furtherance to any efforts to cleanse this politically filthy and corrupt city," Wise told one prominent reformer. He supported Al Smith for the Democratic nomination and later told friends he intended to vote for Norman Thomas in November. He even considered launching a crusade against Roosevelt's candidacy, to advise voters that FDR was a man "of no moral courage whatsoever and no political integrity." When Roosevelt won the White House, Wise complained to Felix Frankfurter, whom he had come to know well through their mutual interest in political reform and Zionism: "There is no basic stuff in the man. He is all clay and no granite."

Once the election was over, however, Wise kept those feelings to himself. A man whose pragmatism matched his passion, Wise realized that with Hitler on the rise in Germany, the welfare of American Jews and his own prestige in that community demanded he rebuild his relationship with the new president. In November 1932 he and John Haynes Holmes sent a conciliatory letter to the president-elect, tendering their "congratulations and good wishes" upon his triumph. In victory Roosevelt could afford to be gracious. "That is a mighty nice letter of yours, and I honestly appreciate the spirit in which it is written," FDR wrote the two clerics. Despite the kind words, Wise was left to heal the damage to the connection that was now, above all others, vital to him. And this would not be not easy.

Without ready access to the White House he was forced to rely on intermediaries, principally Frankfurter. In early April 1933, distressed by the Nazi boycott of Jewish businesses, Wise wrote to Frankfurter almost plaintively, "I am awaiting with eagerness your account of your latest Washington visit," adding, "The pronouncements of the Nazis on the boycott is too awfully shocking in its disclosure of a mentality at once violent and infantile." Ten days later he wrote Frankfurter in gratitude for the fact that Roosevelt had invited him, along with a few others, to attend a conference on Nazi tactics.

But that session proved to be of little benefit. Within a few days Wise wrote Frankfurter again, but in a very different tone. "I have been waiting, I confess, day after day in the hope that you might send me further information about your talk with Headquarters. I do want you to know that I am having an awfully hard time of it with the Jewish masses who cannot be expected to understand why no word has come from the Administration in all these weeks." And he added a warning note: "There are questions on which you or I ought to have the judgment of Headquarters. I would be guided by that judgment if at all possible and I could make that judgment dominant if only I knew it."

A few days later Frankfurter phoned to reassure Wise that the president was indeed fully informed about events in the Reich and the horrors perpetrated by the Nazis. In due time he would give evidence of his feelings. But this did little to ease Wise's frustration and impatience. "Time is of the essence," he wrote Frankfurter. "I prayerfully hope for some word by the president in whatever form he may choose to express his own deep feeling, and that this word will be spoken at once."

When no word came, Wise, near desperation, asked for help from brain truster Raymond Moley, who wrung from FDR a promise to see Wise. Wise rejoiced. But then he heard again from Moley: the White House had called off the meeting since Wise planned to bring a letter of protest, and the White House had decided that such protests could not be submitted in person. For the time being, Wise gave up. Meanwhile he had to submit to the humiliation of an editorial in the *Jewish Daily Bulletin*, an organ of the American Jewish Committee, urging him to avoid contact with the new administration lest he damage the Jewish cause in light of Roosevelt's supposed continuing animus toward him. This triggered a letter from Wise's close friend, federal judge Julian Mack, to Frankfurter suggesting that the latter make clear to the American Jewish Committee leadership that Wise is "not *persona ingrata* [*sic*]" with the president.

While the *Daily Bulletin* may have turned up its nose at Wise, his public esteem otherwise seemed to be at a high-water mark, reflecting his flair for publicity. Thus in June 1933, some twenty years after his *Harper's Weekly* profile, *Vanity Fair* published a similar salute to the rabbi. Underneath a handsome portrait by famed photographer Edward Steichen, the magazine called him the "leader of America's protest against the Hitler anti-Semite campaign," a description Wise would certainly have been glad to accept, though others might have questioned the designation. Wise had his enemies, the magazine acknowledged, but even they "are forced to admit his tremendous gusto and the power of his leadership." Physically the article likened him to a combination of William Jennings Bryan and Gentleman Jim Corbett, with "a leonine head, a voice of muted thunder and the strength of an ox."

For all of that, "the best-known Jew in the country," according to *Vanity Fair*, remained frustrated with his own government. So much so that he allowed himself to be inveigled along with several other Jewish leaders into a meeting with Dr. Hjalmar Schacht, head of the Reichsbank. Schacht had been sent to Washington by Hitler in May 1933 to represent him at an international economic conference. The broadcasting pioneer and prominent Jewish business leader David Sarnoff, who had met Schacht at a similar conclave a few years earlier, arranged the gathering. Its purpose seems to have been only hazily understood by those in attendance. But apparently Wise had the idea that he and his cohorts might impress Schacht sufficiently about the extent of concern among American Jews with the plight of their coreligionists in Germany, so that Schacht might in turn persuade Hitler to temper his tactics.

There was no evidence that Schacht would be sympathetic to such a role. Although he never officially joined the Nazi party, he would eventually be tried as a war criminal at Nuremberg, where John Dos Passos, reporting for *Life*, wrote that he resembled "an angry Walrus." A notably unpleasant man who radiated arrogance, he struck a contemporary as "a compound of a Prussian reserve officer and a budding Prussian Judge who is trying to copy the officer."

The meeting was entirely secret, or as Wise put it to Mack, "graveyard stuff." More than anything else, the initiative signified the desperate outlook of American Jewish leaders. With little else to count on, Brandeis and Mack were both "keenly awaiting" Wise's report on the evening. But so little happened that Wise, who generally recounted in detail anything of consequence, wrote not a word for the record.

Schacht followed that session with a meeting with Roosevelt, who subsequently told Judge Irving Lehman that "at least the German Government now knows how I feel about things." If that government did have such knowledge, it was exclusive information that American Jews would have liked to have shared.

As impatient as Wise, like other Jewish leaders, may have been with FDR's calculated vagueness, the rabbi's willingness to pressure the president seems to have been compromised by his anxiety over the breach in their relationship over Walker and Tammany. In the spring of 1933, a crucial moment for Germany's Jews—and thus for American Jews—Wise appears to have been riven by conflicting concerns. Eager for some gesture from Roosevelt that might slow the Nazis' anti-Semitic splurge, he was also deeply concerned about his own prestige, particularly in relationship to the president. At times his self-concern seemed to overshadow the larger cause. Thus in April 1933 he wrote to Frankfurter: "Frankly, if I were the head of the American Jewish Congress, as I am merely the honorary head, I would resign tomorrow." If he were the actual head of the Congress, Wise explained, he would announce publicly that he had resigned "in order to permit someone else to serve who might have such access to the President of the United States as is denied me. But an honorary presidency is not a job to resign from."

This was a fatuous pretext. Wise had founded the Congress and had been its president for six years. He had resigned in 1929 to get out from under the administrative chores the job required. But he became the organization's honorary president and remained its chief spokesman. To the extent the public thought about such things, Wise was viewed as the leader of the Congress, honorary or not. And if he had quit in protest, it would have created quite a stir. Franklin Roosevelt would certainly have taken note, though how he would have reacted is another question that Wise undoubtedly pondered.

Meanwhile Wise indulged himself in hypothetical near fantasies about the presidential overture he so badly wanted. "I can tell that an open and public move will be made to urge if not practically to compel the president to see some representative of the American Jewish Congress," he prophesied to Frankfurter, whom he knew to be in almost constant touch with Roosevelt. But, said Wise, "I would refuse to see the President under such circumstances. I will not go to the White House as a result of political pressure." And he added, "you will never know how hard my lot has been trying to satisfy an inevitably insatiable constituency."

Notable is that Wise tried, by his own telling, to do all he could to spare the president from the ire of the Jewish populace. "The pressure of wide popular demands for mass demonstrations and organized boycott is becoming increasingly heavy and all but impossible to resist," he warned Frankfurter. "This pressure will undoubtedly be reflected in resolutions in Congress voluntarily offered and insisted upon by Senators. Once this process is initiated and reflected on the Hill, the action may seriously embarrass the White House."

In a similar vein Wise wrote Julian Mack: "You cannot imagine what I am doing to resist the masses. They want organized boycotts. They want tremendous street scenes."

Of course Wise might have viewed these pressures differently. As an advocate for a desperate cause, he might have encouraged the "masses" to make their feelings known and let the White House figure out for itself how to respond. Or he might have at least passed on to FDR the pressure he was feeling.

Despite his frustration, Wise did what he could to smooth Roosevelt's relations with American Jews, sometimes aiding and abetting FDR's own efforts in that direction. In March 1935 Philip Slomovitz, editor of the *Detroit Jewish Chronicle*, a leading Jewish American journalist, wrote to FDR asking him about the truth of a story that he had heard from an old Roosevelt family friend that FDR had Jewish ancestors. Such rumors had been in wide circulation at home and abroad, usually spread by anti-Semitic sources. But Roosevelt responded to Slomovitz as if the journalist was acting in good faith. Actually he knew very little about his ancestors, Roosevelt claimed, and then added a peroration that testified to his own political genius, regardless of bloodlines. "In the dim distant past they may have been Jews or Catholics or Protestants," he wrote. "What I am more interested in is whether they were good citizens and believed in God. I hope they were both." This was a peculiar assertion by the president. A few years later he remarked to Montana senator Burton Wheeler, after mentioning Cordell Hull's wife being part Jewish: "You don't have to go back through your ancestors or mine to find out if there's any Jewish blood in our veins. We're either Dutch or English."

Writing to Slomovitz, he wanted to make a different point, more important to him than his genealogy. At a moment in history when he was being reviled by anti-Semites for his bias in favor of Jews and suspected by some Jews of indifference toward the crisis of their European brethren, Roosevelt had struck upon a foolproof formula that risked little and touched a wellspring of goodwill. Slomovitz promptly made the Roosevelt letter public, and Rabbi Wise saw an opportunity he could not resist.

He wrote to Slomovitz citing a comment by Eleanor Roosevelt at a luncheon in her honor in Wise's home, hosted by his wife, Louise, who provided her husband with a "very accurate" recounting. "Often Cousin Alice [Longworth] and I say that all the brains in the Roosevelt family comes from our Jewish great-grandmother," Louise Wise quoted the first lady as saying. Then Mrs. Roosevelt reportedly added: "Whenever mention is made of our Jewish great-grandmother by Cousin Alice or myself, Franklin's mother gets very angry and says, 'You know that is not so, Why do you say it?'" For Slomovitz's benefit, Wise added, "Mrs. Roosevelt spoke as with knowledge, conviction, authority."

There is no evidence in the Roosevelt family bloodlines to suggest that the first lady had a Jewish great-grandmother, as she supposedly claimed. But the notion was too appealing to Wise for him to discard. "Do you not think," he wrote Slomovitz, "that what President Roosevelt wrote to you is more or less that statement of a man who knows what I have just written to be true but deems it wise and more expedient not to make any public mention of it at this time?" Although Wise advised Slomovitz to "let the matter die down now," he could assume there was a fair chance the journalist would soon find a way to spread this tantalizing tale, to the benefit of both Wise and the president. How, after all, could Jews complain about a president who might be one of their own?

Despite such calculated sleight of hand by both FDR and Wise, as the months passed and conditions steadily worsened for Germany's Jews, Wise's craving for a chat with Roosevelt did not wane. In September 1935 Wise received a suggestion of sorts, through a third party, to ask the White House for an invitation. But he rejected the idea. "If the President desires Dr. Wise to visit him, he will be glad to go to Hyde Park or to Washington, but he can only visit the president if the latter personally and in writing invites him," he wrote, referring to himself in the third person. "I could not do anything else. That time has passed. If he could have me cheaply, that is to say, through a thirdhand verbal invitation, I would not be in a position to secure that for the Jewish case that I am resolved to ask of him."

If Wise expected Roosevelt to be badly shaken by this rejection, he was mistaken. The president did nothing except wait a few months, until early 1936, not coincidentally the year he would seek reelection, and then extend another indirect invitation. Wise received it when he was in Justice Brandeis's office at the Supreme Court, and immediately accepted. No sooner was the meeting done than Wise was on the phone to the *New York Times*, which duly reported that the president and the rabbi had discussed plans for expediting the settlement in Palestine of Jews fleeing Nazi persecution. Roosevelt, Wise told the *Times*, "expressed the deepest sympathy and reiterated his interest in the plans."

To his friend John Haynes Holmes, Wise wrote justifying his decision not to wait for a more direct invitation, that he "might help him [Roosevelt] see the light and the right about the Nazi situation." Whether or not Roosevelt's understanding of the Nazi threat to the Jews was enhanced, he did receive immediate political benefits from the meeting. Two days after Wise's visit to the White House, Al Smith, FDR's onetime ally and more recently a bitter adversary, made a nationally broadcast attack on the New Deal sponsored by the Liberty League, a stronghold of political reaction. Smith's enduring resentment of FDR for winning the prize that Smith felt should be his, and his increasing ties to the titans of big business, had turned him into one of the New Deal's severest detractors. On the day after Smith's broadside Wise suggested in an interview with the *New York Times* that Smith, his erstwhile hero, had blundered by linking himself with the Liberty League.

The long-awaited meeting with the president was the one ray of hope for Wise in an otherwise gloomy landscape. Early in 1936 he had considered proposals to sponsor a committee of Christians who would send speakers around the country to sound the alarm against the Nazis. But he rejected the idea, explaining to his friend Judge Mack that it would be of little value. "Any Christian body must constantly be pushed and driven, and the Christian disguise becomes so thin as to wear off." Besides, Wise said, the American Jewish Congress could not afford it. Unlike the leaders of the American Jewish Committee, who had greater resources, "I have got to work like a dog for every hundred dollars that I get for the Congress, and our budget runs up to seventy or eighty thousand, perhaps ninety thousand."

Adding to his problems, Wise complained of prominent Jews like Bernard Baruch, sometime financial adviser to FDR, who "choose to remain unaware of the danger symptoms of which you and I come upon every day." This attitude was compounded, Wise said, by the article just published in *Fortune* about American Jewry, which minimized the threat of anti-Semitism. "*Fortune*, with the best of intentions, has succeeded in making it still more difficult for me to arouse Jews to an understanding of the truth," Wise observed. "We are repeating the story of Germany during the pre-Hitler years."

While he struggled against these forces at home, new problems loomed in Palestine. In the spring of 1936 violent Arab protests against the projected Jewish homeland stirred anxiety among American Jews for the safety of Jews in the *Yishuv*, as the Jewish community in Palestine was known. The Arab uprisings led the British to establish a royal commission to consider cutting off the flow of Jewish immigration in order to placate the Arabs. In May, Wise turned to his newly refurbished friendship with FDR for help. He chose a roundabout way to raise the issue, expressing concern in a letter to the president about the danger from Arab violence to Americans, both Jew and Gentile, traveling in the Holy Land. In response, Roosevelt promised to protect U.S. citizens. Meanwhile Arab unrest continued, and so did Jewish concerns about a British-ordered halt to immigration.

Encouraged by his earlier correspondence with Roosevelt, Wise wrote again late that summer, this time going at the problem directly. He pleaded with FDR to persuade the British to change their reported plans on immigration restriction. Roosevelt then had Secretary of State Hull let the British know that the United States would regard halting immigration as a violation of the British mandate. Prime Minster Stanley Baldwin agreed to delay the proposed cutback for the time being. But three years later the British imposed severe new restrictions. In the interval some fifty thousand Jewish refugees, all likely future victims of the death camps, were able to flee to Palestine.

Justice Brandeis, not known for lavish praise of others, wrote Wise: "You have performed a marvelous feat. Nothing of more importance has happened to us since the Mandate."

It was indeed a blessing for the Jews. But Brandeis may have given too much credit to his friend Rabbi Wise. In that political season there was abundant pressure on FDR from other quarters, both Jewish and non-Jewish. In early September 1936 the Zionist Organization of America released messages from thirty members of the House and Senate opposing reduced immigration to Palestine. And a Christian organization, called the Federation of America, laid plans to mobilize its members in support of the projected Jewish homeland. "We Christians stand on the side of God if we help the Jew," declared one of the group's leaders.

Whoever else may have prodded FDR to act, Wise was deeply grateful to the president for following through. In October, with the presidential election a month away, Wise wrote a friend traveling in Palestine: "I wish you were here to vote for the Great Man." That same month a presidential invitation to Hyde Park gave Wise the chance to express his thanks in person. Roosevelt's intercession with British prime minister Stanley Baldwin was "a service we [Jews] have no right to forget," he told FDR. What Wise failed to appreciate, as his sympathetic biographer Melvin Urofksy points out, was that Roosevelt as usual was driven more by political calculus than compassion. His gesture was made at "little cost" for his administration. Later, when the political stakes were greater, "Roosevelt would have no compunction about ignoring the plight of European Jewry."

In the midst of Wise's euphoric visit to Hyde Park in October, Roosevelt's conversation should have given him cause for doubts about the steadfastness of the president's backing. In chatting with Wise, FDR mentioned two recent guests who had returned from Germany and told him that "the Synagogues were crowded and apparently there is nothing very wrong in the situational present." Wise tried to explain to Roosevelt that because of the Olympic Games the Germans, eager to make a good impression on international visitors, had reined in their persecution of the Jews.

But the rabbi was in no position to cavil. He had already publicly pledged his support to the president. Earlier in the year, in a letter to Democratic campaign headquarters, Wise had volunteered to spend the entire month of October campaigning for FDR. He suggested he might stump in cities with substantial numbers of Jewish citizens "who seem through the years to have come to attach some weight to my words." He might also appear on the West Coast where he was relatively well known because of his ministry in Oregon.

Roosevelt ultimately accepted this offer, but not without some hesitation. As Wise wrote to David Niles that fall, with anti-Semitism flaring around the country the administration was "a little afraid to put forth Jews too prominently in this campaign." In fact Wise himself shared this concern. When he learned of a campaign fund-raiser attended exclusively by Jewish donors, the rabbi worried about "what hurt it might do to R [Roosevelt] if it leaked to the press in the light of all the foolish things being said about Jewish influence in Washington." Seeking to undercut such talk, Wise in a statement to the Democratic National Committee that fall made a point of stressing that his support for Roosevelt was "not as a Jew but as an American." Even as he campaigned for the president in—by his own reckoning—more than twenty-five cities, this was a theme he kept in mind. "I have never once in all the speeches I have made for President Roosevelt made any allusion to the Jews," he declared at campaign's end, ignoring the reality that his very presence at the podium would be taken by many as an "allusion" to the Jews. And by his own design he targeted cities with heavy Jewish populations. In any event, Roosevelt's unprecedented victory, carrying forty-six states, transcended all demographic boundaries and seemed to make irrelevant the notion of a sectarian vote of any kind.

After the election Wise added his voice to the congratulatory chorus celebrating the victory, and asked a favor in regard to Roosevelt's forthcoming inaugural address. He was greatly disturbed, he wrote FDR, by the statement of Polish Foreign Minister Józef Beck that of Poland's more than 3.3 million Jews, 1 million were "superfluous" and should leave the country. "Oh that you might say one word, dear Chief, on Wednesday," in response to Beck. Such a statement, Wise pleaded, "would bring solace to the hearts of millions who have been terror stricken by the utterance of the Polish government." Roosevelt did indeed include a sentence along the lines of what Wise requested. "We will never regard any faithful, law-abiding group within our borders to be superfluous," FDR declared. Later Wise asserted: "This was only one of many occasions when the word of Franklin D. Roosevelt gave courage if not hope to the victims of Nazis throughout the world." To be sure, Roosevelt had done what Wise asked him to do. But it is hard to see how anyone in Poland or any other foreign country could have taken much comfort from such a cryptic reference.

Whatever benefits Wise believed he gained from his rapprochement with Roosevelt, their improved relationship was at best a mixed blessing. By getting close to the president and offering his unquestioning endorsement in the hustings and wherever the rabbi went in the Jewish community, Wise surrendered part of his independence and the freedom to challenge FDR. His behavior seemed to be founded not only in the faith that Roosevelt, for all his flaws, represented the Jews' best hope but also, and just as important, in the conviction that Wise's own leadership among the Jews depended on demonstrating that he and FDR were on the best of terms.

His attitude was reflected in a note he wrote in early 1937 to the Zionist leader Emanuel Neumann. Wise assured him "that in the District of Columbia we have a great good friend. He is thinking about us and for us. We are on his mind and heart. Thank God for that little *refuah* [balm] in a time of endless *makkot* [plagues]."

Staying true to that message was to lead Wise down a tortuous path in which he often found excuses for not taking the action he was intuitively inclined to take on behalf of Jewish interests. When in 1937 Secretary of State Hull referred to protests by Jews against Nazi persecution as "vituperation," and dismissed their condemnation of Hitler as nothing more than a "row," Wise acknowledged this as "very sad." But in a letter to Julian Mack he added, "In the interests of Palestine, we are going to do what we can to let that pass from the scene." At the time Wise feared that the Peel Commission, established by Great Britain to investigate conditions in its Palestine Mandate, would recommend partition of the country—which indeed turned out to be the case—instead of dedicating the entire territory as a Jewish homeland. "We cannot press the Hitler button and the British and Palestine button at one and the same time!" Wise argued to Mack.

The next year, in the wake of the *Anschluss*, Wise had to press other buttons when Jewish congressman Emanuel Celler of New York announced he would introduce a bill calling for unrestricted immigration for victims of religious or political persecution. Wise's first thought was that the proposal might jeopardize Roosevelt's bootless plan for a refugee conference at Evian. The rabbi viewed Celler's proposal as so harmful "it almost seems the work of an agent provocateur," he wrote Frankfurter. "It simply means that the whole country will go down on the president's proposal with a thud." Under pressure from Wise and other Jewish leaders, Celler backed off. As for the Evian conference, it died of its own weight, without the need of a "thud" from the American public.

Meanwhile Wise had to worry that homegrown anti-Semitism seemed to grow more virulent. In May 1939 a meeting sponsored by the Christian Front and other anti-Semitic organizations gathered in a space fewer than a hundred yards from Carnegie Hall, the headquarters of Wise's Free Synagogue, to extoll the virtues of a "Christian America." Some in the audience of more than seven hundred interrupted speakers with shouts of "throw the Jews out of Christian America." A hundred police officers patrolled the meeting hall and the streets outside to prevent disorder. Afterward, as Wise wrote to a friend, many in the crowd marched outside Carnegie Hall, shouting, "Hang Rabbi Wise to a flagpole! Lynch Rabbi Wise."

"And the police didn't interfere," Wise complained—though it is not clear what the police might have done to prevent citizens from nonviolently exercising their First Amendment rights.

None of these tensions was enough to shake Wise's allegiance to FDR. He again stumped for the president as he sought a third term in 1940. "I had such a charming note from the President who mentions that you told him I was prepared to repeat the 'valiant service' rendered in 1936," he wrote Frankfurter in September 1940. He went on to say that he did not think "anyone's service is necessary," so confident was he of a Roosevelt victory. Wise predicted that the Republican nominee, Wendell Willkie, would get between 100 and 150 electoral votes. Actually he received fewer, only 82; but the election was much closer than that. On election night Roosevelt closeted himself in his study in Hyde Park and literally sweated out the returns from several major states which by narrow popular margins gave him victory, among them New York and other states with substantial Jewish populations.

In 1940, as in 1936, Wise once again worried about the impression among the public of a "Jewish vote" for Roosevelt. This despite the fact that the Jewish vote for FDR was exactly what he hoped to achieve by his campaigning. "There are some Jews, perhaps, who are irrational in their support of Roosevelt, voting for him on the ground that he is friendly or good to the Jews," he wrote to an American Jewish Congress supporter who had voiced concern on this issue. FDR's "friendliness to Jews," Wise argued, "has consisted in nothing more than his championship of the cause of human freedom as against the aggressor nations." Whatever the underlying causes, Jews gave Roosevelt an estimated 85 percent of their vote in 1936 and an even more robust 90 percent in 1940.

The most severe test of Wise's dual loyalty to FDR and to American Jews, and his most dubious decision, would come two years after Roosevelt's victory, and after Ben Cohen had helped pave the way to U.S. involvement in World War II. This was triggered by Wise's receipt of the long-delayed cablegram from Gerhart Riegner with solid information that the Nazis were implementing the total annihilation of European Jewry.

Wise must have realized that the reason he finally got the message by a roundabout route, via Great Britain, was because the cable sent to him had been held up by the State Department. Nevertheless his first response to Riegner's message was to call upon Undersecretary of State Sumner Welles and ask his advice.

In Welles, Wise was confronted with someone who fit the popular stereotype of what diplomats were like. Like Roosevelt, with whom he was linked by family connections, and at whose wedding the thirteen-year-old Welles had been a page, Welles possessed the breeding and background of an aristocrat. He notably lacked, though, the president's leavening humor and bonhomie. The grandnephew of the abolitionist Senator Charles Sumner, he had been educated at Groton and Harvard, where he was a classmate of Eleanor Roosevelt's brother Hall. Encouraged by Roosevelt himself to enter the Foreign Service, Welles was assigned to Buenos Aires where he soon made his mark as an authority on Latin American affairs. Serving as assistant secretary of state under Roosevelt and Hull, he concentrated on Latin American relations and was said to have coined the phrase "Good Neighbor Policy" to define U.S. diplomacy in the Western Hemisphere. As war loomed abroad, Roosevelt promoted Welles to undersecretary of state. In that role, aided by his relationship with the president and despite the growing resentment of Hull, his views commanded attention on a wide range of issues.

Tall, dignified, and aloof, he was a man "of almost preternatural solemnity and great dignity," Harold Ickes observed.

"Just to look at him, one can tell that the world would dissolve into its component parts if only a portion of the weighty secrets of state that he carries about with him were divulged." A British diplomat put it more succinctly: "It's a pity that he swallowed a ramrod in his youth."

When they met on September 3, Welles's response to Wise on the issue of the Riegner cable was what could have been expected, given State Department policy and his own background. Keep the information to yourself, he instructed Wise, until the State Department could confirm it. "He seems to think that the real purpose of the Nazi government is to use Jews in connection with war work both in Nazi Germany and in Nazi Poland and Russia," Wise wrote Frankfurter the day after he met with Welles. He relayed the dreadful news he had gotten from Riegner, but he added, "A moment ago another message came from Berne saying that in the past days one hundred thousand Jews have been killed in Warsaw and their corpses are being used to make soap."

Wise was distraught, and his anguish mounted when new reports from Europe supported Riegner's grim message. "The other day," he wrote his friend Holmes soon after his meeting with Welles, "something came to me that has left me without sleep. One hundred thousand Jews within the Warsaw ghetto have been massacred by the Nazis and their corpses have been used to make soaps and fertilizers. I am almost demented over my people's grief." Now Wise swirled around, asking Frankfurter to pass on Riegner's information to FDR and informing the leaders of the American Jewish Congress of what he had heard and what he had done.

Despite this emotional turmoil, Wise placed his loyalty to FDR above all else and followed Welles's admonition to keep silent. Indeed, he wrote to Roosevelt, "I succeeded together with the heads of other Jewish organizations in keeping it out of the press and have been in constant communication with the state department." In a similar vein he wrote to Frankfurter on September 16 that he had showed the "two awful cablegrams"—Riegner's warning and the news of the 100,000 Jews murdered in Warsaw—to Assistant Secretary of State Dean Acheson and Vice President Henry Wallace. But he could not resist adding: "Have you noted that I have kept the thing out of the press up to this time, thus accept a great responsibility if the threat should be executed."

This "threat" Wise was still reluctant to accept as reality. Hitler might ultimately destroy his Jewish subjects, he conceded in a letter to Frankfurter, but "for the present" there was reason to hope. He pointed out that he had been told by the Polish ambassador—inaccurately as it turned out—that the 100,000 Jews in the Warsaw Ghetto had not been killed by the Nazis after all but instead had been sent to the new Russo-Polish frontier to build fortifications.

Or so Wise wished to believe. In any event, he did not make Riegner's information public until November 24, nearly three full months after he had received it. Wise's defenders have argued that he could not have known that the State Department would hold him to his promise to delay the release of this awful news that long. But for ten years Roosevelt's defenders had used the State Department's attitude, ranging from indifference at best to subtle anti-Semitism at worst, as the *bête noire* for excusing FDR's lack of help for the Jews. How could Wise have expected anything better from that department now?

Earlier, after discussing another of the issues that mixed frustration with impending tragedy, Wise had written to Frankfurter: "Sleep late, go to bed early, never think about the troubles of others, and then you may survive, but you will be damned forever." No one could accuse Wise of not thinking about the troubles of the European Jews. But his choices exposed him if not to eternal damnation then to constant anguish.

On November 24, 1942, Welles called Wise to Washington and told the rabbi that the State Department now had information to "confirm and justify your deepest fears." He added cryptically that "for reasons you will understand," he could not release the information. "But there is no reason why you should not. It might even help if you did."

Released at last from his pledge of silence, Wise called a press conference and made public the gist of the "awful" cablegram from Riegner. But the press response to this long-delayed event had an anti-climactic tone, as if reflecting Wise's own ambivalence about the whole episode. Most striking was the treatment by the *New York Times*, which printed five paragraphs on page ten under the obscure headline "Wise Gets Confirmations. Checks with State Department on Nazi's Extermination Program." Some papers did better by printing a few more paragraphs. But only a few papers played the story on page one. Of more than twenty papers large and small surveyed in a study at the State University of New York, Albany, half did not use the story at all. The study concluded that "In every case that reported the Wise announcement it was presented with language that qualified or left some question as to the mass killing of Jews." This despite the State Department's confirmation of the report.

This coverage reflected the aversion to reports of persecution of the Jews that typified U.S. journalism all through the decade of Hitler's regime. It was an attitude fostered by skepticism about "atrocity" stories left over from World War I, an absorption with coverage of combat between the Axis and the Allies, and perhaps a measure of anti-Semitism. Wise could not be blamed for that. But he had ample time to be aware of this attitude and to prepare for it. Stephen Wise had been holding press conferences for all his adult life, so he had plenty of experience to help him make a convincing disclosure of the Final Solution.

One reason for the uncertainty with which the press treated the story may have been Wise's own reluctance to believe it, as he had acknowledged in his September letter to Frankfurter.*

Testifying to Wise's unpersuasiveness was the remarkable incongruity between the headline over the story "2 Million Jews Slain by Nazis" in the *Chicago Tribune* and its placement in the paper, on page four. Similar evidence could be found on page one of the *New York Times*, which on the same day it placed Wise's announcement about two million Jews on page ten carried a front-page story about a plan devised and carried out by Gestapo chief Heinrich Himmler to murder 250,000 Polish Jews.

Although Wise had had two months to ponder the crisis, he offered no recommendation for rescuing the Jews through some form of ransom. This was an element that might have helped make his press conference newsworthy. It was the issue which, under the leadership of another of the President's Jews, Treasury Secretary Henry Morgenthau, now came to dominate the public and private debate over the fate of European Jewry.

---

*Frankfurter himself was also agnostic about the Holocaust. After a meeting in the summer of 1943 with Jan Karski, an agent of the Warsaw underground who reported eyewitness details of how the Nazis were already beginning their extermination of the Jews, he told Karski, "I am unable to believe you."

VIII

ONE OF TWO OF A KIND

HOWEVER LIMITED the impact of Rabbi Wise's announcement of the Riegner message, it was greater than the State Department wanted. Following his press conference, department officials continued to deny knowledge of Nazi plans for a mass annihilation of European Jewry and to question the credibility of Wise's information. State also resisted a White House proposal for a joint declaration by the Allies condemning the mass murders, arguing on one hand that the reports of the planned extermination were still unconfirmed and on the other hand that a public statement might cause the Nazis to intensify the brutality.

Despite the department's protests, on December 17, 1942, three weeks after Wise's announcement, the United States, Britain, and the Soviet Union along with eight other allies issued a joint declaration condemning the "cold-blooded extermination" of the Jews. The statement cited "numerous reports" from Europe about the mass killings. The *New York Times* carried this story on page one, but most papers ignored it completely. The only other tangible result of Wise's announcement and similar disclosures about the Nazi extermination plan was another international conference, supposedly to deal with the refugee problem, and similar in a way to the Evian conference of 1938. This one was held in Bermuda.

Like the Evian meeting, the Bermuda gathering was doomed to failure from the start. As soon became clear, its main purpose was not to aid the victims of Nazi persecution but to shield the governments of the United States and Britain—who organized the conclave—from public pressure to actually establish some form of refugee rescue program. The two convening powers gave the game away at the start by announcing that discussion would be limited to those relatively few refugees who had somehow already escaped the Nazis on their own, thus leaving the vast majority to their fate. The conclusion of the conference in April 1943, more than four months after Wise's announcement, seemed to end any hope for rescue.

But in the same month that saw the completion of this exercise in futility, a glimmer of opportunity was generated, principally by two men. One was Gerhart Riegner, the German exile who had managed to give the outside world its first real news of the developing tragedy. The other was one of the President's Jews, Secretary of the Treasury Henry Morgenthau.

After gathering the crucial information for his first message to Rabbi Wise in 1942, Riegner had pursued his investigation, despite the resistance of the State Department. Disturbed by the reaction to his earlier message once it was finally released, the department resisted transmitting any more such troublemaking communications. But Riegner overcame these objections and in April 1943 cabled Wise the outlines for a plan for "wide rescue action" in two countries, Rumania and France. In Rumania's Transnistria region, formerly part of the Soviet Union, which included the Black Sea port of Odessa, some 70,000 Jews who had been deported there could be ransomed for some $170,000 and sent to Palestine. In France, children hiding in that country or planning to escape to Spain could be saved if money could be raised pay for their food and clothing. In neither case would the funds fall into Axis hands. Enough money could be borrowed in both Rumania and France to cover expenses if repayment were guaranteed by transferring funds to accounts in Switzerland that would be frozen until after the war.

The French rescue proposal fell by the wayside, a victim of bureaucratic intransigence and foot-dragging in Whitehall and Washington. But the proposal for Rumania remained viable, at least as a possibility. Wise began negotiating with the State Department for approval of the idea while department officials searched for defects. They complained that the plan was too vague. Another concern was that it might be a subterfuge for a scheme by the World Jewish Congress to get ransom money to pay off the Nazis and save more Jews. Not until late June 1943 did the State Department convey information about the plan to Morgenthau's Treasury Department, which would need to issue licenses for any funds to be transferred overseas. And it was mid-July before officials from the two departments met to discuss the proposal.

Representing State was R. Borden Reams, its specialist in Jewish affairs. A Pennsylvania farm boy, Reams had worked as a salesman and hotel manager before passing the Foreign Service examination. After serving in American consulates in France and elsewhere in Europe, Reams joined the Division of European Affairs in 1942 and took charge of its "Jewish questions."

He took his orders from Assistant Secretary of State Breckinridge Long, who with Wilbur Carr's departure in 1937 was the State Department official with the most sway on immigration policy. He supervised refugee and visa questions for Secretary of State Hull and was considered by many to share in the anti-Semitism of which a number of officials in his department were suspected. A journeyman St. Louis lawyer with political ambitions, Long gave his career a jump start by wedding the wealthy granddaughter of Francis Preston Blair, Jr., the unsuccessful

Democratic nominee for vice president in 1868. His wealth allowed "Breck" Long to contribute generously to the 1916 presidential campaign of Woodrow Wilson, who rewarded him by making him an assistant secretary of state, where he naturally got to know the assistant secretary of the navy, Franklin Roosevelt. With Wilson gone from the White House, Long continued to give his wife's money to campaigns of other Democrats, including FDR. When Roosevelt won the presidency, Long's generosity was once again repaid, this time with the ambassadorship to Rome, where he became a great admirer of Mussolini. "The Fascisti are dapper and well-dressed and stand tip straight," he reported to FDR. "The trains are punctual, well-equipped, and fast." Long later revised his opinion of fascism, at least for public consumption, but he consistently fought emergency proposals to save the Jews as diversions from the war effort.

Long's antipathy toward Jews seems to have come out of his background as a Midwesterner striving for social and professional advancement. But his resentment, which may have been part of a generally paranoiac outlook rather than restricted to Jews, intensified as his handling of the refugee crisis triggered criticism from Jewish groups. "They all hate me," he wrote in his diary.

In any event, Long, as Reams knew, was determined to curb any special efforts on behalf of Jews. This restrictive approach, Reams believed, was not only Long's wish but also that of Long's good friend, the President of the United States. Reams himself had no pretensions to being a policymaker; he described himself as a master sergeant. As for recognized specialists in refugee affairs, he referred to them as "people who live off the misery of others." But however humbly Reams styled himself, the fact was that all communications to the State Department dealing with the problems of Jewish refugees were channeled through him. So he was well positioned to shape the fate of millions of victims of Nazism.

Meeting with State Department officials, Reams at first argued that the ransom scheme was not workable because of the complications involved in fund transference, ignoring the fact that hundreds of licenses for such transfers had been issued, though not used. Finally, under questioning by Treasury officials, the truth came out. Reams's fundamental objection to the Riegner plan seemed to be that it might succeed. Seventy thousand Jews were trapped in Rumania, but only thirty thousand places remained available in Palestine for fugitives from Hitler. Reames did not know where else Jewish refugees could be sent.

That was too much for Treasury Secretary Morgenthau. He left the meeting and the next day, July 16, 1943, his department put the State Department on the spot. He informed State that he was ready to approve the necessary licenses for transferring funds. With that action fifty-two-year-old Henry Morgenthau plunged into the fight of his life. It was a battle that dragged on for months, touched off furious conflicts within the administration, and colored the final days of his long career in government. In the course of the struggle Morgenthau, more than any other of the President's Jews, demonstrated a willingness to disregard bureaucratic protocol and personal interest and devote himself to the life-and-death effort to salvage what remained of European Jewry.

For him this was an unexpected role. In the idiom of a latter day Morgenthau might have been considered the Rodney Dangerfield of Roosevelt's Jewish Court. A tall, stolid figure, lacking much in the way of grace or flair, Morgenthau was obscured by the nervy, willful extroverts who populated the leadership echelons of the New Deal. For Morgenthau, this experience was nothing new. From the start of his life he had been overshadowed by his domineering father, whose imperious manner had tried the patience of Felix Frankfurter on their secret World War I mission to Turkey. Despite this personality handicap, Morgenthau went into battle for the refugees with two potent assets—his longtime friendship with FDR, more extensive than anyone else's in the New Deal, and his own powerful resolve. This determination was shaped by a combination of the security derived from inherited wealth and the grit he mustered in rising above his own shortcomings.

Descended from German Jews, Morgenthau, born in 1891, was the only son of Henry Morgenthau, Sr., who made himself a millionaire by shrewd investments in New York real estate. As his wealth increased he became involved with various charities, such as the Ethical Culture Society and the Henry Street Settlement, and ultimately politics, particularly Woodrow Wilson's 1912 presidential candidacy. His wife, Josephine, was as energetic as her husband and deeply involved in social work and in the raising of her four children, though she held more sway over Henry Jr.'s three sisters than over their brother. Young Henry's mother admired her son's deep voice and wanted him to be a singer. But the boy's father thought singing was "sissy" and gave him cello lessons instead.

The elder Morgenthau made his older son his constant companion, which in ways fostered his development but also thwarted it. "His father tried to regulate his life and to dominate his thoughts," his mother later recalled. "He kept him too much with him and away from companions his own age." It was the senior Morgenthau's idea that his son, after preparing for college at Phillips Exeter Academy, should study architecture because it would ready him for the career in real estate his father had laid out for him. But the young man did not take to architecture, or real estate, and soon left Cornell. For a while he tried various other vocational paths that his father suggested. But none satisfied him. Finally, at age twenty-one, determined to enter a field strange to his father, the young man returned to

Cornell to study agriculture. In 1913 he purchased several hundred acres in New York's Dutchess County and settled down as a gentleman farmer.

As it happened, Dutchess County was home to an up-and-coming young politician who also had a distinguished family background. This coincidence would before long bear important fruit for young Morgenthau's career. In addition to presiding over the apple orchards that provided his main crop, Morgenthau and his new bride, Elinor, the daughter of a wealthy New Jersey industrialist, involved themselves in county affairs, serving on school boards and helping run state fairs.

More important for his future, Morgenthau launched a weekly farm journal, the *American Agriculturalist*, which he used to promote such benefits for his subscribers as easier credit, lower taxes, electrification, efficient land use, and more farm-to-market roads. And to help these causes along he naturally became active in New York state politics, an interest that just as naturally brought him to the attention of his neighbor Franklin Roosevelt. After winning reelection to the State Senate in 1912, FDR had gladly answered Woodrow's Wilson's call to serve as his assistant secretary of the navy. But like any ambitious politician, he never forgot the importance of tending to his home base in New York. So it was that in 1915 the squire of Hyde Park invited his gentleman farmer neighbor Henry Morgenthau to lunch and sought to persuade him to run for county sheriff. Although flattered, Morgenthau was still too painfully shy to consider such an enterprise and politely declined, one of the few times in their thirty-year friendship that he turned Roosevelt down.

After the meeting FDR pronounced Morgenthau, who was nine years his junior, an "awfully nice young fellow" and became quite fond of him. For his part, Morgenthau found himself drawn to the older man who was fully as dynamic as Henry Morgenthau, Sr., but whose friendship was not as overwhelming. Over the years the two men grew closer in politics and in personal life. In 1920 Morgenthau chaired the ceremonies at Hyde Park at which FDR was formally notified of the Democratic party's vice-presidential nomination. He then helped run the unsuccessful campaign for the Democratic national ticket in Dutchess County. And during Roosevelt's long recuperation from polio, Morgenthau was constantly at his side, planning the future while playing countless games of Parcheesi with the new invalid.

When FDR did return to the hustings in 1928 as a candidate for the New York governorship, Morgenthau was eager not only to contribute to the campaign treasury but also to serve as chauffeur, advance man, and sampler of the public pulse. It was hardly surprising that after his victory, Roosevelt, who often said that Morgenthau was the only man he knew who had made a profit from farming, named his friend chairman of the newly created New York State Agricultural Advisory Commission. This was only the first in a series of positions he would loyally fill for Roosevelt in Albany and Washington. Morgenthau's commission produced a series of practical and popular recommendations for relieving rural counties of the burden of paying for snow removal, for expanding rural roads, and for improving rural schools.

As he began his second and final term in Albany, Roosevelt named Morgenthau state conservation commissioner. It was the job Morgenthau wanted most. But FDR had reasons of his own for promoting Morgenthau. As he told Morgenthau, he was "getting ready to be president," and he wanted Morgenthau to "get ready" to join him in Washington by gaining experience in running a department.

Soon after he won the White House in 1932, Roosevelt put Morgenthau in charge of unemployment relief, telling him it would be the most powerful agency in the government. But Morgenthau's heart was still in agriculture, so Roosevelt finally satisfied him by naming him to head the Farm Credit Administration, with broad authority over loans to farmers.

In addition to bailing out hard-pressed farmers, Morgenthau got a crack at high-level diplomacy when he helped restore U.S. diplomatic relations with the Soviet Union that had been ruptured by the 1917 Bolshevik Revolution. Roosevelt arranged Morgenthau's involvement because the State Department was hostile to the idea of dealing with the Soviet Union. Morgenthau's role was to negotiate the trade of surplus cotton, grain, and other U.S. raw materials with Amtorg, the Russian trading corporation. It proved to be one stage in a long process that led to U.S. recognition of the Soviet regime. In addition to smoothing the diplomatic path for the Kremlin, Morgenthau's purchases of grain for export were intended to squeeze out speculators and help boost the farm economy.

Along the same lines, FDR ordered Morgenthau in 1933 to buy gold for the purpose of raising commodity prices, then depressed far more than industrial prices. Morgenthau's broad range of responsibilities reflected FDR's disrespect for traditional bureaucratic lines of authority and his confidence in Morgenthau. These views were also illustrated in the president's reaction to Morgenthau's suggestion that the government buy silver for the same reason. Since Dean Acheson, undersecretary of the treasury, who was running the department because of the illness of Secretary William Woodin, was dubious about the idea of buying precious metals, Morgenthau proposed, half-facetiously, getting the attorney general to approve the idea and only then telling Acheson.

"You devil," FDR said. "You're just as bad as I am."

"Well," Morgenthau shot back, "who taught me?" The response delighted Roosevelt.

Given their rapport, Roosevelt in November 1933 named Morgenthau undersecretary of the treasury, the post relinquished by the uncooperative Acheson, and then promoted him to secretary, replacing the ailing Woodin. Morgenthau's greatest asset over the next twelve years was his closeness to the president. FDR once gave Morgenthau's wife of a photo of himself and Morgenthau together in the backseat of an open car inscribed: "To Elinor, from one of two of a kind."

At first glance this appraisal seems off kilter since Roosevelt's apparent optimism and buoyancy contrasted sharply with Morgenthau's dour exterior. What drew them together was that both were wealthy patricians who could afford to look beyond material concerns, a characteristic that helped them share confidences. Roosevelt surely realized that Morgenthau did not measure up to the likes of Brandeis, Frankfurter, and Cohen when it came to intellect. But what mattered more to the president was that without being servile, Morgenthau was absolutely loyal. Roosevelt understood that and trusted him. In the end, the best explanation for their closeness is that Roosevelt believed they were alike, and that judgment overshadowed all differences.

Not every New Dealer shared Roosevelt's admiration for Morgenthau. Some pointed out that he lacked experience in banking or Wall Street. And his introverted personality and lack of verbal skills made it hard for him to communicate with the press or the public. Some colleagues, especially Secretary of State Cordell Hull, resented Morgenthau's intruding on their prerogatives as he ventured into foreign policy. Other objections were philosophical. An inveterate believer in balancing bank accounts and budgets, Morgenthau never accepted the free-spending Keynesian economic theory that became New Deal doctrine, and some branded him too conservative.

Tom Corcoran, who believed that Morgenthau nudged him out of a position he should have received, accused him in a letter to Felix Frankfurter of being "afraid of being a liberal Jew." "Morgenthau was afraid to be associated with you and L.D.B. [Louis Dembitz Brandeis] or have any other disciples in influential places in Treasury," Corcoran wrote. Others were bothered by his taking advantage of his long friendship with the president. Once, when the president was directing the placement of paintings in his office, Marvin McIntyre, an old Roosevelt hand himself, wisecracked: "You are right, Mr. President, you ought to have them hung to suit yourself. After all, you are in this office more than anyone else except Henry Morgenthau." Among those resentful of Morgenthau was Felix Frankfurter, who described him to Brandeis as "a disgrace" and "a stupid bootlick."

Despite this carping from some of his peers, most of Morgenthau's own staff at Treasury appreciated his open-minded approach. "Under Morgenthau, the ordinary jurisdictional bounds were not regarded as applicable," recalled John W. Pehle, a Yale Law School graduate who would show himself to be an aggressive member of Morgenthau's legal staff. "So that staff felt free to start developing programs in any field Treasury was interested."

Roosevelt's trust in his ability and loyalty brought Morgenthau increased international responsibilities. Even before the outbreak of World War II, Morgenthau sought to bolster U.S. ties with its former World War I allies, Britain and France. With Roosevelt's approval, he negotiated the Tripartite Stabilization Pact of 1936, under which American, British, and French treasuries agreed to cooperate in the management of their currencies. When World War II erupted, FDR gave Morgenthau a key role in mustering aid to the Allies.

In selling munitions to Britain and France, Roosevelt sought to bar the big Wall Street banking houses from filling the lucrative and subsequently controversial middleman role they had played in World War I. He turned that task over to the Treasury Department. Under Roosevelt's arrangement the British and French opened special accounts in the Federal Reserve Bank of New York, with Morgenthau in charge of coordinating their transactions. Morgenthau threw himself eagerly into his assignment, which aroused his deepest feelings. "We should learn the lesson which the past seven years have taught us," he had written Roosevelt a few weeks after Munich. "The current claim of an aggressor power is always its last—until the next one."

Morgenthau's hatred of Hitler's regime was deep-seated and personal. In 1938 he took his family, including his two sons, Henry Jr. and Robert, to Europe for a vacation, but also to appraise Nazi Germany from across the border in Switzerland.

Henry Jr. asked if they could cross the bridge into Germany and see the Black Forest.

"What in the world do you want to do that for?" his father demanded.

"Just so we can say we set foot in Germany," the boy explained.

"You are never going to want to say you set foot in Germany," the elder Morgenthau told him.

Two years later Morgenthau had an opportunity to help strike a blow against Hitler that went beyond the financial realm. With representatives of the War, Navy, and State departments, he was called on by FDR to advise on strategy for pushing through the destroyers-for-bases trade with the British that Ben Cohen had helped engineer.

Despite his early determination to oppose Nazism by any means, Morgenthau had not been directly involved in the refugee crisis before the emergence of the Riegner plan for the rescue of Rumanian Jews in 1943. Because Jewish leaders, among them Stephen Wise, who made it their business to know such things did not consider Morgenthau to carry great weight with FDR, he was spared the imprecations aimed at his supposedly more influential colleagues. But he was a regular and generous contributor to the American Jewish Joint Distribution Committee, which was working to find havens for German Jews. He was the only one of FDR's leading Jewish advisers to suggest a specific solution for the problem of Jewish refugees—proposing a haven in British and French Guiana.

After FDR rejected that idea, he suggested that if Morgenthau were to give him a list of the thousand wealthiest Jews in the country, he would tell each one how much to contribute to help the refugees. Now it was Morgenthau's turn to be skeptical. "Before you talk about money, you have to have a plan," he said.

Four years later there *was* a plan to save seventy thousand Jews in Rumania, and Morgenthau was eager to set it in motion. Actually he had learned of the special circumstances in Rumania in February 1943, months before the State Department approached him, simply by reading the newspapers. On February 13, 1943, the *New York Times* had reported from London that the Rumanian government had told officials of the United Nations (the alliance of nations warring against the Axis) that it was prepared to transfer seventy thousand Jews from the Transnistria region to Palestine in Rumanian ships. The ships would use Vatican insignia to insure safe passage. The Rumanians proposed imposing a head tax on each refugee to cover expenses. The offer was complicated, the *Times* reported, by the possibility that spies might mix with the refugees and the likelihood that Arabs in Palestine and elsewhere would protest against such an influx, which would cause Britain to reject the idea.

Morgenthau immediately called Roosevelt. The president knew nothing of the offer and suggested that Morgenthau call Sumner Welles at State. Welles's only knowledge came from the account in the *Times*, but State Department officials abroad soon confirmed the story. The British, as the *Times* story had anticipated, objected to the idea of sending more Jews to Palestine, and Roosevelt suggested North Africa as an alternative. Nothing came of all this until July when the State Department began negotiating with Treasury about ransom, which Treasury approved. As Rabbi Wise explained to Roosevelt, Morgenthau realized that the alternative to the exchange was the death of the seventy thousand Jews. Roosevelt agreed to the plan and so informed Morgenthau. Everything seemed on track.

Despite the president's approval, State Department officials led by Breckinridge Long and his clique found new reason for delay, claiming that the ransom money would somehow fall into Axis hands. Finally, in September 1943, State telegraphed the financial license for the ransom funds to Leland Harrison, the U.S. minister in Bern. But Harrison, remarkably enough, sought further delay. And Treasury learned that the British were also postponing action through their Ministry of Economic Warfare, on grounds that the proposed transaction would supposedly somehow damage the Allied war effort.

In a cable to London countersigned by Secretary of State Hull, Morgenthau asked U.S. ambassador John G. Winant for help. Morgenthau's aide, John Pehle, argued this would do little good because he mistrusted the State Department. But Morgenthau, who normally tried to avoid bureaucratic protocol, insisted that Treasury had no choice but to go through channels. He believed that FDR would want Hull's view before acting. "Unfortunately you are up against a generation of people like those in the state department who don't like to do this kind of thing, and it is only by my happening to be secretary of the treasury and being vitally interested in these things with the help of you people that I can do it. I am all for you." But, he told his aides, "All I can do is to bring this thing and put this thing in Cordell's hands. Then it is up to him to get angry at his own people."

It took the British two weeks to respond, but when the Foreign Office finally offered Winant an explanation on December 15, 1943, it abandoned the excuse of hindering economic warfare and got down to the real truth. It amounted to what Morgenthau described as "a satanic combination of British chill and diplomatic double-talk, cold and correct and adding up to a sentence of death." In essence the British, in an echo of the U.S.

State Department, objected to the plan because it might work. They wrote: "The foreign office are concerned with the difficulties of disposing of any considerable number of Jews should they be rescued from enemy occupied territory. For this reason they are reluctant to agree to any approval being expressed even of the preliminary financial arrangements."

The British response had one salutary effect: it cleared the air of pretense and allowed Morgenthau and his aides to see what they were up against. Morgenthau, Pehle, and Treasury's general counsel Randolph Paul now realized they had been betrayed by British duplicity and State Department indifference. Pehle proposed they try to convince FDR to set up a presidential commission to handle refugee problems. But Morgenthau realized that Roosevelt would want to clear any such move with Secretary Hull first, and that he must see the secretary of state himself.

"I want to go as secretary of the treasury," he told his aides. "Just because I am a Jew, why shouldn't I look after the Jews, or the Catholics or the Armenians?"

Randolph Paul agreed: "You are talking on a broad humanitarian basis—talking as a cabinet member." But when Morgenthau arrived at the State Department for his meeting with Hull a few days later, he was caught off guard. Present with Hull was Breckinridge Long, the durable chief obstacle to any move to ease immigration for Jewish refugees. The Foreign Office's blunt statement as relayed in Winant's cable, however, was too callous even for Long, and now he desperately sought to cover his own tracks.

So Morgenthau, Pehle, and Paul were stunned to learn from Secretary Hull that Long had sent a stinging message to the Foreign Office via Winant. The British statement, Long declared, "had been read with astonishment" by the State Department, which could not agree with its viewpoint. Long added: "It is desired by the department to inform you immediately of the fact that the philosophy set forth in their telegram is incompatible with the policy of the United States Government and of previously expressed British policy as it has been understood by us." In addition, Long had sent Riegner the license to cover the first installment of ransom funds that Riegner had sought eight months earlier. Ultimately about fifty thousand Rumanian Jews would be shifted from Transnistria to safer parts of the country and spared execution.

Talking with Morgenthau, Hull explained that the "trouble" was with "the fellows down the line. I don't get a chance to know everything that is going on." But that did not explain why Secretary Hull made no greater effort to find out what was "going on" with refugee policy. By this time Hull's insensitivity to the impact of Nazism had been well established.

As far back as 1934 he had smothered a Senate resolution protesting Nazi treatment of the Jews on grounds it would infringe on FDR's constitutional powers. Later that same year the secretary unsuccessfully tried to kill a mock trial of Hitlerism at Madison Square Garden, sponsored by the American Federation of Labor and the American Jewish Congress, and made a point of telling the German ambassador that the event did not represent U.S. policy. He took a similar stance in 1937 after New York City's fiery Mayor Fiorello La Guardia referred to Hitler as "that brown-shirted fanatic who is now menacing the peace of the world." When the German embassy officially protested, Hull broke precedent to issue a public apology, leading American Jews and other foes of the Nazis to make protests of their own.

But now, six years later, in meeting with Morgenthau, the State Department sounded a different tune. For his part, Long called Morgenthau aside to repeat Hull's assertion that the failures in refugee policy stemmed from "people lower down in the department." He named one supposed culprit—whom Morgenthau knew in fact had fought other State Department officials to clear the financial licenses required for the ransoming of the refugees—as having spread accusations of anti-Semitism.

Morgenthau, by his own account as recorded in his diary, looked Long in the eye. "Well, Breck," he said, "as long as you raise the question, we might be a little frank. The impression is all around that you particularly are anti-Semitic."

"I know that is so," Long replied. "I hope that you will use your good offices to correct that impression because I am not."

But Morgenthau was unrelenting. "You might as well know that the impression had grown in the treasury that the feeling in the state department is just the same as expressed in the cable from London about the foreign office. There is no difference."

Long protested, but Morgenthau pushed his argument. "After all, Breck," he said, "the United States of America was created as a refuge for people who were persecuted the world over. And as secretary of the treasury I am carrying this out for 135 million people—I am carrying this out as secretary of the treasury and not as a Jew."

Still exuding contrition, Long could not have agreed more. "My concept of America as place of refuge for persecuted people is just the same."

Morgenthau was at first satisfied that with Hull's cooperation there was no need for the special rescue agency that Pehle had proposed. But soon his staff unearthed evidence that after Gerhart Riegner had sent his portentous cable to Wise, the State Department had sought to cut off communication from Riegner to Wise and others in the United States. To convince Morgenthau that State would not operate in good faith, Randolph Paul prepared a memo for the secretary carrying the title, "Report to the Secretary on the Acquiescence of This Government in the Murder of the Jews." The document provided evidence that under Cordell Hull and Breckinridge Long, the State

Department was "guilty not only of gross procrastination and willful failure to act, but even of willful attempts to prevent action from being taken to rescue Jews from Hitler."

Three days after he received Paul's damning report, on January 13, Morgenthau met with Roosevelt with one purpose in mind: the establishment of a refugee relief agency. Aiding Morgenthau in this effort was an important factor of the sort likely to command the president's attention—political pressure on behalf of the refugees.

Much of the pressure was initiated by an inspired agitator named Peter Bergson, whose zeal verged on fanaticism and whose gift for organization and strategy approached genius. Leader of a militant Zionist bloc who had come to the United States from Palestine in 1940, Bergson was a man ahead of his time. A few decades later he could have been a titan on New York's Madison Avenue or one of the brightest stars in the constellation of consultants on Washington's K Street.

But in his own day and age he managed to make a substantial impression anyway. Bergson's first objective was to press for the creation of a Jewish army to fight the Nazis. When that idea was stymied, he concentrated his energies on the rescue of Jews from Nazi terror by any means possible. Bombastic, dogmatic, with a gift for gaining public attention, Bergson defied traditional Jewish leaders, many of whom did whatever they could to keep him from undermining their status. Thus when Bergson, in the wake of the failure of Bermuda conference, convoked the Emergency Conference to Save the Jewish People of Europe in July 1943, Stephen Wise and his allies managed to persuade Sumner Welles not to offer his support.

Wise was less successful with other Bergson allies, among them Democratic congressman Will Rogers, Jr., of California. Wise warned Rogers, as the son of the legendary entertainer later recalled, that by supporting Bergson "I was killing myself with the Jewish community." But Rogers, who did not intend to seek reelection anyway, shrugged off the implied threat.

In a similar vein the rabbi wrote to Interior Secretary Ickes, another Bergson backer, warning him that "the time will come and come soon when you will find it necessary to withdraw from this irresponsible group." Ickes fired a nasty letter back, rebuffing Wise.

Despite Wise's opposition, Bergson was undeterred. He obtained strong statements of support from Morgenthau and from 1940 GOP presidential nominee Wendell Willkie, and even a tacit endorsement from First Lady Eleanor Roosevelt. Upon adjournment the Emergency Conference regenerated itself as the Emergency Committee to Save the Jewish People of Europe. Its aim: to establish a U.S. government agency with the specific mission of rescuing the Jews before they were slaughtered. With Bergson as the driving force, the committee launched a massive national publicity drive with dramatic full-page newspaper ads, most of them written by the playwright Ben Hecht, backed by an intensive lobbying campaign on Capitol Hill.

As part of the effort the committee sponsored "a pilgrimage for rescue" which brought four hundred Orthodox rabbis to Washington on October 6, 1943, three days before Yom Kippur, the day of atonement and the most solemn of all Jewish days of religious observation. Set apart from Washingtonians and ordinary tourists by their beards and long black coats, the rabbis prayed at the Lincoln Memorial, then marched to the White House where they hoped to see Roosevelt and present him with a petition urging immediate efforts to rescue European Jews. But Roosevelt had been advised not to see the rabbis by Sam Rosenman, whose influence had grown steadily during the war years. In the headline over a lengthy profile published, as it happened, on December 7, 1941, the *Washington Post* described Rosenman as the "President's No. 1 Adviser."

But Rosenman had not altered his views on dealing with Jewish refugees. He appeared to agree with the New York Jewish congressman Sol Bloom, who argued that it would do the refugees no good for such an alien-appearing group to represent their cause in the nation's capital. Rosenman explained to the president that the group did not represent the most thoughtful elements of American Jewry.

Through aides, FDR informed the rabbis that he was too busy to see them. Actually his schedule was relatively light that day, permitting him to attend a ceremony at nearly Bolling Field in honor of a contingent of Yugoslavs joining the U.S. Army Air Force. Only five members of the rabbis' group were allowed to enter the White House, where they presented their petition to presidential aide Marvin McIntyre.

Despite Rosenman's attempt to trivialize the rabbis by dismissing their status in the Jewish community, their visit was no small matter. As Rosenman certainly knew, their rebuffed effort to confront the president was part of a far-flung, bitterly fought campaign that had divided not only Jewish leadership but the president's own cabinet over the survival of what remained of Europe's once multimillion-member Jewish community.

Guided by Bergson, the campaign of newspaper advertisements, mass meetings, and endorsements from the likes of the writer Dorothy Parker, Herbert Hoover, Will Rogers, Jr., AFL president William Green, and Ickes helped push both the Senate and the House of Representatives to introduce resolutions calling for "immediate action" to "save the surviving Jewish people of Europe from extinction at the hands of Nazi Germany."

Since the resolutions were only advisory legislation, their passage would not have automatically created the rescue agency Bergson and his cohorts wanted. But they were hoping that even this symbolic gesture would force the president to act.

As might be expected, the State Department, especially Breckinridge Long, fought the resolution tooth and nail. Long demonstrated his determination to stop the proposal when he testified before a closed House committee hearing on November 26. There he contended that the State Department had been doing all it could to help the refugees. To buttress that assertion he announced that the United States had admitted 580,000 "victims of persecution" since Hitler had come to power. For the time being Long's testimony robbed the drive for the joint resolution of its momentum. Many in Congress reasoned that given the work of the State Department claimed by Long, no new entity was needed.

But in his eagerness to block the resolution, Long had overreached and destroyed his own effectiveness in the refugee debate. When his testimony was made public on December 10, supporters of the refugee agency proposal quickly pointed out that the assistant secretary had seriously distorted the facts. Most dramatically, the 580,000 figure, as Long soon was forced to admit, applied only to the total number of visas issued during that period. The actual number of Jews admitted, as official government immigration records showed, was barely more than 165,000. And not all of these were refugees, because, as the American Jewish Congress pointed out, as did the Yiddish Scientific Institute in a letter to the *New York Times*, the overall total included an estimated 30,000 Jews from Austria, Czechoslovakia, Poland, Russia, and the Baltic, Balkan, and Scandinavian countries who arrived between 1933 and 1938 and thus could not be counted as victims of Nazi persecution. To put the matter in perspective, Long's debunkers noted that the total number of immigrants admitted from Hitler's Reich itself during the period 1933–1942 cited by Long amounted to only 123,000, less than half the immigration quota for that country.

The discrediting of Long would eventually lead to his loss of power over refugee visas. More important, in the short run it restored the impetus to the drive for the joint resolution and a new refugee agency. When Morgenthau went to see

Roosevelt on January 17, 1944, a Sunday afternoon, along with Pehle and Paul, he brought with him a condensed version of the staff report accusing FDR's government of acquiescing in the murder of European Jewry, as well as a draft executive order establishing a refugee agency.

Roosevelt, who resisted reading anything longer than a few hundred words, asked for and received a condensed verbal summary of the memo. He glanced at the executive order, then instructed Morgenthau to meet with Edward R. Stettinius, Jr., who had replaced Sumner Welles as undersecretary of state after Welles's forced resignation in 1943.

That same evening Stettinius, who proved much more responsive to Morgenthau's entreaties than Welles, heard Morgenthau out, pointed out that he had already agreed to reduce Long's authority at State, and pronounced the executive order as "wonderful." On January 22, 1944, Roosevelt signed the order to establish the War Refugee Board with a $1 million budget to assist European Jews and other victims of Nazi persecution. What Morgenthau would later refer to as "the terrible 18 months" of anguish and delay that followed the Riegner message had ended. But Morgenthau's battle against the foot-dragging of the State Department was by no means finished.

Following the executive order, all U.S. officials overseas received instructions to comply with goals of the new agency, and the board prepared a presidential declaration condemning the "wholesale systematic murder of the Jews" as "one of the blackest crimes in history." But some at the State Department, led by R. Borden Reams, objected, contending among other things that the statement would help further the Nazi argument that the United States was waging the war mainly for the sake of the Jews. At the White House, Roosevelt said he wanted to clear the declaration with the British. Alerted by Pehle to the stalling, Morgenthau called Roosevelt to urge him to move ahead and to recommend that Pehle be named to head the board.

On March 24 Roosevelt released what was now called a "statement" instead of a "declaration," condemning the systematic torture of civilians by the Nazis and the Japanese. The "wholesale systematic murder of the Jews" was pushed down to the sixth paragraph. The phrase "one of the blackest crimes in history" was retained. And Pehle was given the job he had richly earned as head of the new agency.

It was a dubious reward because it was a next-to-impossible mission. The board's budget was meager; private Jewish agencies provided most of the funds. Although other government agencies offered little cooperation, the board managed to get urgently needed supplies to a few concentration camps behind enemy lines. All told it helped save the lives of about 200,000 Jews, mostly from Rumania and Hungary. Since the board was urging other countries to take in refugees, Pehle felt the United States too should do something. The board thus established a camp in Oswego, New York. But as Pehle acknowledged, this was "largely a symbolic gesture," and the camp had room for only 982 refugees. In addition to its rescue efforts, the board backed a proposal from American Jewish leaders to bomb the gas chambers at Auschwitz, but the War Department refused even though Allied planes were repeatedly hitting military targets nearby.

No matter how hard the board tried, it could not overcome its fatal flaw, its delay in arriving on the scene. "What we did was little enough," John Pehle said later. "It was late. Late and little, I would say."

For those of his colleagues who believed the fight for Germany's Jews carried political risk, Morgenthau's experience provided supporting evidence. Gossip spread in Washington accusing him of acting more out of loyalty to his religion than to his country. And some believed the gentleman farmer's bitterness at his experience led him to draft the Morgenthau Plan for postwar Germany, which proposed stripping the country of its industrial base and reducing it to a pastoral state. Secretary of War Stimson called the plan "Semitism gone wild for vengeance." But by this time many in the West were more concerned about having Germany as a potential ally against the threat of the Soviet Union than about its revival as a warmongering aggressor. Nothing came of the plan except to damage Morgenthau's reputation

After Roosevelt's death, Harry Truman kept Morgenthau at his post. But the secretary, never at ease with himself or others, felt even more uncomfortable without his friend, the Hyde Park squire, in residence at the White House. He quit in July 1945 after Truman refused to let him attend the Potsdam conference.

Although Morgenthau was rarely suspected of eloquence, in a remark to Sam Rosenman he provided perhaps the best epigraph for the labors of the President's Jews. When Rosenman characteristically urged Morgenthau not to take his case against the State Department to Roosevelt, because word might leak to the press, Morgenthau shrugged off the advice. "Don't worry about the publicity," he said. "What I want is intelligence and courage—courage first and intelligence second." If more of his colleagues had followed that formula, the history of the Jews in the twentieth century might not have been quite as tragic as it turned out to be.

That tragedy could not be reversed. But out of the horrors wrought by Nazism and the indifference of much of the rest of the world, the postwar era provided an opportunity to put Morgenthau's principles into practice on behalf of the Jews who survived the Final Solution. The crucial question was how American Jews and their government would respond to this chance.

IX

THE MYSTERY MAN

ABE AND IRVING are facing a Nazi firing squad in the grim joke that Peter Bergson and his followers used to lighten their spirits in the face of the Final Solution. The Nazi sergeant comes forward to offer the intended victims blindfolds and cigarettes. But Abe tears the blindfold off and spits in the Nazi's face.

"Please, Abe," Irving begs, "don't make trouble."

This bit of gallows humor illustrates the attitude common among American Jews that hindered Peter Bergson and others as they sought to rally support for the rescue of what remained of European Jewry. In a larger sense this attitude was simply the latest representation of the quandary that had haunted American Jews for all their time in the *golden medine*: the conflict between their urge to assimilate, to submerge their special identity in the American melting pot and not "make trouble," even as the Holocaust loomed abroad, and the call of conscience that inclined some to spit in the executioner's eye.

Although the quandary was not new, changing circumstances abroad and at home underlined the vulnerability of American Jews. The result was to undercut their traditional response to threats to their brethren overseas, a response that was almost as old as their history in the United States. As far back as 1840, America's tiny Jewish population was roused to protest when the Ottoman government, retaliating for the disappearance of a Capuchin monk, sentenced seventy-two Damascus Jews to death. The Jews had been hesitant to act until President Martin Van Buren, in an election-year gesture, appealed to the Turks as did the British and the French, and the prisoners were set free.

Despite the fact that Van Buren's action preceded their protest, the Jews were heartened by his intervention and encouraged to make further protests over the next hundred years, most often in response to the brutalities of the Russian tsars. Although the response of official Washington was mixed at best, there were some successes, notably the abrogation of the commercial treaty with Russia in 1912. And this sense of obligation had become institutionalized with the formation in 1906 of the American Jewish Committee, whose charter imposed upon its members the responsibility to protect the civil and religious rights of Jews "in any part of the world."

But a generation later when Hitler came to power, attitudes among American Jews had undergone a subtle and complicated change, the net result of which was to constrain the instinct for protest. One reason was the rise in nativist sentiment in the United States, a general antipathy toward foreigners in general, which naturally included Jews. This was painfully manifested by the night riders of the Ku Klux Klan and the invectives of Henry Ford and the *Dearborn Independent*. Perhaps an even more important reason for the dampening of protest was the tightening of the immigration laws. These restrictions not only hurt Jews abroad who might have chosen to come to America but also Jews who were already in the country, by ensuring they would remain a very small minority among many minorities.

Many Jews hesitated to push back against the bigots for fear of heightening Christian resentment. American Jews recognized the shortcomings of their existence in their adopted homeland.

But it remained the best country they had known since the Diaspora, and they were reluctant to jeopardize what they had gained here. Some even blamed what anti-Semites would call their own "pushiness." "We have made a noise in the world far out of proportion to our numbers," said Cyrus Adler, a leader of the American Jewish Committee, traditionally accustomed to looking over its shoulder. "Having thus gotten the world's attention, we could hardly expect that it would all be favorable."

All this strengthened the arguments of the "sha-sha Jews," like Irving facing the guns of the Nazi firing squad, who argued against protest from Jews lest it stir the *goyim* to anger. Still, some sense of solidarity with Jews abroad and outrage at their treatment lingered, as evidenced first by the Jewish War Veterans march in March 1933 and later by the swelling support for Peter Bergson's movement.

Amid this flux and ferment, the President's Jews emerged as a potential influence on the fortunes of American Jews. On the face of things they seemed to offer a tactical advantage to the beleaguered Jewish community, a sympathetic and knowledgeable route to the president, who was himself believed to be sensitive to their circumstances. But this notion led to tragic disappointment. The President's Jews, specifically the three reputedly most influential, Brandeis, Frankfurter, and Rosenman, were not what the Jews outside government wanted them to be. Instead of serving the Jews as conduits, they served the president as buffers, shielding him from the importunings of the increasingly desperate Jews.

The explanation for their conduct lies in their shared experience growing up Jewish on the precarious terrain of late-nineteenth- and early-twentieth-century America, and from particular traits in their characters and intellect. Brandeis was a man most of whose impulses were subsumed by an all-encompassing intellectual vision. Even his fervor for Zionism seems to have been driven not only by the need for a Jewish

homeland as a refuge for persecuted Jewry but also as a labo-
ratory to prove out his theories of progressivism. Frankfurter
was gripped by a mixture of apprehension and ambition that
matched, and sometimes exceeded, even his considerable intellectual gifts. Determined to protect his precious relationship
with Roosevelt and his reputation in the worlds of academe and
politics, not to mention his prospects for a seat on the Supreme
Court, he concluded that vigorously championing the cause of
European Jewry with the man in the Oval Office involved too
much risk. Sam Rosenman, equally determined to protect his
status with the president, dedicated himself to telling FDR what
he believed he most wanted to hear, and which in most cases was
what Rosenman himself happened to believe. Rosenman did not
merely avoid the refugee cause, he actively sought to obstruct
it. If these three felt awkward in the role that advocates for the
refugees asked them to play, they might have gotten out of the
way, as Benjamin Cohen in essence did, and allowed the Jews to
try to communicate with the president on their own. At least
the lines of responsibility would have been clear, and the Jews
would have known where they stood.

As for Cohen, "the brilliant, otherworldly young counsel,"
as *Fortune* called him, he concluded that he could accomplish
nothing by pleading the refugees' case to the president. Instead
he threw his intellectual and political resources into aiding the
British, Hitler's only active adversary at the time, an effort that
he must have seen would ultimately help draw his own country
into the war and thus assure the destruction of Nazi Germany.
He was right about that, but this denouement came too late
for millions.

The president's rabbi, Stephen Wise, too was controlled by
his own ego and ambition. He spent most of Roosevelt's first
term, when the fate of European Jewry was being shaped, trying to make amends for the discomfort that his zeal as a civic
reformer had given then-governor Roosevelt. In the process of

reingratiating himself, he surrendered his freedom of action. Having persuaded himself that Roosevelt was the Jews' only hope, he concluded that his best chance to do anything for the Jews, and to protect his own status, was to remain on the good side of Roosevelt.

Henry Morgenthau provided a striking contrast to the hypocrisy and pusillanimousness that undermined the hopes held by the Jewish community for the President's Jews. He had plenty of self-doubt, but his financial standing, his personal rapport with "the Skipper," and his reasoned judgment gave him the confidence to overcome his weaknesses and take on the State Department and Roosevelt himself. True, he was egged on by an aggressive and dedicated staff. But his aides would not have responded as they did if they had not had faith in their boss. The most serious criticism that can be leveled against Morgenthau is that he was late to the fray. He referred to the time lag between his first knowledge of the Holocaust and his confrontation with the State Department as "the terrible 18 months." But in fact, by the time he emerged as a force in 1943 an entire terrible decade had passed with ruinous consequences.

The initial failure of the President's Jews who were purportedly most influential with Roosevelt was in underselling the Jewish case. They discouraged protest, including the idea of an economic boycott of Nazi Germany, on the grounds that it would be of little avail. But there was strong evidence to the contrary from the very beginning. Thus on March 25, 1933, after the Jewish War Veterans triggered demands for a boycott of German goods and an official protest against the Nazi brutalization of the Jews, the reaction of Herman Göring, then second to Hitler in the Third Reich's hierarchy, reflected the impact. Göring summoned leaders of German Jewry and ordered them to send delegations to the United States and Britain to stop the protests and propaganda against the Nazis or he would not be able to guarantee the safety of their people. The German Jews did as they were told, and the British and U.S. protests were toned down. For their part, the Nazis suspended their anti-Jewish boycott after only three days.

Another strategic error for American Jews, and their supposed allies in FDR's inner circle, was in casting the Nazi persecution of Germany's Jews in narrow terms, as simply another outbreak of anti-Semitism. It would have been more effective, and in the long run more realistic, to portray Hitler's early brutality against the Jews as the tip of a military and political iceberg that not only endangered the Jews but threatened all of Western civilization.

As *Fortune* pointed out: "The connection between Fascism and Jew hatred is not accidental. Fascism having nothing for sale but dictatorship and no selling point but the necessity for force requires civil riots in order to advertise its goods and a civil triumph to complete the sale. Jew hatred, as the Nazis have proved, does very well as an excuse for the first and the Jews as a victim for the second." But for FDR to make such a connection he would have needed foreign policy goals that recognized the nature of the threat Nazism posed to the United States.

On a more tangible issue, the President's Jews and their allies in the American Jewish community failed in rebutting the supposed causal link between immigration and unemployment. There is plenty of historical evidence to the contrary, notably the low employment and rapid economic growth of the United States throughout the nineteenth century, when immigrants flooded the country. Indeed some economists argued that one reason for the economic collapse of the 1930s was the sharp reduction in immigration imposed at the onset of the 1920s. Labor Secretary Perkins tried to make this case within the administration as she fought to ease the "likely to be a public charge" restrictions promulgated by President Hoover. But she could not overcome the resistance of the State Department, based on a low toleration for Jews, verging on bigotry, and bureaucratic rigidity, combined with the reluctance of the president, stemming from indifference and a concern about public opposition. Had the economic rebuttals been advanced publicly, they could have been used by political leaders sympathetic to the cause of the refugees to shield themselves from political damage.

Perhaps the most fundamental error in the approach of American Jewish leaders, due in no small measure to their acceptance of the guidance of the President's Jews, was grossly to underplay a potentially powerful political hand. The Jews comprised a potent interest group which, under the terms of New Deal politics, could compete to advance its interests using its loyalty as a bargaining chip. Leaders in the Jewish community and Jewish members of FDR's inner circle refused to take advantage of their electoral strength to support the concessions they sought in dealing with the Nazis and in easing immigration restrictions, perhaps because they underestimated Jewish political clout. Not only were Jews the most loyal group in the New Deal coalition, regularly awarding Roosevelt 90 percent of their votes, but their concentration in big cities in a few key states with large electoral votes gave them an influence out of proportion to their numbers. Thus in the 1940 elections FDR carried New York, then the nation's most populous state, by a hairbreadth—225,000 votes—an advantage that could reasonably be linked to that state's huge Jewish vote.

Some argued that loyalty to Roosevelt worked against the Jews because it allowed him to take their support for granted and thus deprived them of leverage. But trade union members were roughly just as loyal to the New Deal as Jews. Yet far from taking them for granted, Roosevelt bent every effort to meet their needs, from pushing through "labor's Magna Carta," the Wagner Act, to shrugging off protests over the 1937 sit-down strikes that shook middle-class America. John L. Lewis, Sidney Hillman, and other labor leaders would not allow FDR to forget his debt to their members. If Jewish leaders, instead of heeding the cautious counsel of the President's Jews, had been more forthright about challenging FDR for his failure to respond to the crisis facing European Jews, the president might have been forced to take a different tack.

A case in point was the strategy of A. Phillip Randolph, president of the Brotherhood of Sleeping Car Porters and the most potent civil rights leader of his day. Mindful that Roosevelt had all but ignored black Americans through the first two terms of his presidency, Randolph's resentment boiled over in 1940 as the nation geared for war. Although stepped-up military spending was reviving the economy, blacks were being left out in the cold without jobs. In 1941 Randolph announced plans for a march on Washington by fifty thousand people to demand fairer treatment. Eager to avoid what would have been a national embarrassment, Roosevelt defied the will of the Southern barons who still dominated his party on Capitol Hill. He persuaded Randolph to call off his march by establishing the Fair Employment Practices Committee to curb racial discrimination in war plants.

To put that action in perspective, though it fell short of what Randolph had hoped for, the order helped put nearly two million blacks to work in the defense industry by war's end. Moreover it contrasted with Roosevelt's earlier total resistance to efforts for civil rights, including his refusal even to support federal anti-lynching legislation. It contrasted even more with the record of the previous Democratic president, Virginia-born Woodrow Wilson, one of whose first acts in office was to order racial segregation of the federal civil service.

For Jews the potential payoff for aggressive tactics was demonstrated by the impact of Peter Bergson in his campaign to rescue European Jewry. By pushing both the Senate and the House of Representatives to introduce resolutions calling for immediate action on the refugee crisis, Bergson forced Roosevelt's hand. The threat of Congress stealing his leadership status compelled

Roosevelt to yield to Henry Morgenthau and create the War Refugee Board. Politics, as the Jews learned from this experience, and as Roosevelt well understood, is an exercise in risk and reward. In the case of the War Refugee Board, Roosevelt realized he had to take the risk of dealing with the refugee problem or risk losing the reward of Jewish votes and financial support. It was a lesson too late for six million victims of the Nazi death camps, but one that American Jews would put to good use as they faced their next momentous opportunity, the creation of the State of Israel.

For many American Jews, the revelation of the Holocaust was an occasion for guilt and remorse. They felt that by not acting more forcefully they had been guilty of one of the great sins of history. But American Jews were fortunate in that the struggle to launch the State of Israel offered them a chance to make amends.

By the time World War II ended in Allied victory and the full horror of the Holocaust was revealed, the fight for Israel had been waged for nearly a quarter-century, dating back to the Balfour Declaration. But the struggle came to a head just as the war was ending. It was FDR, still revered by American Jewry, who ushered in the final phase of the fight to establish a Jewish homeland. On his way back from the Yalta conference in February 1945 he met with King Ibn Saud of Saudi Arabia aboard the U.S. cruiser *Quincy* in the Great Bitter Lake at the south end of the Suez Canal. Roosevelt would die two months later, so this turned out to be his final opportunity to fulfill the hopes Jews had for him. But the net result of his meeting was a setback that almost killed the prospects for a Jewish homeland before it was even born.

At first glance the opportunities for successful negotiation with the king seemed bright, because the odds were very much in FDR's favor. He commanded the greatest aggregation of military strength the world had yet seen, its might illustrated by the eight-inch guns of the *Quincy* in whose shadow the two men met. And this was backed by an economic juggernaut that had not only pulled the United States out of the Great Depression, girded the country for battle, and armed its allies to boot but had already laid the foundation for dominating postwar global commerce.

Until fairly recently, Saud's chief claim to renown had been the ruthless stewardship of his tiny kingdom, where beheadings served as the great national public spectacle, along with his self-proclaimed role as protector of the holiest sites of Islam. But in the preceding few years that picture had begun to change as a result of a three-letter word that would dominate the world economic landscape for the rest of the twentieth century and into the next: oil.

As Western entrepreneurs began pumping this precious resource out from under the desert sands, its importance became clear to every general, admiral, industrialist, and statesman on earth. If their countries were to prevail, or even simply survive in the brutal competition the postwar world promised, they could ill afford to be on the wrong side of the Middle East potentates. In the meantime, though, Roosevelt had something else more immediate and specific in mind. As soon as the guns fell silent, he wanted his royal guest to endorse the idea of admitting to Palestine hundreds of thousands of Jews whose lives had been torn apart by the war and persecution.

FDR went to no small effort to soften up his visitor. He had the navy set aside a generous welcome mat on the *Quincy*'s deck, across which were spread oriental carpets, a desert tent large enough to hold a harem, and a sheep pen. If the king was impressed by any of this, he gave no sign. Guarded by bare-foot Nubian soldiers, surrounded by a retinue that included his astrologer, a coffee server, and numerous miscellaneous slaves, cooks, porters, and scullions, he flatly turned down Roosevelt's suggestion.

Speaking for himself, and evidently for the other Arab rulers as well, the monarch made clear his belief that the Jews should stay in Europe where they could be provided with land and funding by Germany. After all, this was the nation guilty of whatever transgressions had been committed against them. He shrugged off the contention that the Jews who had already settled in Palestine had made the desert bloom. Whatever they had accomplished, Saud said, had been made possible by British and U.S. funding. And the Jews had shared none of it with the Arabs. The Arabs, he told Roosevelt in no uncertain terms, would fight and die before they would make room in the desert for the Jews.

Caught off guard by the king's intransigence, and eager to stay on the right side of someone whose goodwill Washington would certainly need in the future, FDR sounded retreat. The United States, he pledged to Saud, would never aid the Jews at the expense of the Arabs.

Roosevelt was not the only putative friend of Israel who would encounter Saud's resistance. When British prime minister Churchill also asked Ibn Saud to back large-scale Jewish immigration, the king told him that would amount to "an act of treachery to the Prophet and all believing Muslims which would wipe out my honor and destroy my soul." But Churchill, as far as is known, gave no reassurances to the king as did FDR.

Moreover Roosevelt followed up his verbal promise to the king with a written pledge. On April 5, 1945, a week before his sudden death, he responded to a letter from Saud with a missive of his own. Their "memorable" discussion had given him a "vivid impression of Your Majesty's sentiments on this question" of Zionism, Roosevelt told the king. And he confirmed what Saud surely remembered, that "I assured you that I would take no action which might prove hostile to the Arab people."

It is not clear whether Roosevelt, with his health collapsing, with the war he was leading nearing a decisive point in battlefronts across the globe, regarded the letter as anything more than a diplomatic courtesy. But whatever he thought, his facile response to the king would immensely complicate the decisions facing his successor in the Oval Office.

Of course FDR never told Harry Truman about his assurances to the Saudi Arabian monarch, anymore than he told his vice president about much else of consequence in U.S. foreign policy, including the existence of the atomic bomb. Given a Senate career that had concentrated on domestic issues, Truman had a lot of catching up to do on international relations—just as world leaders and Americans with strong interests abroad had a lot of catching up to do when it came to understanding Truman.

The new president's mind had a sharp partisan edge, honed by the machine politics of Boss Pendergast's Kansas City but grounded in interest-group liberalism embodied by the New Deal. All his life he had championed underdogs, in whose ranks he counted himself, stemming in part from the dismally poor eyesight that marred his childhood. He was probably close to being legally blind without eyeglasses, and the thick glasses he had to wear cut him off from other children. "Of course they called me four eyes," he later told an interviewer. "That's hard on a boy. It makes him lonely and gives him an inferiority complex."

But young Harry's natural feistiness helped him overcome any such brooding. Hard times in his youth made him the only president since Grover Cleveland not to have attended college. No one had entered the White House in modern times with fewer intellectual pretensions, but no one placed more reliance on the lessons of history, as he understood them. From his childhood Truman had read history, concentrating on the lives of men who had risen to greatness and on models and patterns of behavior that he would later seek to follow. He admired strong presidents who took full advantage of the powers of the office.

As a boy he had been a "hero-worshiper" of Andrew Jackson, the first populist president.

When he assumed the presidency the sixty-year-old Missourian had to contend with obstacles few other presidents have had to face—notably succeeding Franklin Roosevelt in the midst of the greatest war in history, with very little preparation for that office. This was five years after he had brought his political career back from the graveyard by winning a second Senate term when he had little money, few allies, and a host of formidable adversaries. He was a man who had come to terms with himself, which gave him the strength to deal with his foes—who unwittingly helped him by invariably underestimating him.

For all his limited experience in foreign affairs, Truman had given American Jews and Zionists elsewhere in the world reason to feel hopeful about his policy toward the prospects of a Jewish state in Palestine. As a senator he had backed Zionist principles. He had Jewish supporters and friends in Missouri, notably Eddie Jacobson, his erstwhile World War I army comrade and partner in their failed postwar haberdashery business.

In political terms, all the odds seemed to favor Zionism. As Truman reminded a group of American diplomats who warned him that the United States faced trouble in the region if he backed Jewish demands for a homeland, hundreds of thousands of his constituents as president favored the Zionist cause. "I do not have hundreds of thousands of Arabs as constituents."

But actually Truman's situation and the political environment for Zionism was not quite as one-sided as that. For while there were few Arab constituents to speak of, the two most prominent leaders of the American foreign policy establishment, Defense Secretary James Forestall and, more important, Secretary of State George C. Marshall, were bitterly opposed to Zionist demands. They regarded the Jewish push for a homeland as jeopardizing U.S. relations with the Arab states and thereby threatening national security. With cold war tensions mounting steadily, the opposition of Forrestal and Marshall could not be readily dismissed by any president, certainly not by a new, unelected chief executive whose foreign policy credentials were as slim as Truman's appeared to be.

Truman was thus caught in a ferocious political crossfire between American Jews, mourning the victims of the Holocaust, and his leading military and diplomatic advisers who warned that yielding to the Zionists would harm the country Truman was sworn to protect. No wonder in a moment when his patience was near an end he wrote to David Niles, a Roosevelt aide whom he kept on: "I surely wish God Almighty would give the Children of Israel an Isaiah, the Christians a St. Paul and the Sons of Ishmael a peep at the Golden Rule."

It is revealing that Truman wrote frankly to David Niles. For this retread New Dealer and 1930s liberal, almost unknown and unmentioned outside the inner circles of official Washington, would serve as his principal guide through the vortex of pressure that marked the three years leading up to U.S. recognition of the State of Israel. By shrewdly promoting the Zionist cause without compromising the interests of his own country, Niles came to represent the belated fulfillment of the hopes American Jews had had for FDR's trusted advisers. He was in effect the President's Jew of the Truman White House—except that he delivered.

Truman's wishful comments on the Golden Rule were prompted by one of Niles's subtle maneuvers on behalf of the Jewish cause. He had sent Truman a memo calling attention to a report put out by a pro-Zionist group, headed by *Nation* publisher Freda Kirchwey, which branded a major pro-Arab organization as linked to Nazi Germany. The charges, Kirchwey's report claimed, were based on documents leaked by the U.S. State Department. "I think it is important to find out how it got out," Niles wrote of the charges. "It is very damaging evidence that the Arab representatives now at UNO [the United Nations] were allies of Hitler."

In reality, Niles could hardly have been disturbed about how this "damaging" evidence was leaked. His main purpose in the memo was to make sure that Truman did not overlook the Kirchwey report.

The president's reaction was all that Niles could have hoped for. "Thanks, glad you sent it," he wrote back to Niles. "I knew all about the purported facts mentioned and *of course*, I don't like it." It was one of many moves Niles made during this period when the fate of the proposed Jewish homeland hung in the balance. He not only helped build Truman's support for the Jewish cause but enhanced his relationship with the president.

David Niles had been born David Neyhus in 1890 in Baltrementz in Russian Poland to Jewish parents and raised in the slums of north Boston, one of four brothers. His father, Ascher, a tailor, earned only enough for the family to survive. His mother, Sophie, urged him to make something of himself, but there was not the wherewithal to pay for his formal education beyond high school. Niles took a job in a department store and managed to educate himself, relying heavily on Boston's Ford Hall Forum, which offered free lectures and discussion groups and served as a magnet for the city's writers and thinkers. Niles's intense interest in these goings-on so impressed the Forum's director, George W. Coleman, that he made Niles his deputy. And when World War I led to Coleman's taking a federal job in the information office of the Labor Department, he brought his bright young assistant along.

After a brief postwar stint in the nascent motion picture industry, Niles returned to Boston and the Ford Hall Forum in 1921, this time in Coleman's old job as director. His contacts at the Forum gave him access to a variety of liberal causes, among them the 1924 presidential campaign of progressive candidate

Robert La Follette (which in the absence of other dependable leadership Niles more or less managed), the defense of Sacco and Vanzetti, and the 1928 presidential candidacy of Al Smith. Organizing independent voters for Smith, he met FDR and Harry Hopkins, contacts that inevitably led to his becoming an early New Dealer.

As a protégé of Hopkins, Niles was drawn into a number of political skirmishes, including FDR's abortive purge of conservative Democrats in the 1938 midterm elections and in the more successful effort to "draft" the president for a third term in 1940. He had his hand in, too, when Roosevelt ran for a fourth term in 1944, organizing the CIO's political action committee that got out labor's vote.

For his efforts, in 1942 Niles was rewarded by being named a presidential administrative assistant in charge of labor and minorities, particularly for Jews. His post was one of those White House jobs for which Louis Brownlow, the political scientist who helped create the executive office bureaucracy under FDR, famously said that a prime requirement was "a passion for anonymity." In Niles's case, though, colleagues said the passion more nearly approached a mania.

When Truman took over the Oval Office, Niles made the expected pro forma offer of his resignation. Truman's appointments secretary, Matthew Connelly, then advised the president that if Niles were allowed to leave, "he would lose somebody who would be completely loyal to him." Connelly pointed out that Niles had supported Truman for vice president in 1944 when many of his fellow liberals backed the incumbent vice president, Henry Wallace, for a second term. Connelly described Niles as "a very bright political analyst" who in FDR's tenure was known as the "backstairs boy at the White House." Not surprisingly, Truman kept him on.

Niles never married, though for years he had secretly been in love with Stephen Wise's daughter, Justine, whom he had met at a Ford Hall Forum, and through whom he met Rabbi Wise. Niles domiciled himself in a book-filled room he kept for years in the Carlton Hotel, only a few blocks away from his office on the second floor of the distinguished but rickety State, War and Navy Building, next door to the White House. As devoted as he was to his duties, Niles spent a good deal of time outside Washington pursuing official business and his own private affairs. Every weekend he would leave town, first for New York, where he would meet with leaders of liberal and labor organizations and take in one or another Broadway show, in some of which he had modest investments. Then he would go on to Boston to visit his sister and take charge of the Ford Hall Forum's regular Sunday night meeting.

To keep his profile low, Niles rarely wrote letters or memos, preferring to deal with other White House aides and interest-group leaders in person or by phone. After his death his papers turned out to consist almost entirely of material he received rather than anything he sent out. A profile of Niles in the *Saturday Evening Post* billed him as Truman's "Mystery Man" and described him as physically well suited for the obscurity he sought and successfully achieved—"short, plump and altogether unremarkable," with thin hair and pale blue eyes. A protean figure, he left some people with the impression that he was cold and remote; but others found him warm and emotional. Some friends spoke of his weeping openly while walking through a rundown city area. And Truman told another aide that Niles would break into tears when the subject of Palestine came up for discussion.

Niles's "backstairs" operating style irritated some colleagues who resented his influence. "A most secretive individual who slunk rather furtively around the corridors of the White House," is the way Truman aide George Elsey described him. "Niles rarely if ever confided to his White House colleagues what he said to the President or what his recommendations were," Elsey complained. "Part of the influence that Niles liked to have people feel he had on the president was this secretiveness."

Such criticism would scarcely have bothered Niles, given his commitment to the clandestine behavior Elsey grumbled about. What little he said in public about himself was intended to minimize his influence. "I am a man of no importance," he once said. The most he would acknowledge about his role in a letter to a Jewish leader was that he was "an instrument of the president who has been privileged to give my opinion to the president on Palestine, among other things. Decisions are not made by me."

Of course that was literally true. But if Niles did not make decisions, he had a lot to do with shaping the president's crucial choices on Palestine policy. Niles avoided overstating his arguments, which would have undermined his relationship with Truman, who had little patience for overblown rhetoric. But he did not hesitate to offer the president analysis based on his experience. When one U.S. diplomat wrote Truman to warn of Ibn Saud's reaction to U.S. support for a Jewish homeland, Niles told him: "President Roosevelt said to some of us privately that he could do anything that needed to be done with Ibn Saud with a few million dollars"—in other words, don't worry about him. His comment turned to be prescient when in 1945, as Truman began to drift toward the Zionist position on Palestine, Saudi Arabia protested, arguing that FDR had given his word not to support the Jews.

Truman was nonplussed, knowing nothing of the exchange of letters earlier that year between FDR and the king. The administration was forced to release the correspondence, which the State Department argued fell short of an ironclad commitment to opposing a Jewish state. After further grumbling, Saudi Arabia let the matter drop. But the unwelcome surprise caused problems for Truman by undermining the trust he was attempting to build with American Zionists.

To help forge that rapport he came to rely more and more on David Niles. Among the chores Niles performed for Truman, as he had for Roosevelt, was as contact man with the pollster Hadley Cantril. Soon after Truman became president, Niles passed on to him the result of a survey which, to the pollster's surprise, showed that about half of Americans knew of the proposal to establish a Jewish state. Among those who had an opinion, the margin in favor of the idea was three to one, with most of those believing that the U.S. government should help bring about the Zionist goal.

The approval of the general public made it possible for Niles to take advantage of his greatest asset in the struggle over the Jewish homeland, the widespread public support of Jewish Americans. Unlike FDR's Jews, Niles was not at all reluctant to exploit and energize this political muscle. With the encouragement of Niles, who had close relationships with the leaders of Jewish organizations, supporters of the Jewish homeland flooded the White House with some 135,000 letters, petitions, and messages in the crucial year of 1947 as the fate of Palestine was being decided by the United Nations, to whom the British had turned over the problem.

The pressure irritated Truman at times and caused him to resent the Jews who hectored him. "Jesus Christ couldn't please them when he was here on earth," he complained, "so how can anyone expect I would have any luck." But Niles calculated that the president's annoyance would be outweighed by his respect for the political clout the outpouring represented. And Niles took it upon himself to make sure that was the case. In effect he took a risk by becoming an advocate for the Zionist cause, thus jeopardizing his credibility. But he counted on his rapport with Truman, who had come to trust and like him, along with the president's own inclination to support the Zionist goal, to outweigh suspicions of bias.

Like Sam Rosenman, Niles had been a member of the American Jewish Committee, which frowned on Zionism. "Before Hitler came to power I was an anti-Zionist, then after that I became a non-Zionist," he once explained to an interviewer. "After the war I became a full believer in the idea of political Zionism." Another pro-Zionist influence on his views was his friendship with Stephen Wise, whom he met with whenever Wise came to Washington. Also a factor was Chaim Weizmann, then head of the World Zionist Organization. During the war Weizmann was sufficiently farsighted to establish a rapport with Niles and several other Jews in key White House positions in hopes of assuring a line into the Oval Office when the struggle for a Jewish homeland reached its climax.

Niles's role contrasted with the stance of Rosenman, whom FDR had relied on as his chief adviser on Palestine. Immediately after the war in Europe ended, Rosenman helped persuade Truman to urge the British to admit more Jews into Palestine. But as the months wore on and the Arabs and the State Department attacked the Zionist effort, Rosenman backed away from the controversy.

"For obvious reasons it is very embarrassing for me to be in disagreement with the state department on this particular question," he told Truman when asked for advice. "I really think you should have someone else here in the White House handle it— and hope you will." Soon after, Rosenman left the White House for private life. And except for occasionally bearing messages from Truman to Zionist leaders, he was removed from White House decision-making on Palestine.

That left a clear field to David Niles, who made a series of crucial strategic moves to offset the State Department's opposition to Jewish hopes. One of his most important actions came in August 1946 when Zionist leaders chose Niles to accompany Undersecretary of State Dean Acheson to meet with Truman and persuade him to go along with the idea for partitioning Palestine, with one segment set aside for a Jewish state. After his session with Truman and Acheson, when Niles met with the Zionist leader Nahum Goldman, "Niles had tears in his eyes" when he reported "that the President had accepted the plan without reservation and had instructed Dean Acheson to inform the British government." Although the British rejected the proposal, Truman's support was a major milestone on the road to the creation of Israel.

As the 1946 midterm elections approached, Niles realized that Republicans were attempting to take advantage of Jewish dissatisfaction with Truman's apparent indecisiveness on Palestine. He helped persuade Truman to deliver a speech in October 1946, on Yom Kippur, which beat the Republicans to the punch. In the address, which Niles helped draft, Truman not only called for "substantial" Jewish immigration into Palestine but for the first time endorsed creation of a "viable Jewish state" there, the basic Zionist goal. While during the next two years Truman's backing for a Jewish state seemed to waver at times, he never abandoned that promise.

Just as important, Niles used his rapport with Zionist Jewish leaders to shelter Truman from the more aggressive advocates, arranging instead visits from moderates such as Chaim Weizmann, the Grand Old Man of Zionism. As Niles had reckoned, Weizmann's idealism won Truman's heart, and the president instructed the U.S. delegation at the United Nations to back the Zionist position. A few days later, on November 29, 1947, the UN with U.S. backing voted to partition Palestine, dividing the country between Arabs and Jews and setting the stage for the establishment of a Jewish state.

It was a great victory for Zionism, but the celebrations did not last long. The State Department fought back, warning of violence in Palestine and promoting the idea of a trusteeship which would postpone the birth of a Jewish state indefinitely. For a while Truman himself seemed to be leaning in that direction, stirring outraged protests from American Jews. Out of patience, and weary of attacks by supporters of the Jewish homeland and of the controversy that had dragged on throughout his presidency, Truman went into what amounted to a sulk, rejecting further contact with Zionist leaders.

At this pregnant moment, Truman's ex-partner Eddie Jacobson, with Niles's help, wangled his way into the Oval Office to see his old friend and to beg him to meet with Weizmann again. Tearfully Jacobson told Truman he was shocked that he had refused even to talk to any of the Zionists. "It doesn't sound like you, Harry, because I thought you could take this stuff they have been handing out to you."

Truman stared out at the White House Rose Garden for a moment and then turned to Jacobson. "You win, you bald headed son-of-a-bitch," he said. "I will see him."

Within the week Truman did meet with Weizmann, who once again elaborated the Zionist dream of making the desert bloom. Truman's memoirs and those of Weizmann's wife indicate that when the meeting ended both men realized they had reached a common understanding on U.S. support for a Jewish homeland in Palestine. To be sure, there were still twists and turns along the way, due to continued resistance from the State Department and particularly from Secretary of State Marshall. At a crucial meeting in the White House where Truman's political strategist Clark Clifford urged recognition of Israel, Marshall turned red in the face and vented his anger at the president.

"If the President were to follow Mr. Clifford's advice and if in the election I were to vote, I would vote against the President," he declared.

The meeting was stunned into silence, and Clifford remembered thinking that if Marshall made his views public it "could virtually seal the dissolution of the Truman Administration" and break up the Western alliance, not to mention ensuring Truman's defeat in the 1948 election.

Truman himself stayed calm, muttered some placating words to Marshall, and ended the meeting. "Well, that was rough as a cob," he said to Clifford. But he refused to budge. And Marshall, while maintaining his opposition to recognition, promised he would not make his views public. That cleared Truman's way to do what he was determined to do, give the U.S. imprimatur to the Jewish homeland-nation.

On May 14, 1948, at 6 p.m. Washington time, Zionist leaders in what used to be Palestine declared the existence of the State of Israel. Within minutes the United States announced its full and unconditional recognition. And minutes later Truman phoned David Niles to give him the news.

"Dave, I want you to know that I've just announced recognition," Truman told his aide. "You're the first person I've called, because I know how much this would mean to you."

Niles's efforts to help make Israel a reality inevitably aroused criticism from some who felt he was biased. George Elsey contended afterward that Niles served too much as a spokesman for Zionist groups, which were his contacts, instead of simply functioning as a conduit. Elsey added: "When you know what position a man is going to present, it doesn't have any particularly outstanding merit or weight." But that comment seems belied by evidence demonstrating Truman's reliance on Niles's advice and may reveal more about Elsey's resentment of his colleague than about Niles's influence.

Niles's activities raised another and more serious question: whether he was more concerned with protecting the interests of the future state of Israel than of his own country. But for that to have been the case, Niles would have had to consistently mislead his boss, Harry Truman. Given Niles's own prudence and Truman's case-hardened skepticism, it seems unlikely that Niles would have attempted such hoodwinking, or that if he had done so, Truman would have let him get away with it.

The key to understanding Niles's role and his effectiveness is Truman's sympathy with the Zionist cause. The new president's feelings were shaped by a combination of compassion and pragmatism. His heart was stirred by the homeless and stateless European Jews who had been uprooted by Nazi aggression. And his political instincts did not miss the electoral calculus.

Of course Niles was not the only influential friend the Zionists had. Other Jewish leaders and some White House advisers played significant roles in helping gain the U.S. recognition that Israel desperately needed. Particularly important was Clark Clifford, who saw the political weight of the Palestine issue in Truman's bid for reelection.

The contrast between the responses of American Jews to the two crises, over refugees from Hitler and over Palestine, could hardly have been sharper. It can be summed up in one word: politics. The willingness of Jewish leaders and their allies, notably the redoubtable President's Jew in the Truman White House, David Niles, to use the potential of Jewish political strength as a weapon made possible the redemption of the promise for a Jewish homeland. The failure to use that weapon during the long agony of European Jews assured the Holocaust. In the years since 1948, the Jews have learned this lesson. But what is most significant and reassuring is that so have millions of other Americans in a nation where the political balance of power increasingly has come to depend on constructing a majority of minorities. Politics in a democracy is essentially conflict among various interest groups. This is a reality that may trouble upholders of the status quo and that challenges the hypocrisy of many politicians. But it offers a path that all groups might follow toward economic and social justice.

ACKNOWLEDGMENTS

I OWE an initial debt to Professor Gulie Néeman Arad of Ben-Gurion University of the Negev whose *America, Its Jews, and the Rise of Nazism* not only introduced the term "President's Jews" but also provided a trenchant and notably fair-minded analysis of the forces that shaped the nation's response to the crisis of European Jewry.

This book would have been impossible to write without the resources and support of the Johns Hopkins University library staff, particularly Andy Young, Sharon Morris, and Zena Mason of the Washington Center library.

Special thanks are also due Kevin Proffitt, senior archivist at the American Jewish Archives, for helping me gain access to the Stephen Wise papers.

Among the many to whom I am grateful for advice and encouragement are Thomas B. Allen, Ben Ginsberg, Alonzo Hamby, Tom Hannon, Joseph McCartin, Art Pine, Diane Ries, Melvin Urofsky, Brooks Yeager, Bernard Weinraub, and my daughters, Cynthia Diane Shogan and Amelia Ford Shogan. I also thank my publisher, Ivan Dee, for keeping faith.

R. S.

Chevy Chase, Maryland
May 2010

NOTES

Full citations of many of the references in the Notes will be found in the Bibliography that follows.

Abbreviations used in the Notes:
NYT = *New York Times*
WP = *Washington Post*
FF = Felix Frankfurter Papers in the Library of Congress
SSW = Stephen S. Wise Papers in the American Jewish Archives

I. QUANDARY IN THE GOLDEN LAND

page
3 Marchers assembled: NYT, March 24, 1933.
4 The Garden protest rally: NYT, March 28, 1933.
6 FDR's instructions: Feingold, *Witness*, 229.
6 "Three velten": Dalin and Kolatch, 168.
6 The partisan divide: White, 429.
7 Taft's view: Fuchs, 71.
7 The Democratic renaissance: Murray, *103rd Ballot*, 279–284; Josephson, 193.
8 Jews in high-level positions: Kreuger and Glidden.
8 "The President's Jews": Arad, 6, 130–134.
10 The quandary: Arad, 16.
11 The first Jews: Hertzberg, 7; jewsinamerica.org

12 The Puritan view: Hertzberg, 25–26.
13 A great influx: Matthews, *passim.*
14 Tyler's welcome: Arad, 15.
14 View of German jews: ibid.
14 Reform and new tensions: Matthews, *passim.*
15 "Permanent precariousness": Howe, 9.
15 The chaos that followed: Arad, 30.
16 "This Old World soul": Howe, 75.
16 "Curse you immigration": Howe, 67.
16 Jews in the garment industry: Howe, 81.
17 Competing strands: Arad, 31–33.
17 Early anti-Semitism: Hofstadter, 77.
18 Henry Adams's view: "Henry Brooks Adams."
18 "A cross of gold": Dinnerstein, *Anti-Semitism,* 49.
19 Pleas to Harrison, Roosevelt: Arad, 38–39.
19 Kishinev pogrom: NYT, April 28, 1903.
20 Birth of American Jewish Committee: Arad, 40.
20 Marshall background: "Louis Marshall."
21 "A citizen of the Old School": Raider, *passim.*
21 Fight to abrogate the treaty: Arad, 40–43.
22 Congressional action: NYT, December 14, 20, 1911.
22 The Russians were stunned: *Los Angeles Times,* December 20, 1911.
23 The bitter conflict: Urofsky, *Voice,* 59–60.
23 Condemned as stupid: Arad, 50.
24 Wise and Zionism: Urofsky, *Voice,* 17–18.
26 American Jewish Congress meeting: Urofsky, *Voice,* 154.
27 Jews cried out in pain: Arad, 63.
27 "Biological laws show us": Gossett, 405.
27 Hoover's view: Handlin, 159.
28 Ford's campaign: Mulcahay.
29 Libel suit against Ford: Woeste.
29 Mobs looted Jewish stores: Arad, 73.
29 "Greatly exaggerated": NYT, September 27, 1930.
30 Hitler's path to power: Shirer, 170–187; Grobman.

II. THE HIDDEN-HAND SKIPPER

32 Left hand under table: Schlesinger, *Coming,* 583.
32 Best friends anti-Semites: Breitman and Kraut, 245.
33 "I am a juggler": Kimball, *Juggler,* 7.
33 "His mind does not follow": Stimson diary, December 18, 1940.

33 "Close against your belly": Ickes, *Struggle*, 659.

34 "Frictionless command": Freidel, *Ordeal*, 66.

34 "No one could tell": Tugwell, *Roosevelt*, 66.

34 "I was a goose": Freidel, *Rendezvous*, 31.

35 Concealing effects of polio: Maney, 26; Gallagher treats the issue at length and in detail.

36 He enjoyed stumping: Moley, 52.

36 "saving sinners from themselves": Tugwell, *Roosevelt*, 247.

37 "Like a football team": Hurd, 164.

37 "Second-class intellect": Burns, 157.

37 "Psychoanalyzed by God": Leuchtenburg.

38 "Borne a good name": Maney, 2–4.

38 "If we accept": Freidel, *Apprenticeship*, 12.

38 Carefree hours: Maney, 2.

39 "A good chance to be President": ibid., 86.

39 The 1910 campaign: Smith, 62–69.

40 Challenging Tammany: ibid., 76.

41 "A deaf ear": ibid., 81.

41 Wooing Wilson: ibid., 87–98.

42 Traits of Louis Howe: Rollins, 4–5.

42 Love of the sea: Ward, *Trumpet*, 160.

43 Riding up front: Smith, 98.

43 "My fingers in everything": ibid., 103.

43 "The greatest war": ibid., 123.

43 Tarheel temper: ibid., 126.

44 "Stay where he is": ibid., 140.

44 "Bryan is a brewer": *Chicago Tribune*, August 13, 1920.

45 FDR's bragging: Freidel, *Ordeal*, 81–82; Schlesinger, *Crisis*, 364–365; Ward, *Temperament*, 534–535.

46 "Someday Franklin will be president": Smith, 195.

47 Or so Smith believed: ibid., 209.

47 Internal divisions erupted: Murray, *103rd Ballot*, 97.

47 Nominating Smith: Gallagher, 60–62.

48 Reaction to the speech: NYT, June 27, 1924.

49 Deciding to run for governor: Smith, 225–228.

50 The *American Hebrew*'s worries: Fuchs, 20.

50 "An awful class of Jews": Ward, *Temperament*, 250.

50 "A frayed raiment": Cook, 390.

50 "Only Jew gentlemen": Ward, *Temperament*, 59.

51 FDR's heavy-handed humor: ibid., 250–253.

52 New paths for state government: Smith, 237.

52 Twice a day press conferences: Maney, 32.
53 "Little flurry downtown": Morgan, 317.
53 He blamed the legislature: ibid., 33.
54 Unique contribution: ibid., 34; Smith, 250.
55 Lippmann's warning: Steel, 291–292.
55 Backing away from the League: *Public Papers of the Governor, 1932,* 55off.
56 "A corkscrew": Martin, 138.
56 Alliance with isolationists: Cole, 22–25.

III. THE PASSIVE PROPHET

57 The Nazi boycott: Shirer, 203; Grobman.
58 Protests swelled: Arad, 149.
59 Brandeis joined Frankfurter: Stephen Wise to Julian Mack, April 10, 1993, SSW, box 115.
60 Brandeis's hopes for FDR: Strum, 100.
61 Brandeis's rise: Murphy, 18–25; "Louis Dembitz Brandeis," *Encyclopedia of World Biography.*
63 "Separated from Jews": Murphy, 26.
65 Brandeis and Wilson: Strum, 196–210.
66 Attachment to Zionism: ibid., 224–230.
66 The Supreme Court nomination: "Louis Dembitz Brandeis," *Dictionary of American Biography.*
67 Criticism from the *Times*: NYT, July 18, 1916.
67 The Frankfurter connection: Strum, 372–380; Murphy, 32–40.
68 Many at Harvard knew: Strum, 374; Murphy, 44; NYT, February 14, 18, 1982.
70 "Many invisible wires": Lief, 407.
70 Mobilizing the economy: Murphy, 55.
70 Getting Wilson's backing on Palestine: ibid., 55–65.
71 "51 percent sure": ibid., 65.
71 One man think tank: ibid., 74.
72 Brandeis alerted Frankfurter: Strum, 100.
72 "against the bankers": Strum, 181.
72 A broad blueprint: Murphy, 105.
73 "Wolf in sheep's clothing": Tugwell, *Art of Politics,* 247.
73 Placing other disciples: Murphy, 113.
74 "A very satisfactory meeting": Brandeis to Frankfurter, April 12, 1933, FF, box 28.

74 Do something in re German Jews, though Brandeis did not explain what this should be: Brandeis to Frankfurter, April 13, 1933, FF, box 28.

74 Purging Jews from civil service: NYT, April 14, 1933.

75 American Jewish Congress conference: NYT, April 15, 1933.

75 "disgrace to us all": Brandeis to Frankfurter, April 26, 1933, FF, box 28.

75 Hoover's change: Breitman and Kraut, 7.

76 "Something could be done": Wise to Mack, May 4, 1933, SSW, box 115.

76 Hull's background: Hull, 105–106; Gellman, 23–25.

77 FDR's choice: Hull, 150–158.

77 Not entirely above board: Gellman, 31; Novak.

78 Hull's wife: Medoff.

78 "More ashamed than pained": Arad, 165.

79 Reluctant to be involved in controversy: Gellman, 33–34.

79 "Pity Hull was late": Urofsky and Levy, *Letters*, no. 642.

79 "If only LDB had taken hold": Wise to Frankfurter, September 16, 1940, SSW, box 109.

79 FDR offered "Kunstrucke": Urofsky and Levy, *Letters*, no. 536.

80 "Sickening and terrifying": NYT, June 11, 1933.

80 As for Hamilton Fish: NYT, May 26, 1933.

80 Turned down an invitation: Brandeis to Frankfurter, Urofsky and Levy, *Letters*, no. 549.

81 Zionism and Americanism: Arad, 133.

81 The NRA decision: *Schechter Poultry Corp. v. United States*, 294 U.S. 495 (1935).

82 Hillman reaction: Schlesinger, *Upheaval*, 283.

82 FDR's view: Alsop and Catledge, 17–20.

82 Brandeis's scolding: Schlesinger, *Upheaval*, 280.

83 First call on FDR on behalf of Jews: Arad, 258.

83 "FD went very far": Urofsky and Levy, *Letters*, 603.

83 That was sufficient: Brandeis to Wise, November 23, 1938, SSW, box 106.

84 Brandeis's talk with Ickes: Ickes, *Struggle*, 509–510.

IV. THE SOUL OF DISCRETION

86 "He knows best": Wise to Mack, April 2, 1933, SSW, box 115.

86 "More power to you": Wise to Frankfurter, 1933, SSW, box 109.

86 "The most influential": Frankfurter.

87 Frankfurter's early background: Hirsch, 12–18.

89 "Thing that mattered": ibid., 21.

89 He should change his name: ibid., 23.

90 Lawyering not congenial: Josephson, "The Jurist."

90 Stimson background: NYT, October 21, 1950.

91 A stimulating place: Hirsch, 26.

91 "An artist in adulation": Freedman, 27.

91 "No one can testify": Hirsch, 28.

92 "House of Truth": Baker, 67.

92 Courtship of Marion Denman: Hirsch, 10–12, 49–51.

92 "Not a cloistered scholar": ibid., 40.

92 "A happy time here": ibid., 43.

92 Outside activities: Strum, 375.

93 Missions to Turkey and Paris and the Mooney case: Hirsch, 54–57.

94 Letter to Wilson: ibid., 64.

94 Sacco and Vanzetti case: Josephson, "The Jurist."

95 Response to Stimson: Hirsch, 75.

95 "The traffic can bear": ibid., 76.

96 Frankfurter drew the line: Hirsch, 109.

96 "I know his limitations": Freedman, 52.

97 "A stubborn pig": Josephson, "The Jurist."

97 "Shooting ideas into him": ibid.

98 Recruiter-in-chief: ibid.

98 "Eager for service": Frankfurter.

99 Farley's grumbling: NYT, February 23, 1965.

99 "A plague of lawyers": Peek.

99 "Too many Jews here now": Lash, 219.

100 Action followed very speedily: Stephen Wise to Julian Mack, April 10, 1993, SSW, box 115.

100 Perkins's background: "Frances Perkins."

101 She turned to Frankfurter: Breitman and Kraut, 12–13.

101 He sent the proposals to Moley: Frankfurter to Raymond Moley, April 24, 1933, Moley collection.

102 Phillps passed the word: Breitman and Kraut, 14.

102 "Some day" immigration policy may be redrawn: Perkins, 348.

102 No public statement: Perkins to Frankfurter, April 25, 1933, Moley collection.

102 Never mentioned refugees: American Presidency Project.

103 "Rather heartbreaking": Frankfurter to Frances Perkins, April 27, 1933, Moley collection.

104 Jewish leaders not satisfied: Wise to Mack, April 10, 1933, SSW, box 115.

104 "Making their voice heard": Wise to Frankfurter, April 15, 1933. SSW, box 109.

104 "Time is of the essence": Wise to Frankfurter, April 16, 1933, SSW, box 109.

104 Frankfurter added a condition: Arad, 154.

105 "Really is disheartening": Frankfurter to Moley, April 24, 1933, Moley collection.

105 Jewish leaders also censured: Arad, 155.

106 "No application to German situation": Frankfurter to Perkins, April 29, 1933, Moley collection.

106 Carr's anti-Semitism: Breitman and Kraut, 32.

107 Phillips's views: ibid., 36–38.

108 Myth of a "Jewish Hierarchy": Weil.

109 "A more socially just society": Dinnerstein, "Jews and the New Deal."

109 "Most presidents would be allowed": "The Case Against Roosevelt." *Fortune*, December 1935.

110 Frankfurter congratulated his friend: Breitman and Kraut, 101.

111 A group of prominent Jews: Freedman, 481–482.

111 Backing from Norris: ibid.

111 A public statement: Murphy, 187.

112 Dr. Solomon Frankfurter's arrest: Freedman, 472.

112 Frankfurter-FDR exchange: Freedman, 619–620.

V. THE TROUBLESHOOTER

113 "A terrible cry": Wise to Frankfurter, November 12, 1937, SSW, box 109.

114 "Jewishly his influence is bad": Wise to Frankfurter, January 24, 1938, SSW, box 109.

115 "A shameful memory": NYT, June 6, 1933.

115 "Mitigate their distress": NYT, June 15, 1933.

115 "Extremely unfavorable result": Arad, 167, citing records of the American Jewish Committee executive office.

115 Moley's disagreement: ibid., 168, citing memorandum of conversation with Moley, May 14, 1933, Mack's papers.

116 "You should not ask": Ibid., p. 175, citing Wise letter to Mack, June 3, 1933, Mack papers.

116 FDR refused and Hitler torpedoed: Hamby, *Survival*, 132; Burns, 249–250.

116 Rosenman's early years: Hand, 4–19.

117 " A great personality": SIR, 29–32.

118 Rosenman's name never came up: Israel.

119 The 1928 campaign: Hand, 20–24.

119 "Knock out a draft": Rosenman, 16–17.
119 Serving as counsel: ibid., 25–36.
120 "No secretsæ: SIR, 99.
120 "We understood each other": SIR, 51.
121 Considered a blunder: Hand, 46.
121 "A very tight rope": SIR, 77.
121 "Tribute to his devotion": Hand, 53.
122 "cutting off my right arm": NYT, March 12, 1932.
122 "A long memory": NYT, September 30, 1932.
122 Climax of Walker case: Rosenman, 82–83.
122 Creating the "brain trust": Hand, 58–61; but see also Moley, 5–9.
122 Coining the "New Deal": Hand, 61–64.
124 Moley's hostility: Hand, 99.
124 "As he was running the government": Schlesinger, *Coming*, 182.
124 "Almost exclusively social": Rosenman, 94.
125 A special professorship in human relations: Feingold, "Courage First."
125 "The way is to know himself": Israels.
125 Foreshadowed the apocalypse: Grobman.
126 "The apprehensiveness of American Jews": "Jews in America."
126 Asking to be left behind: Rosen, 18.
126 Never addressed anti-Semitism: American Presidency Project.
127 A formidable trencherman: Israels.
128 Watering plants with cocktails: Rosenman, 150–151.
129 "The president is terribly nervous": Rosenman, 154.
129 "A somber verdict": Burns, 116, citing Millis, "The President's Political Strategy."
129 Only one-third would support a third term: *Fortune*, February 1940.
130 Isolationist base of support: Chadwin, 4; Lubell, 140.
130 A silent partner: Beard, 148; Cole, 187ff.
130 Passage of the Johnson Act: Cole, 9.
130 He invited Johnson: ibid., 89–94.
130 "It was Hitler and Mussolini": SIR, 160.
131 Failure of the Evian conference: Breitman and Kraut, 61–64.
132 *Kristallnacht*: Shirer, 430–434.
133 Roosevelt's response: NYT, November 16, 1938.
133 "We have the quota system": American Presidency Project, excerpts from presidential press conference, November 5, 1938.
133 He also recalled the ambassador: NYT, November 16, 1938.
134 "He couldn't understand": SIR, 163.
134 "Produce a Jewish problem": Breitman and Kraut, 230, citing Rosenman to FDR, December 12, 1938, President's Personal File, FDRL.

135 Polling data argued against: Stember, 8–9.
135 A high degree of volatility: ibid., 9–10.
135 "Bold frank leadership": Davis, 267.
136 Rosenman saw colonization: Hand, 140; Breitman and Kraut, 63.
136 "It would take the Jews five to fifty years": Blum, *Roosevelt and Morgenthau*, 518–519.
136 Ickes Background: "Harold Le Clair Ickes"; Shogan, 163–165.
137 "Who would take Hitler's word": Watkins, 668.
137 A double opportunity: Medoff.
138 "Not fully developed": NYT, November 24, 1938.
139 "not sufficient reason": Wise to Frankfurter, October 7, 1939, SSW, box 109.
139 "Would avoid criticism": Ickes, *Clouds*, 55–57.
139 In the end: Medoff.

VI. BUNDLES FOR BRITAIN

142 The gambit overused: Wise to Brandeis, November 11, 1938, SSW, box 106.
142 "They are high moguls": Lasser, 210.
142 Met with Ben Gurion: ibid., 205–206.
143 Cohen's early years: ibid., 9–17.
144 Cohen's Wall Street experience: Lasser, 60.
144 Corcoran and Cohen: Loucheim, 114.
144 The Gold Dust Twins: NYT, August 17, 1983.
144 Curbing the excesses: "Benjamin Victor Cohen."
145 "Go to the movies": Loucheim, 113.
145 Morgenthau complained: Blum, *Roosevelt and Morgenthau*, 258.
145 Cohen passed over: Lash, 184–185; Lasser, 105–107, 182, 201.
146 Goering's order: "Holocaust Timeline."
146 The *St. Louis* affair: Breitman and Kraut, 70–73.
147 The 1936 Democratic platform: *Guide to U.S. Elections*, 83; NYT, June 26, 1936.
147 "Quarantine the aggressors": Freidel, *Rendezvous*, 246.
147 The president dropped the idea: *Presidential Press Conferences, 1937*, no. 400, October 6, 1937, 247–251.
147 The president assured Hitler: Cole, 286.
148 "Good man": Langer and Gleason, 34.
148 He wanted Chamberlain to know: Cole, 301.
148 "I cannot ask": ibid., 320.
150 "The voice and force": Kimball, *Churchill and Roosevelt*, 37.

254 | *Notes to pages 150–166*

150 A great debate: Shogan, 137–139.

150 The Century Group: Chadwin, 70–76.

151 "Substantially more leverage": Alsop, 18.

151 Cohen approached on his own: Ickes, *Clouds*, 233.

152 Cohen memorandum: Cohen to Roosevelt, July 19, 1940, President's Secretary's File, July 19, 1940, FDRL.

153 Another apparent bar: Lasser, "Destroyers," citing act of March 4, 1909, c. 321, sec. 11, 35 Stat. 1090.

153 Did not need congressional approval: Lasser, 222.

154 Off base: Ickes, *Clouds*, 271.

154 Hull shied away: *FRUS*, vol. III, 59–61.

154 "Congress in no mood": Elliot Roosevelt, 1048–1049.

154 Hitler issues order: Churchill, 258–259.

155 Italy invades Somaliland: NYT, August 7, 1940.

155 Only one sentence: NYT, August 3, 1940.

155 Willkie in lead: NYT, August 4, 1940.

155 Dead in the water: Hull, 4.

156 The Right man: Murphy, 210; Lasser, 221, 226.

156 Representing the stock exchange: Louchheim, 132.

157 Acheson's graceful resignation: Acheson, 192–194.

157 A hodgepodge: NYT, August 11, 1940.

158 The Senate survey: Cohen papers.

158 "Not the purpose": Acheson, 222.

159 A one-sentence covering note: Destroyers for Bases folder, President's Secretary File, FDRL.

159 Framing the question: Blum, *Urgency*, 180.

160 Stimson asks Frankfurter for guidance: Stimson and Bundy, 7; Murphy, 36.

161 "After thinking it over": Stimson diary, August 16, 1940.

161 "A fait accompli": PC, 1940, No. 677, vol. 16, 173–190; NYT, September 3, 1940.

162 "A long step": FO 371/24241 A 3793/141/45.

162 "An openly hostile act": Friedlander, 124–125. Also, Conn and Fairchild, 61–62.

162 Pact with Japan: Friedlander, 131; NYT, September 28, 1940.

162 Jackson's opinion: Destroyers for Bases folder, President's Secretary's File, FDRL.

162 Corwin's dissent: NYT, October 13, 1940.

163 "A blueprint for ignoring Congress": Lasser, 231.

164 "Germany may take violent exception": Long, 126.

164 Dubious claim: NYT, September 22, 1939.

164 Hull's argument: Hull, 684.

164 "It seems a pity": Agar, 137.

VII. THE PRESIDENT'S RABBI

166 Unfolding of the Holocaust: "The Nazi Holocaust."

167 Word reached Schulte: Breitman and Kraut, 148.

168 Riegner's response: Wyman, *Abandonment*, 42–45.

169 "It does not appear advisable": Breitman and Kraut, 149.

169 Such "barbaric crimes": ibid., 150; NYT, August 22, 1942.

170 Riegner not naive: Breitman and Kraut, 149–152.

170 Wise's background: "Stephen Samuel Wise."

171 Political and social causes: Urofsky, *Voice*, vii.

172 A dominant motif: Wise, 9–12.

172 The Temple Emanu-El audition and aftermath: Urofsky, *Voice*, 51–55.

172 Division among Jews: ibid., 59–65.

173 Seven pages of *Harper's Weekly*: Inglis.

174 Attracted to Wilson's reforms: Urofsky, *Voice*, 108–115.

174 Fighting Tammany: ibid., 104.

174 Honeymoon with FDR: ibid., 241.

174 The falling out: ibid., 244–248.

175 "A pseudo liberal": Voss, *Rabbi and Minister*, 278.

175 "No moral courage": Wise to Rabbi Louis Newman, July 19, 1932, SSW, box 117.

175 A conciliatory letter: Voss, *Rabbi and Minister*, 281.

175 "A mighty nice letter": Roosevelt to Holmes and Wise, December 16, 1932, SSW, box 68.

176 "At once violent and infantile": Wise to Frankfurter, April 1, 1933, SSW, box 109.

176 Wrote in gratitude: Wise to Frankfurter, April 12, 1933, SSW, box 109.

176 "if only I knew it": Wise to Frankfurter, April 13, 1933, SSW, box 109.

176 "Time is of the essence": Wise to Frankfurter, April 16, 1933. SSW, box 109.

176 Called off the meeting: Wise to Mack, May 4, 1933, SSW, box 115.

177 Make clear to AJC: Arad, 167, citing Mack to Frankfurter, May 22, 1933, SSW, box 115.

177 Salute from *Vanity Fair*: "The Rabbi."

177 Sarnoff arranged the meeting: Arad, 165.

178 "An angry walrus": Lanchester.

178 "graveyard stuff": Wise to Mack, May 9, 1933, SSW, box 115.
178 "How I feel about things": Arad, 166.
179 "I would resign": Wise to Frankfurter, April 15, 1993, SSW, box 109.
179 "He prophesied to Frankfurter": Wise to Frankfurter, April 15, 1933, SSW, box 109.
180 He warned Frankfurter: Wise to Frankfurter, April 16, 1933, SSW, box 109.
180 "Tremendous street scenes": Wise to Mack, April 15, 1933, SSW, box 115.
180 Letter to Slomovitz: American Presidency Project.
180 "We're either Dutch or English": Morgan, 509, citingWheeler's Columbia University Oral History interview.
181 "Our Jewish great-grandmother": Wise to Philip Slomovitz, March 27, 1935, SSW, box 68.
182 He rejected the idea: Wise to David Niles, September 26, 1935, SSW, box 68.
182 Another indirect invitation: Urofsky, *Voice*, 257.
182 "The deepest sympathy": NYT, January 12, 1936.
182 "Help him see the light": Arad, 188.
182 Smith's link to the Liberty League: Josephson and Josephson, 445ff.
183 His erstwhile hero had blundered: NYT, January 15, 1936.
183 "Work like a dog": Wise to Mack, February 15, 1936, SSW, box 114.
183 This attitude compounded: "Jews in America"; see also Ginsberg, 113; Dinnerstein, *Anti-Semitism*, 126–127.
183 Violent Arab protests: NYT, September 1, 1936.
184 Roosevelt promised to protect: Urofsky, *Voice*, 284.
184 Roosevelt had Hull let the British know: Arad, 191.
184 "A marvelous feat": Urofsky, *Voice*, 284.
184 Abundant pressure: NYT, September 6, 9, 1936.
185 "I wish you were here to vote": Voss, *Selected Letters*, 213.
185 Gesture "at little cost": Urofsky, *Voice*, 284.
185 He suggested stumping: Wise to Stanley High, May 28, 1936, SSW, box 68.
186 Roosevelt accepted: Wise, 219–220.
186 "A little afraid": Wise to Niles, October 7, 1936, SSW, box 118.
186 "Not as a Jew": Arad, 290.
186 "Never once": NYT, November 3, 1936.
186 Asked a favor: Wise, 221; Wise to FDR, January 15, 1937, SSW, box 68.
187 "One of many occasions": Wise, 222.
187 "A great good friend": Wise to Emanuel Neumann, June 23, 1937. Voss, *Selected Letters*, 220.

188 "We cannot press the Hitler button": Wise to Mack, March 19, 1937, SSW, box 114.

188 "Down with a thud": Wise to Frankfurter, March 30, 1938, SSW, box 109.

188 "Throw the Jews out": NYT, May 25, 1939

189 "Hang Rabbi Wise": Wise to Rosemary Krensky, May 26, 1939. Voss, *Selected Letters*, 233.

189 "Such a charming note": Wise to Frankfurter, September 19, 1940, SSW, box 109; FDR to Wise, September 18, 1940, SSW box 68.

189 Literally sweated out: Burns, 452.

189 "Cause of human freedom": Wise to "Mr. Friedman," October 18, 1940, SSW, box 68.

189 The Jewish vote: Isaacs, 152.

190 Welles background: Gellman, 59–62.

191 "World would dissolve": Ickes, III, 640.

191 "Swallowed a ramrod": Ward, 473.

191 Keep it to yourself: Breitman and Kraut, 152.

191 "Corpses used to make soap": Wise to Frankfurter, September 4, 1942, SSW, box 109.

191 "I am almost demented": Wise to Nahum Goldmann, September 4, 1942, cited in Urofsky, 321.

191 "I succeeded in keeping it out of the press": Urofsky, 320.

192 "A great responsibility": Wise to Frankfurter, September 16, 1942, SSW, box 109.

192 Still reluctant to accept it as reality: Urofsky, 319–321.

192 "You will be damned forever": Wise to Professor Otto Nathan, September 19, 1940, SSW papers, box 79.

193 "Confirm your deepest fears": Urofsky, 320.

193 Anti-climactic coverage: NYT, November 25, 1942; Drake, 111.

194 fn: Wood and Jankowsky, 188.

194 *Tribune* headline: *Chicago Tribune*, November 25, 1942.

VIII. ONE OF TWO OF A KIND

195 Continued to deny: Breitman and Kraut, 159.

195 "numerous reports": NYT, December 18, 1942.

195 Most papers ignored: Drake, "Manipulating the News," 113.

196 Its main purpose: Feingold, *Rescue:* 190.

196 Riegner pursued: Wyman, *Abandonment*, 179.

196 "Wide rescue action": Breitman and Kraut, 185.

197 Funds frozen until after war: Wyman, *Abandonment*, 180; "America and the Holocaust."

197 Reams's background: Morse.
197 Long background: Morse; Wyman, *Abandonment*, 191.
198 Shared in the anti-Semitism: Wyman, *Paper Walls*, 163, 199.
199 Morgenthau ready to approve: Wyman, *Abandonment*, 180.
200 Morgenthau's early years: Blum, 5–13.
201 "An awfully nice young fellow": Ward, 252–253.
202 Eager to serve: NYT, February 7, 1967.
203 A crack at diplomacy: Blum, *Roosevelt and Morgenthau*, 32.
203 "Who taught me?": ibid., 50.
204 "One of two of a kind": Ward, *Temperament*, 253.
204 "Afraid of being a liberal Jew": Lash, 153.
205 McIntyre's wisecrack: Schlesinger, *Coming*, 541.
205 "A stupid bootlick": Parish, 224.
205 Staff felt free: Loucheim, 269.
205 The Tripartite Stabilization Pact: "Henry Morgenthau, Jr."
205 Morgenthau in charge: Blum, *Urgency*, 94–103.
206 "Until the next one": MD, October 17, 1938.
206 "Deep-seated and personal": Mishkin.
206 A regular contributor: Blum, *Roosevelt and Morgenthau*, 518.
206 Seeking a refuge for Jews: ibid.
207 Promoting the Rumania plan: ibid., 522–523; Wyman, *Abandonment*, 180.
208 New reason for delay: Wyman, *Abandonment*, 180.
208 "It is up to him": Blum, *Roosevelt and Morgenthau*, 525.
208 "A satanic combination": Wyman, *Abandonment*, 182–183.
209 He must see Hull himself: Breitman and Kraut, 187.
209 "Read with astonishment": Wyman, *Abandonment*, 184.
210 Hull's reaction to Nazism: Cook, II, 314.
210 A public apology: NYT, March 5, 1937.
210 One supposed culprit: Wyman, *Abandonment*, 185.
210 Morgenthau pushed his argument: Blum, *Roosevelt and Morgenthau*, 529.
210 Randolph Paul's memo: ibid., 531; Wyman, *Abandonment*, 187.
213 Wise warned Rogers: Wyman and Medoff, 109.
213 A nasty letter back: ibid., 152–153, 221–222.
213 Bergson undeterred: Wyman, *Abandonment*, 145.
213 "A pilgrimage for rescue": ibid., 149–153.
213 Hoped to see Roosevelt: WP, October 6, 1943.
213 Number one adviser: WP, December, 7, 1941.
214 Sol Bloom's view: Wyman, *Abandonment*, 43n.
214 Advised not to see: Hassett, 209.

214 FDR's schedule: Ward, *Temperament*, 254.

215 Fight over the rescue resolutions: Wyman, *Abandonment*, 193–201; NYT, December 11, 1943.

215 Number of Jewish refugees admitted: NYT, December 27, 31, 1943; "Crocodile Tears"; "The State Department and the Jews."

216 Then instructed Morgenthau: Blum, *Roosevelt and Morgenthau*, 532.

216 Signing the executive order: Wyman, *Abandonment*, 204.

216 Resistance to the War Refugee Board: Breitman and Kraut, 193–201.

217 Next to impossible mission: "America and the Holocaust."

217 Saved about 200,000 Jews: Wyman, *Abandonment*, 225.

217 Word spread in Washington: Feingold, *Witness*, 176.

218 "Semitism gone wild for vengeance": Smith, 624.

218 Truman refused to send him to Potsdam: NYT, February 7, 1967.

218 "Intelligence and courage": Feingold, "Courage First."

IX. MYSTERY MAN

219 Abe and Irving: Weinraub, 31.

220 Jews turned to Van Buren: Arad, 16–17.

221 Adler's view: ibid., 66.

222 "The otherworldly young counsel": "The Case Against Roosevelt."

223 Göring's order: Arad, 145.

224 "Connection not accidental": "Jews in America."

224 Evidence to the contrary: "Immigration Causes Unemployment, and Other Economic Fallacies."

226 Calling off the march: Foner and Garraty, 699–700.

226 Wilson's record: Smith, 99.

227 FDR meets with Saud: Hamby, "Instant Recognition"; Radosh and Radosh, 26–28.

229 He confirmed what Saud surely remembered: Snetsinger, 19.

230 "Of course they called me four eyes": Miller, 23.

230 The lives of great men: Truman, 138–139.

231 "I do not have Arab constituents": Hamby, *Truman*, 405.

232 "A peep at the Golden rule": ibid.

233 Niles's background: Donovan, 316; Radosh and Radosh, 44; Pika; Steinberg; Graham and Wander, 294.

234 Secretly in love: Radosh, 45.

235 Weeping openly: Donovan, 317.

235 "A most secretive individual": Pika.

236 "A man of no importance": Snetsinger, 36.

236 Passing on Roosevelt's view: ibid., 19.

237 Three to one in favor: Radosh and Radosh, 69.
237 Flooded the White House with letters: Hamby, *Truman*, 410.
238 Niles and Zionism: Radosh, 45.
240 "It doesn't sound like you": ibid., 412.
240 A common understanding: Donovan, 374.
240 "I would vote against the President": Radosh and Radosh, 333.
241 Truman phoned Niles: Snetsinger, 112.
242 Truman's political instincts: Hamby, 405–406.
242 Clifford's role: Snetsinger, 113.

BIBLIOGRAPHY

Abbreviations used for website sources:
DAB: Dictionary of American Biography (New York, American Council of
  Learned Societies)
BRC: reproduced in Biography Resource Center (Farmington Hills, Mich.,
  Gale Group) http://galenet.galegroup.com/servlet/BioRC

ARCHIVAL SOURCES

American Jewish Archives, Cincinnati. Papers of Stephen S. Wise. Cited
  as SSW.
British Foreign Office Records of communication between its Washington
  embassy and the London Foreign Office for 1940, cited as FO 371 files.
Columbia University Oral History Project. Interview with Samuel I.
  Rosenman. Cited as SIR.
Franklin D. Roosevelt Presidential Library, Hyde Park, N.Y., cited as FDRL.
  Morgenthau diaries, cited as MD. Destroyer for Bases folder. Presi-
  dent's Secretary's File.
Hoover Institution, Stanford University. Raymond Moley collection, box
  68, folder 6.
Library of Congress, Manuscript Division. Papers of Joseph Alsop, Felix
  Frankfurter, and Ben Cohen.
Yale University Sterling Library, New Haven, Conn. Diary of Henry
  Stimson.

BOOKS

Acheson, Dean. *Morning and Noon.* Boston, Houghton Mifflin, 1965.

Agar, Herbert. *The Darkest Year.* Garden City, N.Y., Doubleday, 1973.

Alsop, Joseph, with Adam Platt. *"I've Seen the Best of It."* New York, W. W. Norton, 1992.

Alsop, Joseph, and Turner Catledge. *The 168 Days.* Garden City, N.Y., Doubleday, 1938.

Arad, Gulie Ne'eman. *America, Its Jews, and the Rise of Nazism.* Bloomington, Indiana University Press, 2000.

Auerbach, Jerold. *Rabbis and Lawyers: The Journey from Torah to Constitution.* Bloomington, Indiana University Press, 1990.

Baker, Leonard. *Brandeis and Frankfurter: A Dual Biography.* New York, Harper & Row, 1984.

Beard, Charles. *American Foreign Policy in the Making.* New Haven, Yale University Press, 1946.

Blum, John Morton. *From the Morgenthau Diaries: Years of Urgency, 1938–1941.* Boston, Houghton Mifflin, 1967. Cited as Blum, *Urgency.*

——. *Roosevelt and Morgenthau: A Revision and Condensation of "From the Morgenthau Diaries."* Boston, Houghton Mifflin, 1972. Cited as Blum, *Roosevelt and Morgenthau.*

Breitman, Richard, and Alan M. Kraut. *American Refugee Policy and European Jewry, 1933–1945.* Bloomington, Indiana University Press, 1987.

Burns, James MacGregor. *Roosevelt: The Lion and the Fox.* New York, Harcourt Brace Jovanovich, 1956.

Chadwin, Mark. *The Hawks of World War II.* Chapel Hill, University of North Carolina Press, 1968.

Churchill, Winston. *Their Finest Hour.* New York, Bantam, 1962.

Cole, Wayne S. *Roosevelt and the Isolationists.* Lincoln, University of Nebraska Press, 1983.

Conn, Stetson, and Byron Fairchild. *The United States Army in World War II,* Vol. I: *The Framework of Hemisphere Defense.* Washington, D.C., Office of the Chief of Military History, 1960.

Cook, Blanche Wiesen. *Eleanor Roosevelt,* Vol. I: *1884–1933.* New York, Penguin Books, 1992.

——. *Eleanor Roosevelt,* Vol. II: *1933–1938.* New York, Viking, 1999.

Dalin, David G., and Alfred Kolatch. *The Presidents of the United States and the Jews.* Middle Village, N.Y., Jonathan David Publishers, 2000.

Davis, Kenneth S. *FDR: Into the Storm.* New York, Random House, 1993.

Dinnerstein, Leonard. *Anti-Semitism in America.* New York, Oxford University Press, 1994. Cited as Dinnerstein, *Anti-Semitism.*

Donovan, Robert J. *Conflict and Crisis: The Presidency of Harry S Truman, 1945–1948.* New York, W. W. Norton, 1977.

Feingold, Henry L. *Bearing Witness: How America and Its Jews Responded to the Holocaust.* Syracuse, Syracuse University Press, 1995. Cited as Feingold, *Witness.*

———. *The Politics of Rescue: The Roosevelt Administration and the Holocaust, 1938–1945.* New Brunswick, N.J., Rutgers University Press, 1970. Cited as Feingold, *Rescue.*

Foner, Eric, and John A. Garraty, eds. *The Readers Guide to American History.* Boston, Houghton Mifflin, 1991.

Freedman, Max. *Roosevelt and Frankfurter: Their Correspondence.* Boston, Little, Brown, 1967.

Freidel, Frank. *Franklin D. Roosevelt: A Rendezvous with Destiny.* Boston, Little, Brown, 1990. Cited as Freidel, *Rendezvous.*

———. *Franklin D. Roosevelt: The Apprenticeship.* Boston, Little, Brown, 1952. Cited as Freidel, *Apprenticeship.*

———. *Franklin D. Roosevelt: The Ordeal.* Boston, Little, Brown, 1954. Cited as Freidel, *Ordeal.*

Friedlander, Saul. *Prelude to Downfall.* London, Chatto & Windus, 1967.

Fuchs, Lawrence H. *The Political Behavior of American Jews.* Glencoe, Ill., Free Press, 1956.

Gallagher, Hugh. *FDR's Splendid Deception.* New York, Dodd Mead, 1985.

Gellman, Irwin F. *Secret Affairs: FDR, Cordell Hull and Sumner Welles.* New York, Enigma Books, 2002.

Ginsberg, Benjamin. *The Fatal Embrace: Jews and the State.* Chicago, University of Chicago Press, 1993.

Gossett, Thomas F. *Race: The History of an Idea in America.* New York, Schocken Books, 1965.

Graham, Otis L. Jr., and Megan Robinson Wander. *Franklin D. Roosevelt: His Life and Times: An Encyclopedic View.* Boston, G. K. Hall, 1985.

Guide to U.S. Elections. Washington, D.C., Congressional Quarterly, 1975.

Hamby, Alonzo. *For the Survival of Democracy: Franklin Roosevelt and the World Crisis of the 1930s.* New York, Free Press, 2004. Cited as Hamby, *Survival.*

———. *Man of the People: A Life of Harry S. Truman.* New York, Oxford University Press, 1995. Cited as Hamby, *Truman.*

Hand, Samuel. *Counsel and Advise: A Political Biography of Samuel I. Rosenman.* New York, Garland, 1979.

Handlin, Oscar. *Boston's Immigrants.* Cambridge, Mass., Harvard University Press, 1979.

Hassett, William D. *Off the Record with FDR, 1942–1945.* New Brunswick, N.J., Rutgers University Press, 1958.

Hertzberg, Arthur. *The Jews in America: Four Centuries of An Uneasy Encounter.* New York, Columbia University Press, 1997.

Hirsch, H. N. *The Enigma of Felix Frankfurter.* New York, Basic Books, 1981.

Hofstadter, Richard. *The Age of Reform.* New York, Vintage, 1955.

Howe, Irving. *World of Our Fathers: The Journey of East European Jews to America.* New York, Bantam, 1976.

Hull, Cordell. *The Memoirs of Cordell Hull,* Vol. I. New York, Macmillan, 1948.

Hurd, Charles. *When the New Deal Was Young and Gay.* New York, Hawthorn, 1965.

Ickes, Harold. *The Secret Diary of Harold Ickes: The First Thousand Days.* New York, Simon and Schuster, 1953.

———. *The Secret Diary of Harold Ickes: The Inside Struggle.* New York, Simon and Schuster, 1954.

———. *The Secret Diary of Harold Ickes: The Lowering Clouds.* New York, Simon and Schuster, 1955.

Isaacs, Stephen D. *Jews and American Politics.* Garden City, N.Y., Doubleday, 1974.

Johnson, Walter. *The Battle Against Isolation.* Chicago, University of Chicago Press, 1984.

Josephson, Matthew and Hannah. *Al Smith: Hero of the Cities.* Boston, Houghton Mifflin, 1969.

Kimball, Warren, ed. *Churchill and Roosevelt: Complete Correspondence,* Vol. I. Princeton, Princeton University Press, 1984.

———. *The Juggler: Franklin Roosevelt as Wartime Statesman.* Princeton, Princeton University Press, 1991.

Langer, William L., and Everett Gleason. *The Challenge to Isolation.* New York, Harper & Row, 1952.

Lash, Joseph P. *Dealers and Dreamers.* Garden City, N.Y., Doubleday, 1988.

Lasser, William. *Benjamin V. Cohen: Architect of the New Deal.* New Haven, Yale University Press, 2002.

Lief, Alfred. *Brandeis: The Personal History of An American Ideal.* New York, Stackpole, 1937.

Long, Breckinridge. *War Diary.* Fred Israel, ed. Lincoln, University of Nebraska Press, 1966.

Louchheim, Katie, ed. *The Making of the New Deal: The Insiders Speak.* Cambridge, Mass., Harvard University Press, 1983.

Lubell, Samuel. *The Future of American Politics.* New York, Harper & Row, 1952.

Maney, Patrick. *The Roosevelt Presence.* New York, Twayne, 1992.

Martin, Ralph G. *Ballots and Bandwagons.* New York, New American Library, 1965.

Miller, Merle. *Plain Speaking.* New York, Greenwich House, 1985.

Moley, Raymond. *After Seven Years.* New York, Harper & Brothers, 1939.

Morgan, Ted. *FDR: A Biography.* New York, Simon and Schuster, 1985.

Murphy, Bruce. *The Brandeis-Frankfurter Connection.* New York, Oxford University Press, 1982.

Murray, Robert K. *The 103rd Ballot.* New York, Harper & Row, 1976. Cited as Murray, *Ballot.*

———. *Red Scare: A Study in National Hysteria, 1919–1920.* New York, McGraw-Hill, 1964. Cited as Murray, *Red Scare.*

Parish, Michael E. *Felix Frankfurter and His Times: The Reform Years.* New York, Free Press, 1982.

Perkins, Frances. *The Roosevelt I Knew.* New York, Viking, 1946.

Radosh, Allis, and Ronald Radosh. *A Safe Haven: Harry S. Truman and the Founding of Israel.* New York, HarperCollins, 2009.

Rollins, Alfred B. Jr. *Roosevelt and Howe.* New York, Alfred A. Knopf, 1962.

Roosevelt, Elliot, ed. *FDR: His Personal Letters, 1928–1945,* Vol. II. New York, Duell Sloan, and Pearce, 1950.

Rosen, Robert N. *Saving the Jews: Franklin D. Roosevelt and the Holocaust.* New York, Thunder's Mouth Press, 2006.

Rosenman, Sam. *Working with Roosevelt.* New York, Harper & Brothers, 1952.

Schlesinger, Arthur M. *The Age of Roosevelt: The Coming of the New Deal.* Boston, Houghton Mifflin, 1959. Cited as Schlesinger, *Coming.*

——. *The Age of Roosevelt: The Crisis of the Old Order*. Boston, Hough-ton Mifflin, 1957. Cited as Schlesinger, *Crisis*.

——. *The Age of Roosevelt: The Politics of Upheaval*. Boston, Houghton Mifflin, 1960. Cited as Schlesinger, *Upheaval*.

Shirer, William L. *The Rise and Fall of the Third Reich: A History of Nazi Germany*. New York, Simon and Schuster, 1960.

Shogan, Robert. *Hard Bargain: How FDR Twisted Churchill's Arm, Evaded the Law, and Changed the Role of the American Presidency*. New York, Scribner, 1995.

Smith, Jean Edward. *FDR*. New York, Random House, 2007.

Snetsinger, John. *Truman, the Jewish Vote, and the Creation of Israel*. Stanford, Hoover Institution Press, 1974.

Steel, Ronald. *Walter Lippmann and the American Century*. New York, Vintage, 1980.

Stember, Charles Herbert, et al. *Jews in the Mind of America*. New York, Basic Books, 1966.

Stiles, Lela. *The Man Behind Roosevelt: The Story of Louis McHenry Howe*. New York, World Publishing, 1954.

Stimson, Henry L., and McGeorge Bundy. *On Active Service in Peace and War*. New York, Harper & Brothers, 1947.

Strum, Philippa. *Louis D. Brandeis: Justice for the People*. Cambridge, Mass., Harvard University Press, 1984.

Swanberg, W. A. *Citizen Hearst*. New York, Bantam, 1967.

Tugwell, Rexford G. *The Art of Politics: As Practiced by Three Great Americans*. Garden City, N.Y., Doubleday, 1958. Cited as Tugwell, *Art of Politics*.

——. *The Democratic Roosevelt*. Baltimore, Penguin, 1957. Cited as Tug-well, *Roosevelt*.

Tully, Grace. *FDR: My Boss*. Chicago, People's Book Club, 1949.

Urofsky, Melvin I. *Louis D. Brandeis: A Life*. New York, Pantheon, 2009. Cited as Urofsky, *Brandeis*.

——. *A Voice That Spoke for Justice*. Albany, State University of New York Press, 1982. Cited as Urofsky, *Voice*.

Urofsky, Melvin I., and David W. Levy, eds. *Half Brother, Half Son: The Letters of Louis D. Brandeis to Felix Frankfurter*. Norman, University of Oklahoma Press, 1991. Cited as Urofsky and Levy, *Brandeis-Frankfurter*.

——, eds. *Letters of Louis D. Brandeis*, Vol. V. Albany, State University of New York Press, 1978. Cited as Urofsky and Levy, *Letters*.

Voss, Carl Herman. *Rabbi and Minister.* New York, World Publishing, 1964. Cited as Voss, *Rabbi and Minister.*

———. *Stephen S. Wise: Servant of the People: Selected Letters.* Philadelphia, Jewish Publication Society of America, 1969. Cited as Voss, *Selected Letters.*

Ward, Geoffrey C. *Before the Trumpet.* New York, Harper & Row, 1985. Cited as Ward, *Trumpet.*

———. *A First-Class Temperament.* New York, Harper & Row, 1989. Cited as Ward, *Temperament.*

Watkins, T. H. *Righteous Pilgrim: The Life and Times of Harold L. Ickes, 1874–1952.* New York, Holt, 1990.

White, Theodore H. *The Making of the President 1960.* New York: Pocket Books, 1962.

Wise, Stephen. *Challenging Years: The Autobiography of Stephen Wise.* New York, Putnam, 1949.

Wood, E. Thomas, and Stanislaw Jankowski. *Karski: How One Man Tried to Stop the Holocaust.* New York, John Wiley and Sons, 1994.

Wyman, David S. *The Abandonment of the Jews.* New York, Pantheon, 1948. Cited as Wyman, *Abandonment.*

———. *Paper Walls: America and the Refugee Crisis.* Amherst, University of Massachusetts Press, 1968. Cited as Wyman, *Paper Walls.*

Wyman, David S., and Rafael Medoff. *Race Against Death.* New York, New Press, 2002.

PERIODICALS, JOURNALS, AND WEBSITES

"America and the Holocaust: Deceit and Indifference," American Experience, www.pbs.org/amex/wgbh/holocaust

American Presidency Project, www.presidency.ucsb.edu

"Benjamin Victor Cohen," *Scribner Encyclopedia of American Lives,* Vol. 1: *1981–1985,* New York, Charles Scribner's Sons, 1998. BRC.

Dorothy Borg, "Notes on Roosevelt's 'Quarantine' Speech," *Political Science Quarterly,* Vol. 72, September 1957.

"The Case Against Roosevelt," *Fortune,* December 1935.

Edward Corwin, "Executive Authority Held Exceeded in Destroyer Deal," *New York Times,* October 13, 1940, letter to the editor.

"Crocodile Tears," *The Nation,* December 25, 1943.

Leonard Dinnerstein, "Jews and the New Deal," *American Jewish History,* June 1983. Cited as Dinnerstein, "Jews and the New Deal."

Henry L. Feingold, "Courage First and Intelligence Second: The American Jewish Secular Elite, Roosevelt and the Failure of Rescue," *Publications of the American Jewish Historical Society*, Vol. 72, June 1983. Cited as Feingold, "Courage First."

"Frances Perkins," *DAB, Supplement 7, 1961–1965*. BRC.

Felix Frankfurter, "The Young Men Go to Washington," *Fortune*, January 1936.

Gary Grobman, "Adolf Hitler," Remember.org/guide/facts

Alonzo Hamby, "Instant Recognition: Israel's Debt to Harry S. Truman," *Weekly Standard*, July 11, 2009. Cited as Hamby, "Instant Recognition."

"Harold Le Clair Ickes," *DAB, 1977*. BRC.

"Henry Brooks Adams," *Wikipedia*, citing *Letters of Henry Adams II*, Worthington Ford, ed. Boston, Houghton Mifflin, 1946, p. 33.

"Henry Morgenthau, Jr.," *DAB*. BRC.

"Holocaust Timeline," Historyplace.com

"Immigration Causes Unemployment, and Other Economic Fallacies," amateurassetallocator.com

William Inglis, "Celebrities at Home: Rabbi Stephen S. Wise, Ph.D.," *Harper's Weekly*, December 5, 1908.

Josef Israels, "The Saga of Sammy the Rose," *Saturday Evening Post*, December 8, 1942.

"Jews in America," *Fortune*, February 1936.

Matthew Josephson, "Profiles: The Jurist: I," *The New Yorker*, November 30, 1940.

"Jews in America: Our Story," http://jewsinamerica.org

———, "Profiles: The Jurist: II," *The New Yorker*, December 7, 1940.

Thomas A. Kreuger and William Glidden, "The New Deal Intellectual Elite: A Collective Portrait," in Frederic Cople Jaher, ed., *The Rich, the Well Born and the Powerful: Elites and Upper Classes in History*, Urbana, University of Illinois Press, 1973.

John Lanchester, "Heroes and Zeroes," *The New Yorker*, February 2, 2009.

William E. Leuchtenburg, "The First Modern President," in Fred I. Greenstein, ed., *Leadership in the Modern Presidency*, Cambridge, Mass., Harvard University Press, 1988.

"Louis Dembitz Brandeis," *DAB, Supplement 3: 1941–1945*. BRC.

"Louis Dembitz Brandeis," *Encyclopedia of World Biography*, 2nd ed., 1998. BRC.

"Louis Marshall," *DAB, 1928–1936*. BRC.

Rev. Terry Matthews, Wake Forest University, Religious Life in the United States, Lecture Series, www.yahoo.com/ Society_and_Culture/ Religion/Judaism

Rafael Medoff, "Senator Allen's 'Jewish Problem,'" David S. Wyman Institute for Holocaust Studies, http://wymaninstitute.org. Cited as Medoff, "Senator Allen's Jewish Problem."

———, "Thanksgiving Plan to Save Europe's Jews," *New Jersey Jewish Standard*, November 15, 2007. Cited as Medoff, "A Thanksgiving Plan."

Walter Millis, "The President's Political Strategy," *Yale Review*, September 1938.

Bud Mishkin, "One on 1: Manhattan District Attorney Robert Morgenthau," NY1.com, January 7, 2010.

Arthur D. Morse, "How the Indifference of the U.S. State Department Aided the Nazi Murder Plot," www.fdrheritage.org/fdr&holocaust

Robert Mulcahay, "Henry Ford and His Anti-Semitism," www.wsws .org/articles/2003/apr2003

"The Nazi Holocaust 1938–1945," Historyplace.com

Robert Novak, "Secret Affairs," *American Spectator*, September 1995.

Jerome Peek, "In and Out: The Experiences of the First AAA Administrator," *Saturday Evening Post*, May 16, 1936.

Jopseh A. Pika, "Interest Groups and the White House Under Roosevelt and Truman," *Political Science Quarterly*, vol. 102, no. 4 (Winter 1987).

"The Rabbi: Dr. Stephen S. Wise," *Vanity Fair*, June 1933.

Mark A. Raider, "Vigilantibus non dormientibus: The Judicial Activism of Louis Marshall," *Jewish Social Studies*, vol. 14, no. 1 (Fall 2007).

"The State Department and the Jews," *New Republic*, December 20, 1943.

Alfred Steinberg, "Mr. Truman's Mystery Man," *Saturday Evening Post*, December 21, 1949.

"Stephen Samuel Wise," *DAB, Supplement 4, 1946–1950.* BRC.

Arthur T. Weil, "Exploding the Myth of a Jewish Hierarchy," *American Hebrew and Jewish Tribune*, May 1934.

Victoria Saker Woeste, "Suing Henry Ford: America's First Hate Speech Case," Americanbarfoundation.org./research/project

GOVERNMENT DOCUMENTS

Department of State. *U.S. Documents on German Foreign Policy, 1918–1945*, vols. IX and X. Washington, D.C., Government Printing Office, 1957. Cited as *DGFP*.

Department of State. *Foreign Relations of the United States, 1940.* Washington, D.C., Government Printing Office, 1941. Cited as *FRUS.*

Department of State. *Peace and War. U.S. Foreign Policy 1931–1941.* Washington, D.C., Government Printing Office, 1942. Cited as *Peace and War.*

Navy Department. *Fuehrer Conferences on Matters Dealing with the German Navy, 1939–1945.* Wilmington, Del., Scholarly Resources, 1983. Cited as *Fuehrer Conferences.*

Roosevelt, Franklin D. *Complete Presidential Press Conferences, 1933–41.* New York, Da Capo, 1972. Cited as *PC.*

———. *Public Papers and Addresses, 1933–1941.* New York, Macmillan. Cited as *PPA.*

———. *Public Papers of Franklin D. Roosevelt, Forty-Eighth Governor of the State of New York, 1929–1932,* vol. IV. Albany, J. B. Lyon, 1939. Cited as *PPG.*

SCHOLARLY PAPERS

Robert George Drake, "Manipulating the news: The United States Press and the Holocaust, Ph.D. dissertation, State University of New York at Albany, 2003.

William Lasser, "The Destroyers for Bases Agreement and the Origins of the Imperial Presidency," paper delivered at the American Political Science Association Meeting, Washington, D.C., September 1993. Cited as Lasser, "Destroyers."

PLAYS

Bernard Weinraub, "The Accomplices," typescript.

INDEX

Ickes, Harold, 33, 72, 83–84, 111,
136–37, 154, 190, 213–14; and
Alaska plan, 138–39, 145; and
destroyer deal, 151
immigration laws: as exclusionary,
15; Jews, effect on, 27; and
"LPC" clause, 75, 101; national
origins law, passage of, 27; and
quotas, 27
Israel, 24, 70, 83, 142, 227;
creation of, 239; recognition of,
232, 241. *See also* Palestine

Jackson, Andrew, 231
Jackson, Robert, 111, 159, 162–63
Jacobson, Eddie, 231, 240
Jamaica, 11
Japan, 137, 147, 162
Jellinek, Adolf, 171
Jewish Agency for Palestine, 142
Jewish conspiracies, 78
Jewish Daily Bulletin
(publication), 177
Jewish Education Committee, 125
Jewish refugees, 136, 206–7, 222;
and Alaska plan, 136–40;
Congressional resolutions,
214–15; and immigration
restrictions, 74–76, 78, 83,
102–6, 110, 115–16, 131, 133–
34, 139–40, 198; persecution
of, reluctance to respond
toward, 85–86, 99–106,
110; pilgrimage for rescue
petition, 213–14; refugee
relief agency, 212; rescue
ransom plan in, 196–97, 199,
206–7; resettlement of, and
Alaska plan, 136–40. *See also*

American Jewry; European
Jewry
Jewish War Veterans of America,
4; economic boycott, demands
for, 223; march of, 221
Jews: in America, arrival of, 11;
and Ashkenazim Jews, 13;
Ashkenazim v. Sephardim,
12; background of, 12–13;
discrimination against, 6,
13; fear of, 17; and Final
Solution, 193, 218–19; as
Germans, identification with,
13; Harvard University,
admissions policy toward,
95; and Holocaust, xi–xii;
identity of, and assimilation,
10; immigration of,
restrictions toward, 15, 27;
mass immigration of, 15–17,
23; in New World, reluctant
acceptance of, 12; pogroms
against, 15; and Franklin D.
Roosevelt, xi, 5. *See also*
Jewish refugees; President's
Jews; Roosevelt, Franklin D.
Jodl, Alfred, 162
Johnson, Hiram, 56, 130
Johnson, Hugh, 86, 109
Johnson Act, 130

Karski, Jan, 194
Keynes, John Maynard, 156
King, William, 138–39
King-Havenner Bill, 139
Kirby, Rollin, 123
Kirchwey, Freda, 232–33
Kishinev (Bessarabia, Russia):
pogrom in, 19–20, 31

A NOTE ON THE AUTHOR

Robert Shogan is a former prizewinning national political
correspondent for *Newsweek* and the *Los Angeles Times*.
Born in New York City, he studied journalism at Syracuse
University. After reporting for newspapers and magazines
and writing books for more than forty years, he turned
to teaching. He has been professional in residence at the
Annenberg School of Communications of the University of
Pennsylvania, and is now adjunct professor of government
at the Johns Hopkins University. He lives
in Chevy Chase, Maryland.